The Building of London
from the Conquest to the Great Fire

The Building of London

from the Conquest to the Great Fire

John Schofield

A Colonnade Book
published by British Museum Publications Ltd
in association with The Museum of London

Colonnade Books
are published by British Museum Publications Ltd
and are offered as contributions to the
enjoyment, study and understanding
of art, archaeology and history.
The same publishers also produce
the official publications of the British Museum.

Published by British Museum Publications Ltd,
46 Bloomsbury Street, London WC1B 3QQ.

British Library Cataloguing in Publication Data
Schofield, John
    The building of London.
    1. Building – London (England) – History
    I. Title
    690'.9421   DA677
    ISBN 0-7141-8053-X

Designed by David Challis and Donald Rooum.

Text set in 11/12 pt Linotron 202 Baskerville, printed
in Great Britain at The Pitman Press, Bath.

Frontispiece: A miniature from an edition of the poems
of Charles, Duke of Orleans, painted in England,
c. 1500. Charles was captured at Agincourt and
imprisoned in England from 1415 to 1440. This is one
of the earliest representations of medieval London.

Below: Floor-tiles from the chapter-house of
Westminster Abbey, mid-13th century.

Contents

Preface   vii

Map of London, *c.* 1550   viii

Introduction   1

1. Roman and Saxon origins 50–1066   14

2. Norman London 1066–1200   36

3. The emergent city 1200–1300   58

4. The London of Yevele and Chaucer 1300–1400   80

5. Stability and consolidation 1400–1500   106

6. London in the 16th century   130

7. To the Great Fire 1600–1666   156

8. Postscript   178

Map and gazetteer   182

Bibliography   184

Acknowledgements   186

Index   187

Preface

I think the idea for this book (or indeed books, since there is material for a whole series), on the buildings of medieval and Tudor London, first occurred to me while leafing through the superb collections of antiquarian prints and drawings in the Print Room of Guildhall Library. Since then, several years ago, many people have helped me write the book. It grows from my Ph.D research into the medieval buildings of London, and first thanks must go to my supervisor Caroline Barron not only for allowing this deflection from the straight and narrow but for her continued interest and criticism of the text. The research upon which it is based has been carried out in a number of places where I have always been received with kind attention: by Miss Betty Masters and her staff at the Corporation of London Record Office, Chris Cooper and his staff at the Guildhall Library Manuscripts Room, and by David Wickham at the Worshipful Company of Clothworkers. For the research, and for this book, the help and advice of Ralph Hyde and John Fisher at the Print Room of Guildhall Library have been invaluable.

I have drawn upon a wide range of published and unpublished work by colleagues and friends; all of whom, I hope, are sufficiently credited in the bibliographical notes on pp. 184–6. My colleagues at the Museum of London have been a great help in providing references, information, and corrections. My major debt is to Charlotte Harding and Richard Lea; the manuscript has profited beyond recognition from comment by John Clark, Tony Dyson, Gustav Milne, Frances Pritchard and Rosemary Weinstein. Parts of the text have also been fruitfully criticised by Richard Gem, Vanessa Harding, Derek Keene, Frank Kelsall, Richard Morris and David Palliser. The libraries and institutions which have kindly allowed reproduction of figures are listed in the Acknowledgements on p. 186. For production of the photographs I would like to thank especially Trevor Hurst, Jon Bailey and Jan Scrivener of the Museum of London, and Godfrey New for work at Guildhall Library. The maps and line drawings are by Richard Lea, David Bentley, Chrissie Milne, Annie Upson, and Chris Unwin. And finally two people have been closely concerned with this book from the beginning, and by their efforts have brought it forth: Jenny Chattington at British Museum Publications, and Janet Taylor, who typed the text with a critical eye.

Left: Glean Alley and Vane Street, Southwark, in a watercolour by J. C. Buckler, dated 1827. Even in the 19th century traces of the 16th-century London townscape remained, in the form of jettied buildings, gutters spouting into the street and poles for hanging out washing.

Overleaf: The City of London about 1560–70. The woodcut panorama known as the Agas map. The general topography and notable buildings are shown in sketch form, but the houses are conventional shapes and drawn larger than they should be. The map is, however, extremely valuable as a research tool and for giving a vivid impression of the late medieval city. The Walbrook stream, which divided the Roman and Saxon city, had by this time been canalised underground. Superimposed on the map are the names of some of the buildings discussed in this book.

CIVITAS LONDINVM

Clerkenwell Nunnery

Charterhouse

Priory of St John

St Bartholomew's Priory

St Giles

Cripplegate

Aldersgate Street

St James's Hermitage

Elsing Spital

Clothworkers' property

Ely Place

St Bartholomew's Hospital

Aldersgate

St Alban

Moor

Holborn

Precinct of St Martin le Grand

Site of Goldsmiths' Hall

Milk Street excavation

Guildhall

Staple Inn

Barnard's Inn

Newgate

Greyfriars

Site of St Nicholas Shambles

Cheapside

Eleanor Cross

St Mary le-Bow

Mercers Hall

Fleet

Ludgate

St Paul's Cathedral

Temple

Whitefriars

Blackfriars

Site of first Baynard's Castle

Site of Gerard's Hall

St Michael Paternoster

Bridewell

Thames Street

Vintry

St Martin Vintry

Baynard's Castle

Trig Lane excavation

Queenhithe

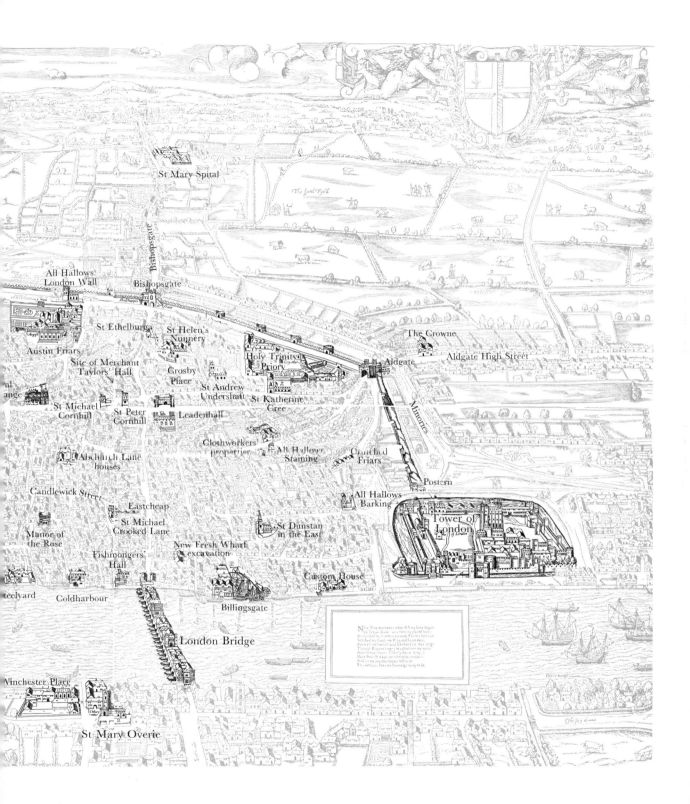

St Mary Spital

Bishopsgate

All Hallows
London Wall

Bishopsgate

The Crowne

St Ethelburga

St Helen's
Nunnery

Aldgate High Street

Austin Friars

Holy Trinity
Priory

Aldgate

Site of Merchant
Taylors' Hall

Crosby
Place

St Michael
Cornhill

St Peter
Cornhill

St Andrew
Undershaft

St Katherine
Cree

Minories

Leadenhall

Clothworkers'
properties

Abchurch Lane
houses

All Hallows
Staning

Crutched
Friars

Candlewick Street

Postern

Eastcheap

All Hallows
Barking

Manor of
the Rose

St Michael
Crooked Lane

St Dunstan
in the East

Tower of
London

Fishmongers'
Hall

New Fresh Wharf
excavation

Steelyard

Coldharbour

Custom House

Billingsgate

London Bridge

Winchester Place

St Mary Overie

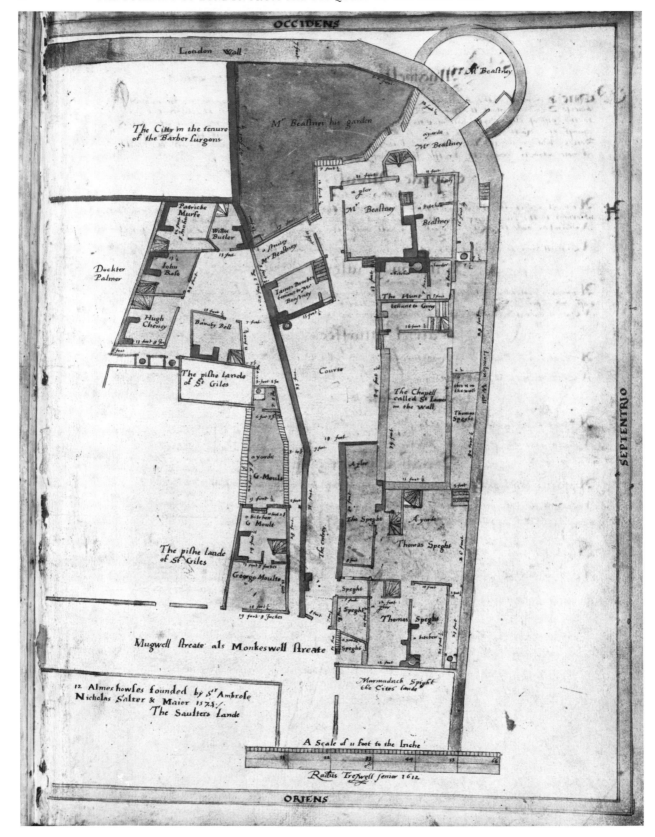

Introduction

Why are towns interesting? And why choose London to study? There is hardly anything standing in London today which has a medieval or Tudor air about it. Walking down the streets of York, or Tewkesbury, Lavenham or Canterbury will give the visitor an idea of medieval buildings in their modern settings. This has not been possible in London for over a century, as the conurbation we know as the Greater London Area filled out the remaining fields and transformed rural villages and small towns into suburbs of the capital city. At the heart of the metropolis, the City of London is known to more people for the Stock Exchange and the Bank of England than for its Roman and medieval past.

And yet it is the digging of foundations for those skyscrapers which are the symbols of London's present prosperity which unearths the houses, shops and wharves of the former city [1]. Should we merely look over the wall and satisfy our curiosity, or attempt to save a few potsherds from the spoil-heap as mementoes? This book is written to assist people who want something more: to understand how London and other towns were formed and grew into their present appearances, and thus perhaps to comprehend their present surroundings.

London should not be taken as a paradigm or blue-print of English towns; but London is best recorded, both in documentary material and in the amount of modern archaeological excavation, and so may serve to illustrate the growth of a city. Towns, and especially a city comparable with other great European centres such as London, can claim to have in them more traces of the society which created and used them than any other type of human settlement. In the town we find evidence of local and long-distance trade, specialisation and technological advances, well-developed regulations governing all aspects of social and political life, and greater evidence of the religious aspirations of the population. And the best indicators of the fortunes of a city, of economic growth and decline, and often of the fears and ambitions of the people are the buildings which they erect. Today, the biggest acquisition most people will make will be their house; and it will be the object on which they pour most of their personalities, in decoration and construction. Their notions of privacy will be displayed in the height of walls with their neighbours, or the distance between houses; their idea of status by the size of their garage.

That towns are not only interesting, but actually beneficial and character-forming, was a view put forward with enthusiasm by London's two great observers of the medieval city: John Stow, who published his *Survey of London* in 1598, and William Fitzstephen, who wrote a description of his native city as a prelude to a life of St Thomas Becket about 1174. Not only is good behaviour called *urbanitas*, says Stow, but

. . . at once the propagation of religion, the execution of good policy, the exercise of charity, and the defence of the country, is best performed by towns and cities;

Property at Monkwell Street in the City, bequeathed by William Lambe to the Clothworkers' Company and surveyed by Ralph Treswell in 1612; from the planbook which still survives in the archives of the Company. The plan shows a variety of houses and the former chapel of the medieval Hermitage of St James. The city wall and corner-tower are still visible today in the Barbican estate.

1. Excavations on the site of the GPO Headquarters Building, Newgate Street, in 1976, within a hundred yards of St Paul's. The late Saxon and medieval church and graveyard of St Nicholas in the Shambles is under excavation.

and this civil life approacheth nearest to the shape of that mystical body whereof Christ is the head, and men be the members . . . and to change it were nothing else but to metamorphose the world, and to make wild beasts of reasonable men.

And whatever could be said of cities generally, could be said of London in particular. Fitzstephen opens his description with the words:

Amongst the noble and celebrated cities of the world, that of London, capital of the kingdom of England, is one of the most renowned, possessing above all others abundant wealth, extensive commerce, great grandeur and magnificence.

What was it about this city that produced such fierce civic pride? How did the Londoner regard his city? These are the questions we can ask of the evidence, both in the ground and in documents. Some elements in the world-view of the medieval Londoner, such as his belief in a mythical origin for the city, need not detain us long; but it is important to distinguish some of the underlying themes of our enquiry before we begin to untangle the evidence.

Old age bred respect; and old cities were to be honoured for their longevity. An important ingredient in the outlook of medieval citizens of London was a body of myths and legends about the city's origins and early history which had become woven into the fabric of urban life. Over the west gate of the city, Ludgate, stood statues of King Lud and his two sons [2]. Lud was supposed to have repaired the city in the years before the invasion of Julius Caesar. According to the chroniclers, Fitzstephen reported, London is even more ancient than Rome: both derive their origin from the same Trojan ancestors, but London was founded by Aeneas's

2. Statues of King Lud and his two sons, from the inner facade of Ludgate. Dating probably from the rebuilding of the gate in 1586, they were removed in the late 18th century and now stand in the porch of St Dunstan in the West in Fleet Street.

descendant Brutus, before Rome was founded by Romulus and Remus. Stow introduced his *Survey* with Geoffrey of Monmouth's calculation that the founding occurred in 1108 BC; but added carefully: 'herein antiquity is pardonable, and has an especial privilege, by interlacing divine matters with human, to make the first foundation of cities more honourable, more sacred and, as it were, of greater majesty'.

Certain buildings, particularly those which lasted several generations, assumed a spurious Roman antiquity in the popular imagination. It was common opinion that the Tower of London was originally built by Julius Caesar, its mortar tempered with the blood of beasts. Excavation for a chapel on the south side of St Paul's in 1316 produced a hundred ox skulls, confirming the contemporary view that the cathedral lay upon a Temple of Jupiter, and that there had been daily sacrifices. Some 'wise and learned men' connected this with ceremonies on the saint's day at the end of June in each year, when the priest of every parish in the diocese of London came to St Paul's, followed in procession by a fat buck whose horns were borne aloft on a pole.

Stow would not commit himself on whether he believed the mythic origins of London; it suited his purpose to use them to introduce London's undoubted great age. Other fables, about giants, he dismissed. But at the same time he could repeat, with simple faith, his father's story about ugly shapes seen in the steeple of St Peter Cornhill by a group of bell-ringers one night, and claw-marks three or four inches deep found afterwards, cut through the stones as if they were butter. To the medieval generations which preceded Stow the Virgin Mary and all the saints, as well as the Devil, were almost tangible forces at work in the city. There was a parish church on almost every street corner: one hundred and seven all told. A person walking across the city from Newgate to Aldgate, a distance of about a mile and a quarter, would pass the doors of sixteen of them. The churches are worth study because they took up much of the attention of the contemporary mind.

From its Saxon beginnings, the church provided its own leadership in the imposition of order in civic life and in the development of the city and its fabric. The various physical ways in which the two main groups of religious buildings – St Paul's and the monastic communities on the one hand, the parish churches on the other – moulded or affected the shape and appearance of the city will be examined throughout this book. Beyond the effects of being constantly surrounded by fine monuments, imagery, coloured glass and architecture which made the city a living pattern-book for English patrons and craftsmen [3], the citizen was moulded by the propagation of religion. The doctrine of God, says Stow, is more fitly delivered in towns, by reason of the frequent assemblies possible; by often hearing, men are better persuaded in religion, and because townspeople live in the eyes of others, they are by example more easily trained to justice.

Further: 'whereas commonwealths and kingdoms cannot have, next after God, any surer foundation than the love and goodwill of one man towards another, [these qualities] are also closely bred and maintained in cities, where men by mutual society and companying together, do grow to alliances, commonalities, and corporations'. There was a natural tendency in the medieval world to form groups in order to counter the problems of urban life, or improve it, and therefore to prefer the corporate to the

3. Fragments of stained glass from St Stephen's Chapel, Westminster, inserted in 1349–52. Some ordinary 'white' glass came from Chiddingfold in the Weald, from Shropshire and Staffordshire; coloured glass probably came from abroad.

individual. That is why one of the first steps in an investigation is to try to define the characteristics of these groups in society – their homes and places of work, their relationship with the religious organisations of their day, and the other physical trappings of their distinctive lifestyles.

Stow, however, does not finish here: only in peopled towns, he says, do the liberal sciences and learning of all sorts flourish – 'without the which a realm is in no better case than a man that lacketh both of his eyes' – and both manual arts and commerce have their origins in towns, thus producing the major share of wealth and riches. The needs of the poor can be easily assessed and relieved, and the towns are surer refuges in time of foreign invasion. In all these claims, except perhaps the last, we would think that there is no more than a grain of truth. More to the point is that development of the crafts and trade emphasised the inequality which was deeply rooted in men's minds. As towns, and especially a large and well-endowed town like London, took part in local and international trade, and as they developed markets or industries dependent upon distant materials, or upon trade with other towns, so the merchants who controlled foreign commerce rose in power and tended to control the community. In London, their houses were in the same class as those of the nobility, from whom they had often been bought. The 'more sufficient', the abler or more powerful citizens were the merchant aldermen whose authority grew largely from their wealth. They governed the city, and at the same time, as officers or senior members of their own trade guilds, saw that the organisation of industry dovetailed into their concept of the well-ordered city.

Even in Fitzstephen's day, the customs of the city, the largely unwritten laws, were probably already formidable in number, forming the backbone of urban life; ceremony not only bound men together, but reinforced the status quo:

I think there is no city in which more approved customs are observed – in attending churches, honouring God's ordinances, keeping festivals, giving alms, receiving strangers, confirming espousals, contracting marriages, celebrating weddings, preparing entertainments, welcoming guests, and in the arrangement of the funeral ceremonies and the burial of the dead.

The need for custom to be observed was a powerful force in the shaping of buildings throughout the medieval period, from the design of a company hall to the inability of a citizen to close up a door in his own house because it lay on the route taken by parishioners beating their bounds through the house.

We can suggest that the buildings of the city themselves, by their association with its institutions and customs, were instrumental in handing down certain traditions over the centuries, and that this in turn influenced the attitudes of its citizens to their world both inside and outside the city walls. This book will outline how this question can be approached through the records and fragmentary remains of its buildings.

First, we must begin with the existing medieval buildings, or fragments of them, which remain in the City. Their survival has been sorely affected by two devastations: the Great Fire of 1666 and German bombing in 1940–4. In between, and since, commercial redevelopment passed in wave after wave over the various parts of the city, so that buildings which escaped one phase of redevelopment were enveloped by the next. Almost all the medieval and Tudor masonry or timberwork now visible in the city has been greatly restored, but with great skill and respect. Each year archaeological work adds another unearthed portion to the catalogue of scattered fragments which may be inspected by the curious, the intrepid and the privileged. Some pieces lie in underground cellars or car parks, and others are in private possession; a summary is given in the map and gazetteer at the end of this book (see pp. 182–3).

The several timber-fronted buildings in and around the City – the frontage to Holborn of Staple Inn [4], Prince Henry's room in Fleet Street, the building above the entrance to St Bartholomew's churchyard at West Smithfield – are all virtually modern fakes, though sound enough in character. Staple Inn recalls many genuine late sixteenth-century buildings in its details, but there is no evidence that it was built to look as it does now, after restoration in 1894 and 1936; indeed, the evidence points to a more humble appearance (see below, pp. 154–5). The western suburb of the city, formed by Holborn and Fleet Street, is comparatively rich in old buildings despite severe war damage to almost every one: the halls of Staple Inn and Lincoln's Inn, Gray's Inn and Barnard's Inn, the Middle Temple and the Templars' church. To the north-east lie St Bartholomew's priory church and the Charterhouse.

All these buildings lay to the west and north of the area devastated by the Great Fire. Within the city walls, the same rule applies: with the

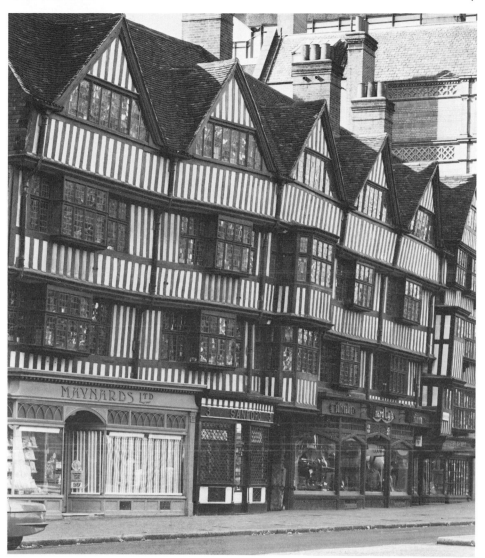

4. Frontage of Staple Inn, Holborn, built in the late 1580s, but completely restored in 1936. All the windows are modern reproductions of styles common around 1600. The buildings may not have had the close-set studs (vertical timbers) in their original form; only every fifth stud is pegged into the frame.

exception of Guildhall, medieval buildings survive only in the eastern third of the walled area, untouched by the Fire. Of the six pre-Fire churches in this district, two (St Olave Hart Street and All Hallows Barking) were badly bombed. As St Katherine Cree was rebuilt in 1628–31, the three remaining – St Ethelburga, St Andrew Undershaft and St Helen Bishopsgate – stand as precious intact remnants of the host of 107 churches which thronged London's medieval streets. Beyond the city boundaries, we shall examine the surviving portions of the priories of St Mary Overie in Southwark (now Southwark Cathedral), St John of Jerusalem, Clerkenwell, and the royal palace and abbey of St Peter at Westminster.

The great majority of these buildings have been recognised and discussed for many years. It was paradoxically the Second World War itself which generated the discipline of medieval urban archaeology which forms the second source of our information. Since the end of the seventeenth century antiquaries had been recording destruction or modifications brought about by redevelopment [5]; but the availability of large areas of blitzed rubble, and the extreme thoroughness of destruction from buildings built after the War, forced archaeologists to tackle the problems of urban excavation everywhere in the post-War years. Belatedly, resources came to hand. Following the creation of urban research and rescue units in towns such as Winchester, York and Lincoln, the Museum of London (at that time, the Guildhall Museum) set up the Department of Urban Archaeology in 1973.

Pre-Fire domestic and religious buildings have been excavated on a number of sites, especially where the survival rate was high on the waterfront. Inland early medieval buildings and rubbish pits have been recorded at Milk Street, thirteenth-century houses overlain by the gardens of the Greyfriars at the GPO Headquarters site, Newgate Street, and traces of undercrofts or stone buildings at Well Court (Bow Lane) and Lovat Lane. But the chief emphasis of archaeological study, at least since 1972, has been the waterfront zone south of Thames Street, which today runs a

5. Discovery of an undercroft dating to about 1300 at the junction of Leadenhall and Aldgate Streets in the late 18th century. The original floor is several feet below the accumulated (archaeological) debris. Drawn in 1784 by John Carter, one of the earlier antiquaries concerned with redevelopment in London.

short distance to the north of the present river along the entire length of the city's river bank. It is now known that the rising river, eroding and silting up the latest Roman quays, reached its furthest point northwards in the Saxon period, and from the tenth century, in areas around nodal points such as Billingsgate and Dowgate, wharves composed of narrow plots divided by fences began to push out into the river. This process is described in detail in chapters two to five. By the early thirteenth century buildings were appearing on the reclaimed land, usually at the street end, and in several cases adapting the underlying Roman riverside city wall as their frontage to Thames Street. On most waterfront sites these buildings can be studied until their violent demise in the Great Fire of 1666; in some cases the destruction wrought by the fire itself is graphically visible [6].

The archaeological study of buildings in London, which is just beginning in earnest, hopes to make its contribution by analysing the surviving physical evidence in the ground: floors, walls and foundations, cesspits and cellars, roads and wharves. Timber buildings leave few traces, but there may be evidence of posts driven into the ground, preparation of defined areas for flooring, or differences at the same level between 'interior' surfaces and rougher 'external' yards or alleys. From the thirteenth century timber frames were laid on low walls to counteract damp, and the raising of successive floor levels often kept these underpinning walls intact when the frame was eventually taken down and the building otherwise destroyed. Larger stone buildings such as churches and prominent houses had deep foundations, often three feet wide (a width demanded by the early thirteenth-century building regulations), and these naturally form the base of many rebuildings, each of which can be detected by careful survey. The walls are therefore described very carefully: is the stone in square blocks, laid with very thin joints (ashlar), or rough rubble poured into shuttering? Are the courses of equal height, or uneven? Are the corners stressed with larger blocks, and are there any decorative features such as bands of

6. A medieval building revealed by modern archaeological excavation: cellar of a 16th-century house in Lower Thames Street (New Fresh Wharf) in 1974. The building collapsed in the Great Fire, which started a hundred yards away in Pudding Lane, in September 1666. The collapse saved the pine flooring from destruction.

knapped flint or courses of roof-tile fragments laid between the stones? The wall or foundation might include reused Roman building material (such as Roman tile, and often, in early medieval buildings, stones from Roman buildings with the characteristic brick-speckled mortar still adhering to them); or moulded stones, taken from an earlier building, often the nearby parish church. The wall must be drawn in elevation at the scale of 1:10, and scrutinised for evidence of the tools used – marks of the axe or chisel – and possibly masons' marks. The stones will be sampled to find out, if possible, where they were quarried. Brick walls, which become common by 1500, are described in similar ways, but with special attention paid to the way the bricks are laid (bonding) or pointed; each style of bonding has its own life-span, and the method of pointing can provide further information about the wall or its immediate surroundings.

Timbers survive only in deep waterlogged deposits such as along the waterfront or in the valleys of streams now covered over by buildings; but they represent a wide variety of structures, such as wells, drains, wooden-framed buildings, bridges and quayside revetments. The timbers, carefully recorded, not only provide us with a corpus of medieval carpentry which has otherwise been almost totally lost in London, but individual timbers can be dated by dendrochronology (tree-ring analysis). If sapwood is still present on the timber the date of felling can be calculated; and this is usually very near the date of use. Thus structures or buildings can be given a date of construction from their timbers; and associated artefacts, such as the hundreds of objects in domestic rubbish dumps used to reclaim land behind each of the successive waterfront revetments, are arranged for us in dated groups.

What questions can archaeology answer? They concern the use of the land by different groups or individuals in society. Excavation can detect improvements in house form (such as stone houses with lavish under-crofts), as the city grew more urban in late Saxon and Norman times, or changes in diet as markets specialised, from the food debris left in rubbish- and cesspits. Other scrap may be from industrial processes, or the workplaces may themselves be excavated. Given the conservative nature of pre-modern planning, the skeleton of a town or an area within it – the walls, streams and roads – would change very slowly, but *land-use* might change comparatively quickly, as the area was subjected to social and economic pressures. A residential street might become a street of shops, an old house might be broken up into small tenancies or change into a factory. Only the larger buildings, often of more durable material such as stone, would preserve links with their former functions and surroundings. London has been used as a town by different peoples – Romans, Saxons, Vikings, Normans, and immigrants from many European countries, each with different notions of what constituted a city. And within each period, different groups used the land within the city boundaries for various military, religious, commercial, industrial or cultural purposes.

How did these various purposes fit together in the comparatively confined space of the town? Here archaeology can make a major contribution, for excavation and subsequent analysis of both buildings and finds can suggest how problems of organisation created by economic and physical growth were dealt with. The city authorities would in time provide drinking water, public privies and market spaces or buildings, at the same time removing noxious practices such as the slaughtering of beasts and leather-preparation to the fringes of the built-up area. It would order the clearing of debris from streets and watercourses, and make rules about the deposition of rubbish. In common with other major medieval cities of Europe, London had by the thirteenth century formulated building regulations which sought to improve standards of construction and prevent fires. This might be deduced from the archaeological evidence alone, but for London the availability of documentary records enables us to ascertain how far specific regulations were observed in practice.

The documentary evidence for medieval and Tudor London is vast. Scattered charters of the Saxon and Norman periods are supplemented from about 1250 onwards by the survival of many thousands of deeds and wills, especially a long series enrolled or copied in the main London court of Husting, and therefore called the Husting Rolls. The main documentary sources used in this book have been the city's administrative and judicial records, medieval building accounts (especially those in livery company records), plans of property owned by corporate institutions, wills and deeds (either selling or leasing property). Churchwardens' accounts and the cartularies (charter-collections) of religious houses with property in London fill out the picture.

The administrative and judicial records of the city are especially full after about 1300; from 1301 to 1437 survive the very important judgements of the *Assize of Nuisance*, in which the mayor and aldermen, informed in many cases by the specialist advice of appointed masons and carpenters known as viewers, decided in cases of complaint about building operations brought by one neighbour against another. In this way, the buildings of London, and their occupants spring suddenly to life: even within a single generation a prominent family might have several brushes with the law over its property in the city.

The functions of the four sworn viewers continued throughout the fifteenth century, though their judgements are found scattered through the records of cases heard in the mayor's court. Their actual reports are preserved for the periods 1509–53 and 1623–36. The cases are still concerned with boundary disputes or encroachments. The viewers occasionally put stones or stakes in the ground themselves to record an arbitration; in suburban Moor Lane, for example, they could use two elm trees as markers.

At the same time, the Repertories and Journals of the Court of Aldermen, the latter surviving from 1416, show the control by the Court of Aldermen and Court of Common Council of many other aspects of town life: trade and industry, hospitals and poor relief, markets and the Thames, water supply, sanitation and building. They were especially concerned with the state of the roads, the city wall and gates, and the prisons. They were careful, for instance, to instruct the alderman of Portsoken to set up a boundary stone to divide the bounds and liberties of the City from the shire of Middlesex. When Ludgate was repaired in 1585, the court ordered that signs on houses at the west end of St Paul's churchyard were to be taken down and rehung under the lower jetty, with stalls in front of the houses being only ten inches in front of their 'principals', i.e. the main timbers of the building; apparently the frontage was being cut back to give a proper view of the gate.

The next most useful sources of documentary information are records of
land-owning institutions. The richer craft guilds or livery companies
became, by the mid-sixteenth century, administrators of large amounts of
property; the Goldsmiths' Company had so much property that by 1478
they created a kind of Clerk of Works to supervise craftsmen carrying out
repairs. The company had its own builders' yard for materials and in 1496
even appointed an official carpenter, with seven pence a day and a house
rent-free. Several other companies appointed one of their wardens to collect
the substantial rents. In many cases the history of a specific property can
be reconstructed by correlation of city and company records, which often
include title deeds stretching back long before the company's acquisition of
the property.

Until about 1560 the onus for repairing, and even rebuilding, the
property generally lay with the landlord, and so building accounts often
survive in company records. They also survive when the company repaired
or rebuilt its communal buildings. A remarkable amount of detail can be
gleaned when a fastidious clerk has noted down payments for labour and
materials, often in an order which must reflect the progress of the work. In
1423, for instance, the Clerk of the Brewers' Company recorded the
expenses in converting houses at the company's gate into a block of
almshouses 'for poor brethren and sisters of the craft', together with the
repair of a tresaunce, or cloister (a covered way), between the kitchen and
the hall, retiling of all the buildings except the hall, the making of a
cupboard ('almarye') to stand in the kitchen and the construction of a
hen-coop in the yard. Here are some of the opening payments:

First, for sawing of diverse pieces of timber . . .   17d.
Paid to Jankyn Pekker, carpenter, for all the workmanship
  as in carpentry . . .   40s.
Item, for ale to the carpenters . . .   1d.
Item, for 400 oak laths at 8d. [a hundred]   2s. 8d.
Item, for 400 sap laths at 6d. [of inferior quality, taken from the
  outer sapwood of the tree]   2s.
Item, to Nicholas Fuller for 1½ lbs of iron, called Stiropes   4d.
Item, to Robert Cok, labourer, for ½ day in the breaking of a wall in the
  tenantry called the Alms House   1d.

Payments to other labourers follow. Walls of lath and daub were built,
and John Crowston (Croxton), then building Guildhall nearby, was paid
16d for 'four foot of hard stone, to be the foot of the door'. The freestone for
the sides of the door came from other masons. An old privy was cleaned out
and its plumbing serviced; the kitchen of the almshouse received new stone
paving and its chimney was refurbished with tile from Flanders. The future
inmates seem to have had individual chambers since there is much concern
over locks, bolts and keys for several doors; one chamber even had a lock on
its privy. The total cost of the works came to £10 2s 6½d, just over the £10
budget created by a bequest specifically for the purpose.

The final source for the reconstruction of the medieval and Tudor city is
cartographic and pictorial. From the mid-sixteenth century survive panoramas and bird's-eye views of the city, almost all from the south; the first
large-scale street-map of the city is by Ogilby and Morgan in 1677 (i.e.
after the Great Fire; see 124, 144). From the latter part of the century there
are also a good number of ground-plans of individual houses, made by

7. Watercolour by T. Shepherd of the hall of Crosby Place (1466) in the early 19th century. Being outside the area of the Fire, the medieval building survived to suffer drastic changes; a modern stair leads to a entrance in the oriel, from which another stair led to a mezzanine floor inserted just beneath the ornate roof (shown by the adaptation of the windows on the right).

surveyors for leasing or other legal purposes, or simply for record; the work of Ralph Treswell [118, 131, 132] between about 1585 and 1613 will figure largely in later chapters. In addition many old buildings were the subject of engravings, sketches or watercolours in the eighteenth and nineteenth centuries [7], usually on the eve of demolition. We owe the early antiquaries a great debt for making these records, for without them we would find it very difficult to visualise the buildings in three dimensions. Often, also, an engraving or picture is the vital link which brings together scattered pieces of evidence in other documents. At the same time we must tread warily, for artistic licence can alter the shape and even position of doors and windows, remove later accretions and 'restore' to a state of noble originality present only in the artist's mind.

The evidence, therefore, is of several different kinds: actual buildings, conclusions drawn from archaeological research, documentary sources, maps and plans. No one source is sufficient by itself. We must sift and compare, and sift again.

Roman and Saxon origins 50-1066

1

The City of London is nearly two thousand years old. That in itself is worth remembering as we start our enquiry. This book will deal mostly with the city between 1066 and about 1600, but before the entry of the Normans an introduction to the previous ten centuries is required; we must go back to the foundation of the city about twenty years after the death of Christ.

If balloons had been invented, and if we could have been in one high above the Thames, we would have seen the great river looping lazily to the sea through easily-flooded marshes. On the north side lies a gravel plateau, sporadically capped with a loess or silty clay. At the point where the plateau fades out and the marshes begin, a slight eminence is emphasised by the marsh on one side and a stream on the other, cutting a small valley down to the Thames. This is the place the Romans chose; they made approaches to it by building causeways over the boggy ground on the south side of the river. The eastern eminence is still called Cornhill, though much of the natural rise in the ground has been obscured. The stream, later called the Walbrook, still attempts to flow underground from Moorfields to Cannon Street, where its ancient valley causes the road to dip. Beyond lies a second hill across which the Roman town quickly expanded, to a further tributary stream we call the Fleet.

On this empty slate history has drawn, rubbed out and drawn again many times. The city of 1066 owed its form largely to three previous periods of occupation and their products: the more durable remains of the Roman provincial capital, the partial erasure of the Dark Ages, and the re-establishment of a very different city within the Roman hulk by Alfred and his successors.

Despite occasional prehistoric finds in and around the City of London, such as a single Bronze Age urn excavated on the site of the GPO Headquarters building, Newgate Street, in 1975, or a possible Iron Age burial of a young man found in the Tower in 1978, there is no direct evidence of settlement in the city before the Roman invasion of AD 43. This part of the Thames Valley seems to have been a comparative backwater in economic and political terms; the Thames itself probably formed a tribal frontier.

It is natural to think of London as central to the military conquest of the province. Certainly the roads which were quickly laid out to communicate between new fortresses and towns all led from the crossing over the Thames, a few yards downstream from the present London Bridge. But the establishment of the converging roads on the southern, Southwark, side can be dated only to about AD 50–65; absence of coins and distinctive pottery forms of the decade after AD 43 strongly suggests that London was not founded until about the year 50. There is moreover little evidence for a purely military foundation; there are very few relics of an invasion force. But there *are* roads and buildings, shops and houses laid out over an

8. The city wall at Tower Hill. Here the Roman work, albeit repaired in medieval and modern times, survives up to parapet level.

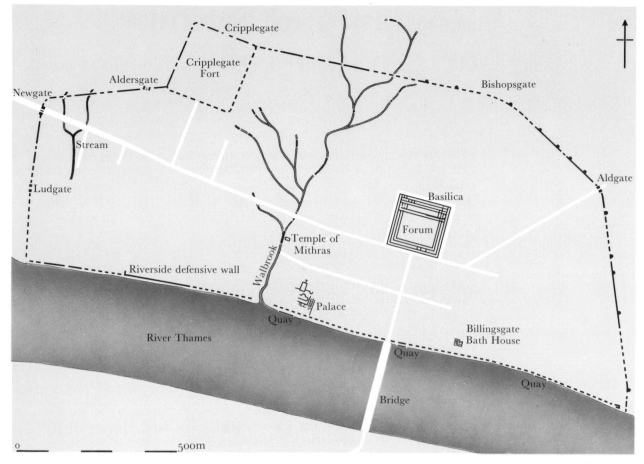

9. The main features of Roman London.

ambitiously large area. London may, therefore, have begun life as a port and trading centre of merchants and services both for the army and the new province.

London's history has been punctuated by a series of disastrous, widespread fires. The first, the only certainly malicious burning, occurred in the rebellion of Boudica in AD 61. In the rebuilding which followed London grew in status; over a period of forty years were built a forum and basilica, together with the provincial governor's palace, a stone-walled enclosure or fort to the north-west of the growing town, probably for the governor's staff and bodyguard, and in the early second century a second forum and basilica complex on the site of the first, but four times larger. A hundred years later the city received its first stone defences, a wall [8] with five (later six) gates.

These and the other public buildings of Roman London, such as temples, warehouses, and buildings for public entertainment, were constructed almost totally of stone and building tile. The city of London has no true building stones, for the subsoil is gravel or the tan-coloured loess called brickearth. The Romans were the first to import large quantities of stone, a cretaceous sandstone called Kentish Ragstone, from the Lower Greensand Bed, principally around Maidstone in Kent. It was shipped down the Medway and brought by river to the city; one of the barges, with a load probably for the early third-century city wall, foundered in the river at Blackfriars perhaps after a collision and was discovered there in 1962. The Roman method of construction was to build courses of squared ragstone on the outsides of the wall and fill in the middle with rubble and concrete. At intervals the wall would be brought to a level and the two faces tied together by double or triple courses of tiles. The Romans were expert tilers: in and around the city the earliest Roman strata are often found to overlie backfilled brickearth quarries, in the form of large shallow scoops in the ground. Recent tests show that the brickearth used in London's Roman tiles is identical to that on which they stand.

The second, much less durable but probably more widespread material available to Roman builders was wood and, in particular, oak. Most of the private houses, shops and inns of the port would have been timber-framed above stone, clay or tile footings. Occasionally, when fire debris is excavated, the burnt-out position of the frame can be seen holding together the wall of fired or partly-fired brickearth blocks [10]. Some indication of

10. Collapsed mud-brick wall, with spaces left by charred vertical timbers or studs, part of a Roman building destroyed by fire *c.* 125 AD. Excavated on the site of the GPO Headquarters, Newgate Street, in 1978.

the power of Roman engineering and building skill with timber has come to light recently in the excavations of the Roman waterfront. During the rebuilding after the destruction caused by Boudica in the late first century, the sharp slope down to the bridge was terraced for long distances along the bank; the hillside was squared up into a series of steps with walls and timber revetments. At the foot lay the quay, its front a timber wall composed of five tiers of squared oak trees, braced back with anchorbeams. Succeeding quays extended along the bank in both directions and out into the river by stages; Roman wharves have been traced from the south-east corner of the city (near the Tower) for a distance of three-quarters of a mile to the terracing below the provincial governor's palace, now beneath Cannon Street railway station. Fortunately the waterlogged conditions by the present river have preserved the timbers, their joints, marks and differences in details of construction [11].

11. The front of the early 3rd-century Roman timber quay, excavated at New Fresh Wharf, Lower Thames Street, in 1975. Five or six squared oak beams formed the quay-wall; the Roman river lay to the right. The post-Roman city was probably littered with such large timber structures. Scale is 0.5 m long.

Thus the Romans bequeathed to their successors a city of large stone buildings and monuments – how many we do not know – and timber constructions such as wharves, bridges and drainage schemes which would survive only if buried by enveloping silt. The majority of buildings would have been of much slighter construction, and could quickly decay or be dismantled. Within their houses, whether of timber or stone, the people of Roman London enjoyed a high degree of civilised comforts; mosaics were common [12], even within less substantial timber buildings, and there were bath-houses, especially on the slope above the Thames where springs issued out under the gravel and above the impermeable London clay. Decorated wall-plaster, imported marble, and window-glass were features of the better sort of buildings. To the Romans, the town and its civilising influences were a potent symbol of colonial authority; and the fortunes of towns mirrored those of the province as a whole.

12. Mosaic from a 2nd-century building excavated at Milk Street in 1977. It shows a stylised vase (cantharus) in a setting of round and square cable pattern. The areas of damage are caused by later pit-digging from a higher level, when the building had long been forgotten.

The two-hundred-year period after the Romans left London, and Britain, in 410 is the largest gap in the city's history. Information about the fate of other Roman towns in Britain is hardly better. Some scholars argue that towns did not last until the end of Roman Britain, and that, as markets and institutions, they were distinctly on the wane after 350. Perhaps the large fourth-century villas in the countryside offered the services of a town, such as centres for buying and selling produce, or luxuries like baths, and it is to these rural places that we should look to understand the structure of late Roman Britain. Others suggest, on the contrary, that many Roman towns were equipped to withstand the barbarian attacks of the fourth and fifth centuries, and that they did survive, often greatly changed, to become focal points in a new landscape.

In London there is contradictory evidence for the nature of the late Roman city. In the early 200s the emperor Severus, with an ambitious building programme which included the great city wall, temples, public buildings [13] and some of the grandest port facilities in north-west Europe, restamped London on the imperial map with an assurance of expectation which was not to be fulfilled. Inside the walls, traces of more everyday life are difficult to find. On several sites the desolate 'dark earth' more typical of the Saxon period (and described below, p. 23) is found to overlie buildings which did not survive long after 200, or were by then in decay. Others were already dismantled. There may have been fields, or market-gardening, within the great arc of the city wall. Down by the waterfront, which was silting up and was not being cleared, several houses

13. Early 3rd-century relief of four mother-goddesses, reused in the 4th-century riverside wall at Blackfriars. It probably comes from a complex of Roman public buildings in the south-west corner of the city.

near Billingsgate have shown signs of occupation possibly into the fifth century, but the associated bath-house was decaying, unused.

On the other hand, the inhabitants still buried their dead in traditional cemeteries outside the wall; third- and fourth-century burials were excavated, for example, beneath buildings of St Bartholomew's Hospital in 1979. Londoners were numerous enough, or frightened enough, to build a mile-long riverside city wall from Blackfriars to the Tower in the three or four decades after 350. This was a prodigious operation, involving piling on a large scale, and demolition of temples and monuments for their large blocks – often with sculptures or inscriptions on them – to act as foundations. The line of the wall ran between the quays on the south and the warehouses they served to the north; presumably there were gates or passages for communication, but none have yet been found.

These troubled times are also the likeliest date for the addition of interval towers, or bastions, to the landward city wall. Sites of thirteen bastions are now known [9]; they are so regularly spaced that an original group of eighteen can be suggested, guarding the eastern approaches to the city from the south-east corner of the defences to the boggy headwaters of the Walbrook, which probably formed a marsh as the stream was increasingly dammed up by the clogging of the culverts through the wall. The bastions share two building techniques with the riverside wall: a foundation raft of rammed chalk, and reuse of large sculptured blocks, taken mainly from prominent tombs in the cemeteries beyond. It is possible that the nearer parts of the cemeteries, perhaps crowded with monuments like Highgate cemetery today, had to be cleared to improve the field of fire from the walls and especially from the new towers, which were for bolt- or stone-throwing artillery. The western group of interval towers, which resume beyond Cripplegate, are probably medieval in origin; we do not know why the fourth-century builders stopped at Bastion 11, now under All Hallows London Wall church. Perhaps they thought the marsh of the upper Walbrook sufficient deterrent; perhaps the crisis they sought to prevent had passed.

London, despite barbarian pressures, seems to have remained Romano-British, for the *Anglo-Saxon Chronicle* records that in 457 the British fled there after being defeated by the Saxons at *Crecganford*, which is usually taken to be Crayford, in Kent. We next hear of London about 600, by which time the seat of power in south-east England lay in Kent, where King Ethelbert may well have been *bretwalda*, or chief king of the Saxons. Yet his court was fully imbued with the culture of the Franks, a people who brought their own version of sub-Roman living standards from northern France. The import of Frankish metalwork, pottery and glass was followed in the first half of the seventh century by the introduction of Frankish currency and thereafter Saxon imitations of coins. Old stone-walled Roman forts such as Richborough and Reculver, which have produced coins of this period, may have been used as open-air markets.

These hints are all we can assemble to make a picture of London at this time. The main Roman roads led to it; if the Roman bridge was still standing, it formed the only real crossing for miles. In the time-gap between the old city and the formation of the new, its walls provided a meeting-place of roads, refugees and traders.

Throughout this book, the continual influence of religious leaders in helping to create towns and erect their buildings will be stressed. The greatest of these formative acts was the establishment of a new Christian church in London by the missionary Mellitus in 604. The first St Paul's was established on the western hill, on or near the main Roman road leading out of one of the west gates, some distance from the great basilica of the Roman forum which no doubt still stood on the eastern hill. The original intention of this mission, sent from Rome by Pope Gregory, was to make London the seat of an archbishop (although in the event the archbishopric remained where it was first established, at Canterbury in Kent). This may imply that Pope Gregory knew London to be a centre of population. Popes have often been, by necessity, shrewd politicians, and the choice may have been helped by the existence in London of some kind of royal encampment, either of the East Saxons or of Ethelbert himself, to whom the East Saxons were subject. By 673–85 at least a hall for Kentish merchants is known in London, where transactions were overseen by the king's reeve or representative. On the other hand, it may be that Pope Gregory merely knew London to have been the major city of southern Britain in the Roman Imperial period.

During the two centuries after the foundation of St Paul's in 604, glimpses of London become clearer and a little more frequent. Gold coins, on Frankish lines, were in use by 640, inscribed LONDUNIV; in 672 a 'place where ships tie up' is mentioned opposite land on the south bank, probably in what was later to be Southwark. The energetic Bishop Erkenwald, who was later to be regarded as a saint and whose bones formed the greatest medieval tourist attraction to St Paul's, founded two important abbeys at Chertsey in Surrey and Barking in Essex. Possibly as early as the eighth century a church we call All Hallows Barking, because it belonged to Barking Abbey, was built on the crest of the slope above the silted-up

Roman quays in what is now Great Tower Street, in the south-eastern corner of the city. Its great age was made apparent only when wartime bombing disclosed an arch of reused Roman tiles on the south side of the church, which probably led to a side-chapel or *porticus* [14]. In the present first-floor vestry the original north-west corner of the church, also of Roman tiles, survives twenty feet above the ground. These form London's earliest post-Roman building fragments, and must act as representatives of other, lost early churches – the first St Paul's, of which nothing remains, and its possible companions in a rough line on or beside the Roman road which led westwards towards Ludgate: St Augustine Watling Street, St Gregory (later to form part of the west front of the medieval cathedral) and St Martin Ludgate, just inside the Roman west gate.

From the seventh to the ninth centuries London formed the principal outlet for various Saxon kingdoms to the economic empire of the Frisian

14. Arch of reused Roman tiles at All Hallows Barking, Great Tower Street, looking from the nave of the 8th-century church into the chapel, or *porticus*.

traders of the Low Countries; the economy of England was fuelled largely by cross-Channel trade. Wool from the midlands kingdom of Mercia must have entered international trade during the eighth century, and from at least 730 the port of London was probably controlled by Mercian kings. A reeve protected the royal interests in London, and a number of tax-gatherers collected royal tolls on ships.

The city at this period would have had four main components: a royal residence, a cathedral church, a small number of private estates of high social status, and a street market of traders both native and foreign. The royal palace, it has been suggested, may have lain within the walls of the Roman fort in the north-west corner of the defences. The west gate of the fort, now preserved beneath London Wall, was closed up with rubble sometime in the late Roman or Saxon period; the north gate survived to be known as Cripplegate, the 'low, cramped' gate (did it remain substantially Roman and gradually submerge?), by 1000. Excavation of St Alban's Wood Street, within the fort area, in 1962 found a first church of stone, certainly Saxon but not demonstrably of the eighth century (see 21); Matthew Paris, a thirteenth century monk of St Alban's Abbey, which the great Mercian King Offa (757–96) founded, believed that the London church adjoined Offa's palace.

Between Westminster and the City, Saxon farms of this period have been found, or suggested, at Whitehall, the Savoy, and Arundel House in the Strand. But within the city walls there is little significant archaeological evidence of buildings, plots, or even traces of settlement such as rubbish pits, before the ninth century. On many sites the entire Saxon period is represented by a thick layer of dark earth, sometimes with faint traces of occupation surfaces within it. On the site of the present new GPO Headquarters building in Newgate Street in 1975, for instance, 700 small stakeholes were found cutting down from somewhere in this deposit into the underlying Roman layers. The stakeholes were not in any perceptible patterns apart from occasional concentric configurations. The dark earth itself continues to frustrate analysis. At the sites where detailed examination has been possible, no patterns of gradual change in soil colour or concentrations of stones or pottery can be discerned. The layer is usually seen as a single deposit, containing late Roman material, the pottery fragments with well-rounded, abraded edges, and occasional Saxon finds. Preliminary results of soil analysis suggest it was homogeneous (i.e. not laid by natural actions such as wind), probably cultivated soil, and possibly ploughed – though this cannot have been during the first quarter of its gradual accumulation, because ploughmarks would have gone through to the underlying Roman strata. In part, no doubt, it represents rubbish disposal from a reduced community over a long period.

The enigma of the dark earth epitomises the problem of the nature of London in the two hundred years before Alfred. For Bede, writing in the 730s, London was 'a mart of many nations coming by land and sea'; its use as the principal port by the otherwise land-locked Mercian kingdom established its pre-eminence over seventh-century rivals such as Ipswich and Hamwih (the predecessor of modern Southampton). But the buildings of this formative period have still to be found. Largely they will already have been destroyed, for modern cellars remove between twelve and fourteen feet of the latest deposits, and on the majority of sites archaeologists lift the basement floor to find Roman buildings beneath. In the absence of hard evidence, we must again resort to surmise and speculation. Apart from the market areas such as Cheapside there can have been little pressure on space within the Roman walls. The layout of the holdings – the major ones called *hagas* or fenced enclosures, as in the case of *Ceolmundingchaga* not far from the west gate (probably Ludgate), granted by King Burgred of Mercia [15] to the bishop of Worcester in 857 – may have resembled contemporary rural villages such as that recently excavated at West Stow in Suffolk, where a number of timber halls were surrounded at a respectful distance by groups or rings of smaller sunken-floored buildings.

15. Coin of Burgred, king of Mercia 851–73, found in the Thames upstream of London. The use by Mercian kings of London made it an attractive prey to the Vikings in the mid-9th century.

From about 800 Mercia was being overtaken by the rising kindom of Wessex to the south; but potential rivalries were forgotten in face of a common enemy, Viking pirates, who in 842 raided Canterbury, Rochester and London itself, causing many casualties. After many campaigns of mixed warfare and negotiation, triumph and frequent setback, Alfred of Wessex ousted the Vikings from a fourteen-year use of London in 886. He probably restored the city in some way, as he restored Roman towns such as Winchester and Chichester, or laid out new towns such as Cricklade and Wallingford; but only recently have suggestions about the nature of his achievements been forthcoming.

No positively Alfredian alteration or restoration to the defences has been identified, though rough patching of the Roman wall at Cooper's Row, Tower Hill, preceding the twelfth-century work, has been attributed to him. Alfred's designs for the improved defence of his town-strongholds, or *burhs*, included a street running round and just inside the wall at the foot of the bank. This emphasised the military overtones of his town-planning, for it is a feature found in Roman forts, but not in Roman towns. An intramural street of this kind is still found between Aldgate and Aldersgate (now partly obscured by the post-War Barbican estate), and in the early medieval period it probably ran as far as Ludgate.

Reorganisation of Winchester in the late ninth century involved a new grid of streets, watercourses and the apportioning out of land in large blocks which varied in size. In London a grid of streets could be found to the east and south of St Paul's in the medieval period, but few of them can be traced back in documents before the twelfth or thirteenth centuries. When sampled archaeologically, the streets themselves are found to be severely damaged by the insertion of modern services such as gas, water or electricity. At sites alongside Milk Street and Bow Lane, however, buildings which must have lain along tenth- or eleventh-century predecessors of the modern streets have been found; and the general development of the grid may be dated to this period, perhaps as early as the last decades of the ninth century, on evidence from one of the grid-squares by the river at Queenhithe.

Here a 'mercantile shore' was promoted by two awards of land by Alfred to two leaders of the church who were engaged with him in an apparent programme of re-establishing towns as market centres. The awards can be shown to refer to the area north of Queenhithe, then called Etheredeshythe after Alfred's son-in-law Ethelred, who governed Mercia. Measurements are used to specify the ground in the first grant of 889, but roads evidently surrounded the plots in the second of 898/9, suggesting the establishment in the interval of streets [16].

The area around Billingsgate, which is first mentioned in about 1000, is now also producing evidence of the creation of trading installations to match this probable development of Queenhithe. At New Fresh Wharf (now St Magnus House), immediately upstream, excavations in 1974–8 provided evidence of tenth-century works. Some of the upper beams of the old Roman quay were removed, while others formed the basis of a new embankment of stones and timber. On this embankment boats would be drawn up; and stakes driven into the river silt at its western end suggest a jetty or access to the embankment through the ruined Roman riverside wall [17, 18].

The first mention of Southwark in about 915 suggests that the Roman bridge was reopened either by Alfred or his successor Edward. The main north–south route of Bishopsgate and Gracechurch Street, now bisecting instead of passing the Roman basilica and forum, would probably then be established, and with it a second grid of streets, of different proportions to the first, around the bridge-head and especially on both sides of the market of Eastcheap. Billingsgate would serve this market area as Queenhithe served the streets around West Cheap and St Paul's. That this development is of the ninth century has been strongly suggested by recent work on one side of Botolph Lane, near its junction with Thames Street, where part of the ancient lane has been destroyed for a modern office block. Several layers of compacted gravels, stones and cobbles formed the first road surfaces; the lower surfaces incorporated more reused Roman building material, the upper used increasingly more waterworn flint cobbles. Alongside the street three property plots could be discerned, though the excavation was only of small areas within them. Domestic hearths and ovens were found; the buildings' destruction debris suggested that the walls were of wattle and daub. A row of small timber buildings along the lane is indicated. The dating evidence suggests provisionally that the buildings are likely to be late ninth or tenth century.

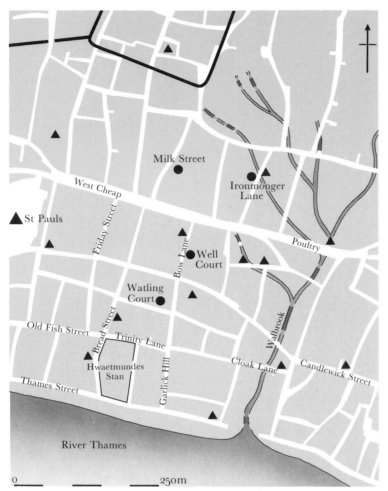

16. Medieval streets to the east and south of St Paul's. Some are 10th century in origin, others may be earlier.

● Excavated site
▲ Church known in late Saxon period

17. Partial reconstruction of the Saxon bank and stakes at New Fresh Wharf, with the 10th-century Graveney boat drawn up on it to show how it functioned. The stakes may have supported a jetty which led to the bank.

18. Grid of stakes placed around the Roman quay at New Fresh Wharf in the early 10th century (compare 17).

These developments are principally dated by associated pottery; and the study of Saxon pottery in London has only just begun, mainly owing to lack of material. Thus several Saxon buildings can only be safely placed in the late Saxon period (*c*.850– *c*.1100) or, slightly more precisely, to the ninth or tenth centuries. This problem means that the growing number of Saxon buildings found in London must be presented as a single group which ranges in date over 250 years. Such a grouping does however assist study of the building traditions they represent [19].

Three distinct types of domestic building are to be expected in late Saxon towns: 'sunken-floored', 'large-cellared', and ground-level buildings (i.e. without any sunken area). These types may reflect either different degrees of sophistication of construction, or three generally different functions for buildings; they do not yet indicate any sophistication of construction techniques over time.

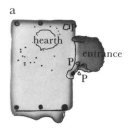

The simplest type, involving the least carpentry, is a rectangular hole in the ground with the ends, and sometimes the sides, retained by planks laid horizontally on edge, and posts to support the roof. These have been found on many Saxon sites in south-east England from the fifth century onwards, and have been interpreted most often as weaving sheds, from the presence in their destruction debris of clay loom-weights; but other functions suggested have included living houses, or when boarded floors occur at the sunken level, the cellars of houses; barns, byres, store-houses, bake-houses, industrial workshops or even loom-weight manufactories. A London example was recently excavated at Milk Street [19a]. Provisionally of ninth-century date, measuring 4.5 by 3 m (14¾ by 9¾ feet), it was sunk into the contemporary ground surface by at least 0.5 m (1½ feet), and was entered by a ramp down to a door from the edge of a still-used Roman street. Within the hut were stakeholes perhaps for furniture, though their positions were not in set patterns; a hearth and traces of planking near the threshold imply a floor and thus occupation at the lower level. Refuse accumulated in the hut to such a height that partial removal was necessary later to keep headroom and enable continued use. Related, and possibly slightly better, forms of this type have been found near Cannon Street and fragmentarily at Addle Street, within the Cripplegate fort area; both examples went out of use sometime in the late Saxon period. Another lay beneath the late Saxon church of St Mildred, Bread Street[19b].

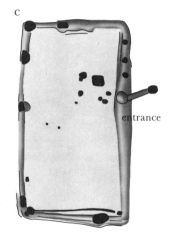

A second, more sophisticated form of cellar, generally of the tenth or eleventh century, covered a greater area. Examples are known from the commercial area around Cheapside in Cannon Street, and at Watling Court. Plank linings are held in place by posts set into a trench, which permits a greater accuracy in setting out. The best example, from the Financial Times site in Cannon Street, was 9.9 by 5.18 m (32½ by 17 feet) [19c] and possibly had a porch in the middle of the longer, southern side; it had gone out of use by the eleventh century. A cognate development which allowed even larger subterranean storage space involved placing the vertical posts or studs in a sill-beam; thus the building was truly timber-framed, like a large rectangular box let into the ground. This form is known possibly at Well Court, Bow Lane, and certainly across the street at Watling Court, where two examples were found. The larger [19d] was 15 m (49¼ feet) long and about 6.6 m (21½ feet) wide. The cellar it formed was at least 2.2 m (7¼ feet) deep, and it had a floor of planks on joists. Its smaller companion had two layers of plank lining, perhaps as insulation. These large-cellared buildings are generally to be found away from the medieval, and presumably late Saxon, street frontages, implying they were at the rear or in the middle of properties; perhaps their cellars were for storage of valuable commodities, or they supported timber buildings of higher status.

Ground-level buildings fall into two groups. Small ground-level structures have been found, or inferred, along Botolph Lane and along roughly

19. Four examples of late Saxon (*c.* 850–*c.* 1100) sunken buildings, from excavations at:
a) Milk Street
b) St Mildred Bread Street
c) the site of the Financial Times building, Cannon Street
d) Watling Court, Cannon Street.

the present line of Bow Lane at Well Court in the ninth century, possibly predating any Alfredian replanning. One building at Well Court may be a bakehouse. Tenth-century buildings overlay the dark earth at Milk Street and indicated the establishment of that street. In both cases a nearby Roman road was built over and forgotten. Grander structures are to be expected but, apart from traces of one on the GPO Headquarters Site in Newgate Street, have not been found. These buildings would be properly framed, with their sill-beams either laid directly on the ground or in trenches. Alternatively, the walling was of regular posts with panels of wicker and daub between, so that the building is only seen as a rectangular shape of dotted holes. These buildings may reach considerable lengths, and are sometimes aisled; they normally represent living accommodation, sometimes with a byre attached but more often not. Both types of ground-level buildings will have been greatly depleted by the ubiquitous digging of medieval pits and foundations along the same boundaries, whereas the lower parts of sunken buildings have at least a small chance of survival.

From a small number of widely-spaced sites in the city it now seems a fair conclusion that the tenth and eleventh centuries saw the laying out of several streets and the establishment of property boundaries which were to last throughout the Middle Ages. This is the case, for instance, along Thames Street near Billingsgate, where the stakes and bank of the ninth or early tenth century were overlain by a second embankment of timber and clay [20]; tree-ring analysis indicates this was roughly sixty-five years after the first embankment. It comprised at least five properties extending 20 m ($65\frac{1}{2}$ feet) into the river from the street, divided by fences and with slight differences in individual construction. Timbers from the boundary fences were cut down in 964 ± 9, 976 ± 9, and 1000 ± 9. This would imply wharves in the late tenth century, with boundaries which coincided with later medieval divisions between properties in the strata above, and in one case with an alleyway known from documents in the mid-twelfth century.

The larger estates of prominent individuals, implied in documentary references from the ninth century, now become identifiable in the eleventh. Street names and medieval house names recall both *hagas* (enclosures) and *burhs* (fortified residences). Recent work has unravelled the complex history of part of the Cripplegate fort area [21]. *Staeningahaga* can be identified with the parish of St Mary Staining, recorded in 1190, which overlapped the southern wall of the fort. Mentioned in Domesday Book (1086), it seems to represent the common practice of a manor (Staines) holding a town house or estate in the nearest urban centre. So also might *Basingahaga*, first documented in 1160–80, now represented by both the ward and parish of Bassishaw, which uniquely occupy exactly the same area, to the east of the fort. To stand by the ward notice-board in Basinghall Street today is to stand at the centre of this well-defined area, in Saxon times well away from the commercial centres of the city but near the possible site of the royal palace within the fort.

A third area of interest lies between, in the street called Aldermanbury, which, before the removal of its northern part after the Second World War, not only coincided with the east wall of the fort, but went past the site of the east gate. Before it was applied to a street, the name denoted a *soke*, or private estate, and a prominent tenement. In the medieval period the estate

had rights over the adjacent church of St Mary Aldermanbury (now a public garden), to which it was connected in 1347 by a postern door. Here the coincidence of the Roman gate (probably of stone), a notable late Saxon estate and a name meaning 'fortified residence of the alderman' is significant. We know that Edward the Confessor (1042–66) established a new royal palace at Westminster, possibly after a confrontation with the anti-Norman lobby among his earls in 1052 which involved him in embarrassing scenes in the city of London. Whatever connections Saxon kings may have had with the Cripplegate fort, Edward seems to have thereafter sold or granted away much of the fort site. Perhaps the internal south and east walls of the fort had already disappeared as effective defences. We can suggest that the eastern gatehouse survived to form the nucleus of a reduced official residence for the alderman, a royal official representing the king's interests in the city. When the first Guildhall was established in the twelfth century by the leaders of the wards, themselves called aldermen, a new site was found, a short distance away to the south-east.

The origins of the ward and the parish, units of organisation at the local level of secular and religious life respectively, are probably to be found before the Norman Conquest. There were twenty-four wards until Farringdon was divided into its present two parts in 1394. Except for the eastern side of the city, where Portsoken may represent an earlier defensive or administrative unit outside the wall, the wards of the outer areas lapped over the wall and gates for which they had to provide watchmen. Within

20. Tenth-century land reclamation and/or wharf construction at New Fresh Wharf: the stakes shown in 17 and 18 were overlain by logs, stones and earth to form an embankment upstream of Billingsgate, which is first mentioned c. 1000.

the walls, the wards were arranged around principal streets, as some of their present names show; the Walbrook stream, cutting the city into two almost equal halves, was used to divide them into two administrative groups from at least the thirteenth century. Its smaller contributory channels defined parts of the boundaries of seven wards as it flowed to the Thames; in the north of the city few houses can have been far from one of its streams.

Parish rights – for a priest to baptise, bury and to gather financial support (tithes) from a local community – became fully defined in London by 1200. Some churches began as chapels to the larger estates, whether *hagas*, *burhs* or sokes. Others began as neighbourhood churches, and can be found at crossroads. Yet others were founded by groups of tradesmen or merchants. Parish boundaries often ran along the backs of properties which fronted on to separate and parallel streets; occasionally a parish boundary can be shown to follow an old Roman wall or even a submerged Roman street. At Lambeth Hill, for instance, the boundary between the parishes of

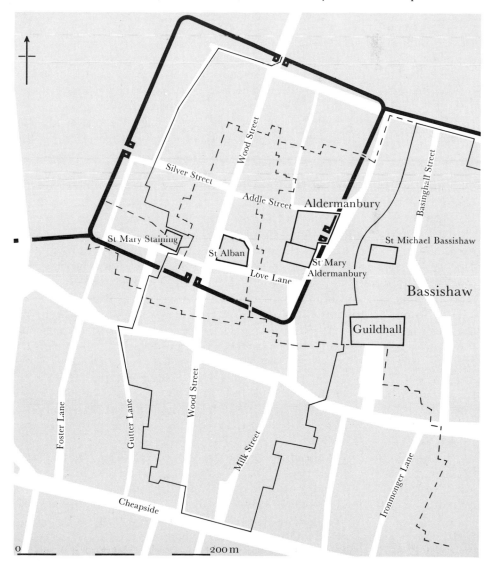

21. Medieval topography of the Cripplegate fort, Aldermanbury and Guildhall. Addle Street sweeps north to avoid the urban estate called Aldermanbury, which lies over the east gate of the Roman fort. Today the site of the fort is sliced in two by the post-War London Wall carriageway.

St Mary Mounthaw and St Mary Somerset, established as late as the thirteenth century, was made along a length of Roman walling which may well have been still visible above ground.

By 1300 the existence of nearly all the 107 parish churches in London is known; the origins of 10 have been sought archaeologically, and in nearly every case remains dating to before the Conquest have been found [22]. Although some Saxon churches, like St Andrew Holborn mentioned in a charter of 959, were of timber, the excavated examples have been stone structures. In London there was much Roman building material, chiefly ragstone and tile, available until the twelfth century; but there was also a thriving stone industry in southern England by the late Saxon period, with coastal transport from the Isle of Wight and bulk overland transport for up to seventy miles. The main Saxon building stones of the south-east were, as in the medieval period, limestones and sandstones, and there is much evidence of careful quarrying and skilful selection. Saxon walling is usually uncoursed, or occasionally coursed, rubble, but ashlar walls are known, with blocks weighing up to a ton, implying sophisticated lifting gear. Semi-circular arches would have needed timber centring, and traces of scaffolding can sometimes be found in the wall fabric. Unfortunately, apart from the arch at All Hallows Barking, no pre-Conquest church fabric in London has been recorded above ground. Only the outlines of the churches can be discerned from their foundations.

Study of these small neighbourhood churches can tell us much about the communities they served. The church is nearly always the oldest building in the locality which can be identified from records; its site is often the best preserved, the older parts encapsulated within the later church. The situation of a church in a certain place indicates that there was a local community to serve either before or shortly after its foundation. Thus if we could find out the date of origin of the three churches dedicated to St Botolph which still lie outside London's gates, we would have a clue to the date of development along the suburban roads in the late Saxon and early medieval period. Similarly, the positions of four churches south of Thames Street (see 23) are of great interest. The first references to each of the four date from soon after the Norman invasion. They were located close to the sites of eleventh-century embankments discovered at Dowgate, near the pre-Conquest establishment of foreign merchants, and between the bridge and Billingsgate, which reinforces the suggestion that large-scale encroachment into the river had taken place at these points by the late eleventh century.

By 1000 London was uniquely powerful among English cities.. The revival of the port over the previous three hundred years had helped reopen regional and international trade routes. Its connection with the royal court and cathedral provided a wide market for surplus commodities, particularly luxuries. Foreign dignitaries and ambassadors passed through the port; the Icelandic poet Gunnlaug, for instance, visited Ethelred's court twice, apparently in 1001 and 1003–4. On the first occasion he and his companions disembarked at London quay, where the port regulations of the time reveal a bustling international trade:

If a small ship came to Billingsgate, one half-penny was paid as toll; if a larger ship with sails, one penny was paid. If a barque or merchantman arrives and lies there, fourpence is paid as toll. From a ship with a cargo of planks, one plank is given as toll. On three days of the week toll for cloth is paid, on Sunday, Tuesday, and Thursday. A merchant who came to the bridge with a boat containing fish paid one half-penny as toll, and for a large ship one penny. Men of Rouen who came with wine or blubber fish paid a duty of six shillings for a large ship and 5% of the fish. Men from Flanders and Ponthieu and Normandy and the Isle of France exhibited their goods and paid toll, as did men from Huy, Liège and Nivelle [Flanders] who were passing through London. And subjects of the Emperor who came in their ships were entitled to the same privileges as ourselves; besides wool which had been unloaded and melted fat they were also permitted to buy three live pigs for their ships . . .

It was this cosmopolitan wealth which no doubt drew the attention of the Vikings once more. In 980, Viking fleets resumed their coastal raids and in 982 London was burned; attacked again in 994, it became the target for sporadic raids until Swein of Denmark came in earnest in 1013. The forces of Ethelred II, the 'Unready', at first resisted attack, but later in the year submitted, and Ethelred fled to Flanders. After Swein's death in 1014 Ethelred joined with Olaf, the future saint and king of Norway, and together they sailed to retake London. *Olaf's Saga*, though possibly embroidered in detail, tells how the Danes had made great fortifications around Southwark:

. . . and built inside them walls of wood, stones and turf [compare 20], and there had a large force. Ethelred caused a fierce attack to be made on it; but the Danes defended it, and the king could not capture it. There was such a broad bridge across the river between the city and Southwark that wagons could pass each other on it. On the bridge were bulwarks which reached higher than the middle of a man, and beneath the bridge piles were driven into the bottom of the river.

Olaf's forces covered their ships with hurdles against missiles from the bridge, rowed up under the bridge:

. . . and tied ropes around the supporting posts, and rowed their ships downstream as hard as they could. The posts were dragged along the bottom until they were loosened from under the bridge. As an armed host stood thickly on the bridge and there was a great weight of stone and weapons upon it, and the posts beneath were broken, the bridge fell with many of the men into the river; the others fled into the city or into Southwark.

The triumph of Ethelred and Olaf was short-lived; Ethelred and his son Edmund were gradually out-manoeuvred by Swein's son, Cnut. In 1016 Ethelred and then Edmund died; resistance collapsed and Cnut exacted an enormous tribute from the country, of which London paid one-eighth.

Evidence of the second Viking occupation of London during the reign of Cnut (1016–35) is very scarce. There had probably been peaceable Viking influences at work over the previous century; from the late tenth century comes a reference to a well-established court for testing silver in London, called the *Husting* ('indoor court'), a Scandinavian term. A sprinkling of church dedications to St Olaf show that the city's friend of 1014 was not forgotten; the five churches in the city and one in Southwark which bear his name must date from at least the middle years of the century. London probably absorbed the new invaders as one of many foreign elements; meanwhile Saxon life went on around them [22].

From this city (see 23), in October 1066, the new king Harold II and a rapidly-collected army issued forth to meet another invader, Duke William of Normandy. A few days later, the survivors struggled back in disarray. One account of the battle implies they were so ill-equipped they had taken

22. Two examples of sepulchral sculpture from 11th-century London. *Above:* the famous Viking tomb-stone found in the south-east corner of St Paul's churchyard in 1852. It marked the grave of a Viking buried about the time of the death of Cnut in 1035. The runes along the edge read: *Ginne had the stone laid and Toke . . .*
Below: fragments of a Saxon stone cross built into later medieval walling at All Hallows Barking, revealed by bomb damage, which are now on show in the church crypt. The sides (*left to right*) show Christ in Majesty, St Peter and St Paul, a man named Werhenworrth and a Saxon cable pattern. This free-standing cross, perhaps a grave monument, would have stood near the church, and is rare evidence of a school of sculptors in 11th-century London, only slightly influenced by Viking fashions.

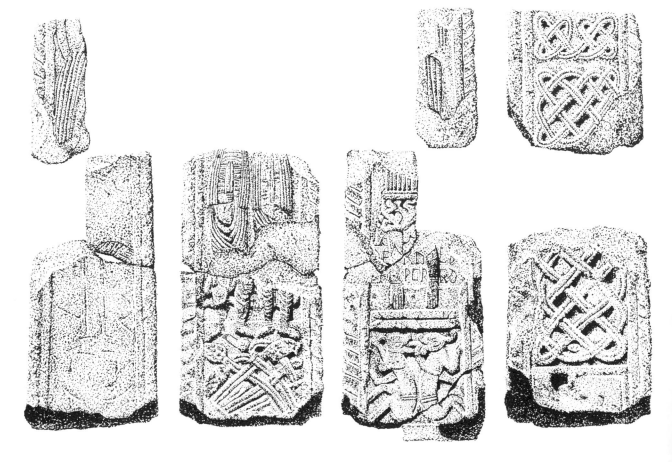

23. London on the eve of the Norman conquest, showing known features, and sites of recent excavations mentioned in the text. There were probably more churches than those known to exist.

window-shutters as shields. In London they were at least safe, as the mid-twelfth-century *Song of the Battle of Hastings* testifies:

London is a great city . . . richer in treasure than the rest of the kingdom. Protected on the left side by walls, on the right side by the river, it neither fears enemies nor dreads being taken by storm. The obdurate people conquered in battle sought this place, believing that in it they could dwell for a long time masterless . . .

But William knew he had to have London in order to win the country. He took it by diplomacy heavily tinged with threat, and lost no time in clamping down on 'the vast and fierce populace'.

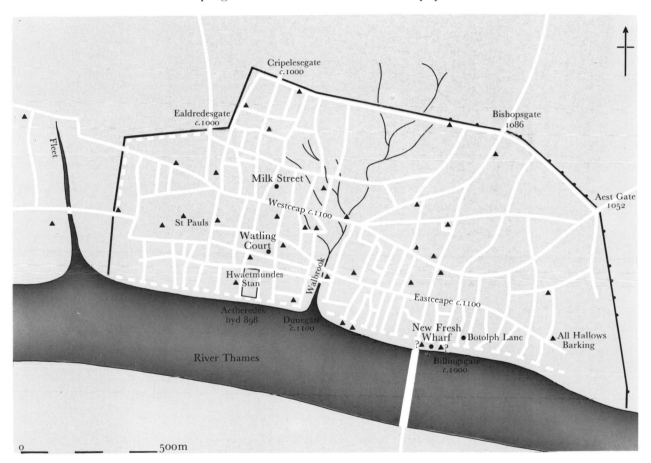

● Excavated site
▲ Church known in late Saxon period

Norman London 1066-1200

2

In 1066, the city of London was already a thousand years old. Romans and Saxons, and possibly even Vikings, had contributed to a conglomerate townscape of different shapes, sizes and materials. By comparison, Norman development came with a rush; in the century and a half following the Conquest, London received three castles, a new cathedral, several large monastic houses and numerous hospitals, priories and nunneries. Each was a major undertaking which had a lasting effect upon its surrounding topography. As a group, these monumental buildings underlined the Norman determination to dominate and endure, for they were largely of stone. Outside the city at Westminster William Rufus built a great stone hall for his seasonal palace, next to the church of St Peter, where henceforward kings were to be crowned. Though the Norman kings, like their Saxon predecessors, governed while being continually on the move, rather than from fixed places – the seat of government was where the king happened to be – the royal palace at Westminster gradually began to house the more elaborate organs of government such as the Exchequer and other judicial courts, and assumed a continuity of use which became permanent in the reign of Henry III in the thirteenth century.

Norman architecture, like Norman politics, reflects a union of church and state. William's invasion of England, blessed by the Pope, was a holy war. Castles and greater churches shared a style of architecture called Romanesque which spread over all Europe: solid, overpowering, and thick. The establishment of monasteries, like that of castles, was often a political act, and the treatment of London should be seen against the background of the Norman kings' attitude to towns elsewhere. Like the Romans, and like Alfred, the Normans appreciated that the founding of towns could be an instrument of government. In the forty years after the Conquest, therefore, the Crown 'planted' towns throughout the country. The majority were established under the shadow of a castle; in other cases (as at Battle or St Albans) the town was allowed to grow at the door of a major monastery. In existing Saxon towns such as Norwich, Bury St Edmunds or Oxford, the buildings of the new overlord, whether religious or secular, were imposed upon existing street-patterns, often resulting in the destruction and clearance of previous housing. William's attitude to London was the same; its commercial and political strength, drawn from its national and international status, had to be contained.

In 1077 occurred one of London's most serious conflagrations; there would be much waste ground when in the next year Gundulf, Bishop of Rochester, arrived to supervise the building of the White Tower [24, 25]. By analogy with other keeps planted in former Saxon towns, we might expect traces of previous buildings to have been found in the many modern excavations within the Tower, but so far there have been none. The new keep, a fortress based ultimately on the castle-palaces of the Norman dukes

24. The chapel of St John in the Tower of London, dating from the late 11th century. The chapel forms a semicircular projection at the south-east corner of the fortress, as in the larger keep at Colchester.

of the tenth century, was of a size not seen before in this country. It dominated the river and the city, lying in the south-east corner of the defences, and at first contained by the Roman wall and its bastions. Ninety feet high, it had foundations up to 26 feet wide. Above the basement vaults, the rooms of the castle were on two floors; on the lower, entered from a timber stair at the point used today, lay a large guard-room, a chamber, and a crypt below St John's chapel (for the use of the garrison), and, above, a two-storeyed hall, a great chamber and the chapel [24], with a gallery running round all three. Both hall and chamber had privies, hidden in the thickness of the walls. South of the keep lay the bailey with its service buildings, at first defended on the city side by a ditch; but by 1097, when the Tower was approaching completion, the Anglo-Saxon Chronicle reported that 'men from many shires in fulfilling their labour service to the city of London were oppressed in building the wall around the Tower'.

The Tower was both a royal palace and a protection for London against invasion, for the threat of Danish attack was still potent. The design was copied at Colchester, where the castle keep is even larger, but stone keeps did not become widespread until the following century. The English citizens of London must have regarded it with fear and astonishment, visibly dominating their city and controlling the access to the sea.

At the western end of the city, matching the position and effect of the Tower at the eastern end, lay two smaller castles, probably also William's foundations: Baynard's Castle and Montfichet's Tower. Both lay within the area later given for the building of the Blackfriars' friary, and so their precise sites are not known, although suggestions can be made [26].

Castle Baynard preserves the name of Ralph Baignard, a major tenant in eastern England in 1086, whose seat was at Little Dunmow in Essex. A castle seems to have existed in the western part of London by 1087, when a serious fire which burnt 'the palatine tower in the west' is recorded. The soke, or area of private jurisdiction, of the castle was said in Edward II's reign to be co-terminous with the parish of St Andrew (also known in the medieval period as St Andrew Castle Baynard, now by the Wardrobe). We know from deeds that the castle lay within Ludgate and south of Ludgate Hill, and in about 1114 Henry I granted to Richard, Bishop of London, as much of the ditch of 'my *castellum* on the south side [of St Paul's] as was needed to make the [precinct] wall of St Paul's, and as much of the ditch as was required for making a way outside the wall, and, on the north side of the church, as much as the bishop destroyed of the same ditch'. This indicates that the south-west corner of the precinct of St Paul's was formalised, or extended, along the ditch of the castle. The reference to a continuation of the ditch on the north side of St Paul's does not seem to fit until we realise that an ancient stream flowed across Newgate and what is now Paternoster Square in a southerly direction. It was open in the Roman period, and must have been also in the late Saxon or early medieval period, since it coincided with a ward boundary for a considerable distance. The stream has been traced south of Ludgate Hill, and was aiming for an exit point into the river at Puddle Dock. It seems possible that this stream bed may have contributed to a defensive ditch of a castle which lay between St Andrew's Hill and the city wall to the west.

Another shred of evidence can be gleaned from the earliest scaled street map of the city, drawn by John Leake in the days after the Great Fire of

A Doctor Vsher, Lord Prima
te of Ireland,
B the Sherifes of London,
C the Earle of Strafford,
D his kindred and friends.

25. The White Tower, as
seen by Hollar in 1641 at
the public execution of
the Earl of Strafford
(*right*). The Tower is
shown with its original
windows, before the
restoration of the late
17th century. The onion-
shaped turret caps of the
16th century (which
survive) replaced earlier,
conical structures.

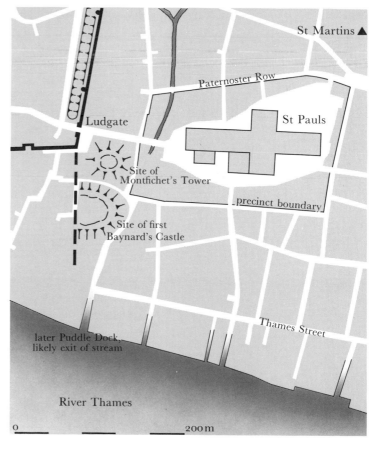

26. St Paul's and its surroundings in the
13th century, showing suggested sites for
the first Baynard's Castle and
Montfichet's Tower.

1666. In the area of interest the junction between what are now St Andrew's Hill and Carter Lane is rounded on the west side. It is the most circular corner in the whole map. In a town such as Southampton or Oxford a curving street like this would have a clear message: it followed a castle defence, either a bank or a ditch or both. We can suggest that this is the most reasonable site for the bailey of Baynard's Castle, its moat fed by the stream to the north. The castle was rendered unusable by King John in 1212 and the Blackfriars seem to have removed any previous buildings when they built their church on the suggested site of the motte.

Into the space left between Baynard's Castle and Ludgate must be fitted another, smaller fortification known as Montfichet's Tower. William de Munfichet was a witness to Henry 1's charter to London between 1108 and 1122, and the tower existed before 1136, when its lord was concerned in a plea over rights on the Thames. A poem of 1173–4 mentions it being strengthened in the rebellion at that time. It may be the 'old and ruined tower' lying between Ludgate and Castle Baynard in 1272, and it was certainly transferred with the Castle in 1275 to the Blackfriars. If the suggestion for the site of Baynard's Castle is accepted, then Montfichet's tower must have lain in the space west of Creed Lane, in the north-east corner of the Blackfriars' precinct. Unfortunately there has been little modern excavation in any part of the Blackfriars precinct.

Before turning to the major churches of Norman London we must continue westwards, beyond the city, to look at the largest complex of Norman buildings: the palace and abbey of Westminster. The origins of the place are wrapped in mystery, confused by the strenuous efforts of the medieval monks to claim as their founder first King Sebert in 604 and then the legendary King Lucius of Roman times. Certainly the church lay on an island called Thorney, surrounded by two mouths of the Tyburn stream. According to a writer of about 1075, this meant that at the consecration in 604 tents had to be pitched half a mile from the church. The abbey was either founded or refounded by Offa, in the eighth century; about 959 King Edgar gave a piece of ground which may be the basis of Scotland Yard, near the abbey, to Keneth, King of Scotland, so there may have already been a close royal connection by this time. The abbey was certainly the burial place of Harold 1 in 1040, his body being brought from Oxford where he died. Edward the Confessor presumably had this connection in mind when he began to make there his own mausoleum, a new abbey in the Norman style in about 1050–65 [27].

Of the church nothing survives, but details can be gleaned from small excavations, from contemporary descriptions and from the representation on the Bayeux tapestry. It derived its style from Romanesque architecture in Normandy and was probably related to the (? slightly later) abbey at Jumièges. The grand scale of the church reflected the prestige and resources of the late Anglo-Saxon monarchy while its style shows the influence of Norman culture even before the Conquest. It is a shame we cannot compare its details more closely with the other great Norman churches of London. Of the monastic buildings of Edward or his Norman successors there remain parts of the dormitory with the undercroft beneath, of the reredorter and latrines, and of the refectory. Arches along the dormitory wall featured alternating blocks of deep yellow sandstone and chalk, similar to others in William Rufus's Westminster Hall.

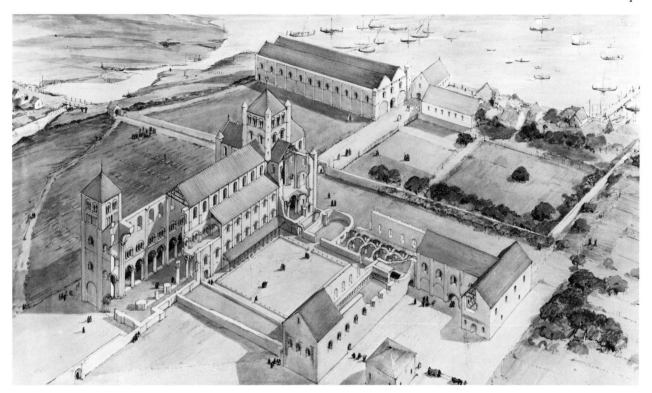

27. Reconstruction of Westminster Abbey in the late 11th century by Richard Gem and Terry Ball. It is based on surviving fragments, excavations, descriptions and comparative material. Beyond is an impression of the late Anglo-Saxon palace, and a reconstruction of the Hall built by William Rufus. These buildings give some idea of architectural style in and around late Saxon London.

Alongside his abbey, Edward the Confessor built a palace. Rufus rebuilt the hall in the 1090s; it was the largest of its date in England, and possibly in Europe, being 240 feet long and 67 feet 6 inches wide. The king thought it 'too big for a chamber and not big enough for a hall'. The rebuilding by Richard II in 1394–1402 which produced the present hall heightened and remodelled the walls, but much of the walls and windows of the Norman hall remains in the later masonry. Twelve bays were lit by Romanesque windows in an arcaded wall gallery which ran round the building; the roof was probably supported on timber or stone pillars, dividing the hall into either two or three aisles. The building is slightly bow-sided, like earlier great timber halls such as that of the Saxon kings at Cheddar. The two side walls are also, bay by bay, slightly out of line with each other; this implies the new building was set out around an existing hall which was only dismantled when the new one was complete. Nine sculptured capitals from the palace, possibly from the hall itself, were found in 1835 built into the later medieval fabric, and are now on show in the Jewel Tower nearby. To the south of the hall lay other buildings, of which traces survived to the nineteenth century. A smaller hall, later the Court of Requests, is known from at least the mid-twelfth century, and may be earlier; projecting at right angles from its southern end, bordering the river, was a third, smaller chamber (later the Painted Chamber of Henry III) and probably a chapel on the site of the later St Stephen's, also lapped by the Thames. Secure in his semi-rural palace, the king could warily contemplate the city downriver – a view then, as now, dominated by the cathedral church of St Paul.

Before the Norman Conquest, the successive Saxon cathedrals of St Paul, expanding from the tiny church of Mellitus (and all now equally without trace or record), must have been the most imposing stone buildings in the city. By 1087 the royal emphasis had moved to Westminster; and considerations of rivalry and a wish to re-assert pre-eminence may not have been absent from the motives of Bishop Maurice, who began a total rebuilding of St Paul's in that year. Though he was bishop for another twenty-two years, he saw only the laying of the foundations and completion of part of the work; it was still in progress even in 1136, when one of the periodic serious fires provided a further setback.

The Norman nave survived until the Great Fire of London, though it was by then in serious decay. Wren, reporting on the possibilities of restoration to a committee just before the Fire, said:

... the work was both ill design'd and ill built from the Beginning: ill design'd, because the architect gave not Butment enough to counterpoise and resist the weight of the Roof from spreading the Walls: for the Eye alone will discover to any man that those Pillars, as vast as they are, even eleven Foot diameter, are bent outwards at least six inches from their position. This bending of the Pillars was facilitated by their ill Building, for they are only cased without, and that with small stones, not one greater than a Man's Burden; but within it is nothing but a Core of small Rubbishstone, and much mortar, which easily crushes and yields to the weight.

He is describing the usual Norman method of building pillars, which led to several major collapses among large churches in the ensuing centuries.

The cathedral had been surveyed by Hollar a few years previously [28–29]. The effect of the enormous eleven-bay nave can now be appreciated only by combining Hollar's print [29] with details from other large

28. Ground-plan of medieval St Paul's, surveyed by Hollar in 1665. Compare 29, 42 and 65.

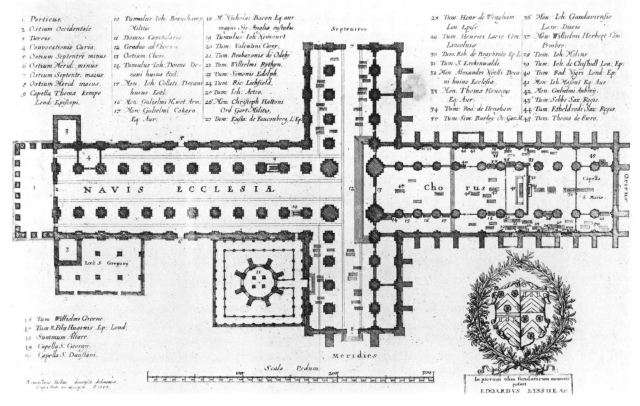

NAVIS ECCLESIÆ CATHEDRALIS   S. PAVLI.
PROSPECTVS   INTERIOR.

29. Nave of St Paul's, by Hollar (1656). The style is of the 12th century; most of the work probably dates from after the fire of 1136.

Norman churches which have survived in London and elsewhere. The arches were recessed in two rings or *orders* as at St Bartholomew the Great, Smithfield; the piers were basically cruciform and enlivened with attached columns, resembling those in the nave of Peterborough Cathedral. The Norman choir did not (or could not) extend as far eastwards as the thirteenth-century replacement, for Wren found a row of nine wells beneath the later choir which strongly suggested a north-south street incorporated into the body of the church only in rebuildings of 1255. A reconstructed section of the choir by Edmund Ferrey [51] suggested that four bays of a Norman crypt survived to support the thirteenth century choir.

A short way down Cheapside Bishop Maurice would have seen another remarkable new building; for about this time, and probably during the primacy of Lanfranc (1070–89), the Archbishop of Canterbury was establishing St Mary le Bow as his administrative centre in the heart of the city. The crypt, beautifully restored, survives beneath the Wren church; it comprised a nave and two aisles [30]. The nave was subdivided into three bays separated by circular columns, of which three survive, with cushion-capitals. The side walls, with some diagonal tooling and wide joints between the stones, give a good idea of Norman work at its best. The nave roof was rebuilt in brick by Wren, but the vaulting of the north aisle is original, showing that the whole crypt was vaulted in stone. Some of the arches leading from the nave to the aisles use Roman bricks, which is hardly surprising for the late eleventh century. In the north wall are four filled-in original round-headed windows, and in the north-west corner the remains of an original stair-turret. The crypt is now below street level, but would have been almost at ground level in the eleventh century; recent excavations in Bow Lane to the south, at Well Court, confirmed that the early medieval street level must have lain only a foot or two above the level of the crypt floor.

Even nearer St Paul's, just outside St Paul's gate at the west end of Cheapside, lay a third important religious establishment which today is remembered only by a street name: St Martin-le-Grand. This was a royal chapel founded, or refounded, in the reign of Edward the Confessor; around it, as at Westminster, the fugitive found sanctuary from pursuit by civilian law. It was in a large area between Foster Lane and a boundary wall to the west of the present St Martin-le-Grand; curiously, this street ran through the precinct to Aldersgate. In 1818 the houses to the west of Foster

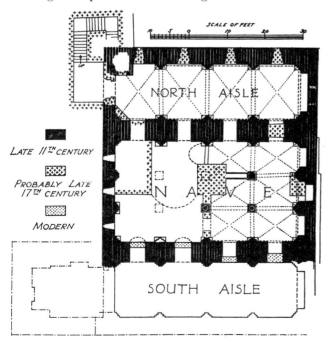

SCALE OF FEET

LATE 11ᵀᴴ CENTURY

PROBABLY LATE 17ᵀᴴ CENTURY

MODERN

NORTH AISLE

NAVE

SOUTH AISLE

30. Plan of the crypt of St Mary le Bow, Cheapside, by the Royal Commission on Historical Monuments in 1929. Post-war reconstruction has opened up the south aisle, and a spiral stair was found in the north-west corner in 1959.

Lane were being cleared when two connected undercrofts were discovered. The smaller, eastern crypt was of the thirteenth century, but it was evidently an extension of a much larger structure which in many respects resembled the crypt of St Mary le Bow. It seems quite possible that this structure was another eleventh-century undercroft, part of a religious establishment with a diminished but continuing royal connection in the north-western part of the city.

During the decades that followed the strengthening of the Norman grip upon the city another wave of continental influence arrived: the religious orders which had sprung from reform of the continental church in the eleventh and twelfth centuries. The medieval clergy were organised in two quite distinct ways: the secular priests who worked in a network of parishes and were subordinate to the bishop of the diocese; and the monks and regular canons living in self-contained establishments under their own rule and customs (Cluniac, Augustinian and so on) and often exempt from the bishop's jurisdiction. The importance of this second, monastic group for the building of London, as for other towns, lies in three factors. First, the building of their precincts first developed the outskirts and outlying parts of the city, and then fossilised or restrained further developments until the Dissolution in the sixteenth century. Secondly, the large churches, like castles, displayed the achievements of builders on a scale not possible except with major royal or noble financing. And thirdly, monastic houses epitomised the medieval idea of the well-ordered community; a monastery, behind its high gatehouse (as formidable as that of the town) was a little town, with its own church, legislative centre (the chapter-house), accommodation for eating, sleeping and working, storehouses and a water supply (see 32). The standards of building were high. When the civic leaders thought about improvements to the city at large, they must have been influenced by the existing models in their midst provided by the religious communities.

Edward the Confessor's Benedictine abbey of St Peter at Westminster was already flourishing. Next to arrive in London were the Cluniacs, owing allegiance to Cluny in Burgundy. They were given the manor of Bermondsey by William Rufus in 1089, on which (or perhaps, on an adjacent piece of ground) they had already built a 'new and beautiful church'. This was the only monastery which the normally disrespectful Rufus founded; was it perhaps his intention to be buried there, as Edward had intended at Westminster and William at Caen in Normandy? Any such plan was thwarted eleven years later when he died mysteriously in the New Forest and was buried at Winchester. The priory continued to enjoy much royal favour in the twelfth and thirteenth centuries as a stopping-place for the court, and two queens spent their declining years within its walls. A large number of pilgrims were also attracted by the cross or rood which by tradition had been found near the Thames in 1117. This contributed to the priory's function as a kind of upper-class hotel, so that in 1238 there was complaint to the king that the monastery had heavy expenses of hospitality which it could not reduce without scandal or commotion, as the house was set as a 'gazingstock' or prestige symbol for king and kingdom.

Fragments of the priory were recorded in the nineteenth century and the east end of the twelfth-century church was excavated in 1956, at the junction of Tower Bridge Road and Abbey Street. The church was 310 feet long, in the same general form as the mother-church at Cluny, with an east end of five rounded chapels and further chapels off at least the northern transept. Three capitals, probably from the twelfth-century cloister, are preserved in the adjacent parish church of St Mary Magdalene. One is scalloped, the others are decorated with a crow-stepped pattern and foliage. Other fragments of the priory buildings no doubt lie beneath the surrounding houses.

William Rufus's successor, Henry I (1100–35), was a master of political intrigue. He would appreciate that the church found it essential to support the king and increase his authority in order that it might carry out its own work in a peaceful and orderly fashion. Henry married Matilda, daughter of St Margaret of Scotland, who also had English ancestry; and joined with her in the foundation of many religious houses. In London, Matilda was popular; Etheredeshithe became Queenhithe in her honour. Henry must have given his approval for her foundation in 1108 of Holy Trinity Priory, Aldgate, the largest of three Augustinian houses in London.

The triangular precinct of Holy Trinity, just inside Aldgate, was based upon a site already containing a church attached to the religious house at Waltham Holy Cross. The queen endowed the house with the gate of Aldgate, and considerable property in the neighbourhood to generate income from rents; after her death in 1125 Henry I added Portsoken Ward, an immense tract of land outside the walls. Except perhaps for the king, the priory must have been the largest landowner in twelfth-century London. Throughout the medieval period the monastery held an important place in London's daily life: its prior was an alderman. The richness of the priory and of its buildings must have been awe-inspiring. Though savagely despoiled at the Dissolution, the buildings can be reconstructed [32] thanks to two historical accidents – the survival, in the papers of Elizabeth I's Lord Treasurer, Lord Burghley, of a plan of the church and priory buildings in 1591, and a fire of November 1800, which to the surprise of the antiquaries of the day disclosed that the destroyed sixteenth- and seventeenth-century timber buildings had been hiding several piers and arches of the twelfth-century church [31]. In addition, most of the precinct was bought by the city in or shortly after 1582, when it was already broken up into several tenancies. Lease-plans of the late seventeenth and eighteenth centuries show fragments of the priory buildings incorporated into contemporary premises. The area around Aldgate has also been redeveloped in piecemeal fashion over recent years, allowing archaeological investigation of various parts, most notably the west range of the cloister, which lay to the north of the church.

It is known that work, probably on the choir, was interrupted by a fire of 1132, and it is therefore no surprise to see two slightly different styles in the details recorded in 1800. The east end of the choir comprised five single-storey chapels. Near the high altar would be tombs of royalty – two children of King Stephen, Baldwin and Matilda, were buried here. Excavations in 1979 near the west end of the church found early medieval chalk-lined burial cists of men, women and children, later built over by further expansion. Here also were twelfth-century foundations of the west range of the cloister, which faced a great yard to the west; this range later probably comprised accommodation and a hall on the first floor over storage vaults.

31. Arches of the choir of Holy Trinity Priory, Aldgate, drawn after the fire of 1800 by David Thomas Powell. For reconstruction of the houses built above the arches, see 121.

A member of the royal court, probably a clerk, named Rahere founded two connected houses outside the city wall in fairly open ground near the horse-fair at Smithfield in 1123: the Augustinian priory and hospital dedicated to St Bartholomew. Work on the priory church, which was to reach 350 feet in length, began at once and most of the choir and crossing which survives today is of the mid-twelfth century. The apsidal east end of seven bays had three radiating chapels; those to the north and south were double-apsed, and the third located beneath the Lady Chapel in 1905 was probably also apsidal, giving an effect like that at Norwich Cathedral. By the early thirteenth century the nave of ten bays, the cloister and chapter-house were completed. The undercroft below the dorter, also of the twelfth century, was photographed before demolition in 1870; it extended for 135 feet and was 35 feet wide, and the vault was supported on a central row of octagonal columns. None of the buildings of the medieval hospital survive, apart from the little church of St Bartholomew the Less.

The third Augustinian house, and the one that has survived best though in greatly altered form, was founded in 1106 as St Mary Overie (over the water), now the Anglican cathedral of Southwark. The founders were two Norman knights, William Pont d'Arch and William Dauncey; they are said to have received much help from the Bishop of Winchester, especially in the building of the nave in 1107. The Bishops of Winchester had their London house immediately west of the priory, and were linked with its

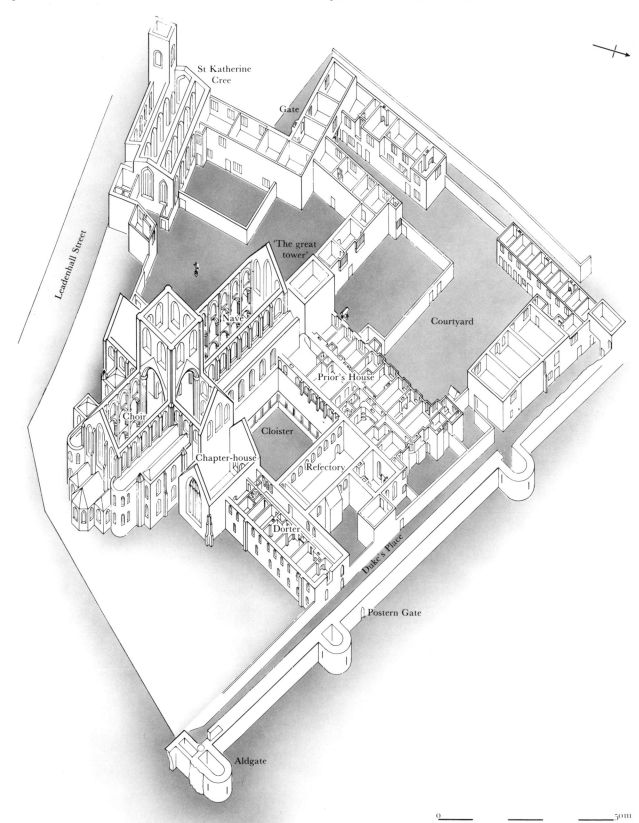

St Katherine
Cree

Gate

Leadenhall Street

'The great
tower'

Courtyard

Nave

Prior's House

Choir

Cloister

Chapter-house

Refectory

Dorter

Duke's Place

Postern Gate

Aldgate

0   50m

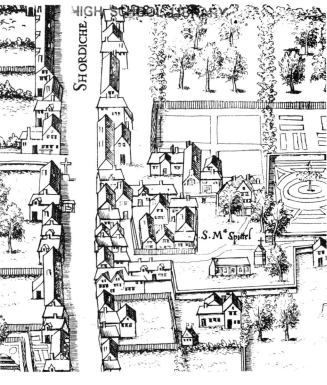

33. The eastern of two Norman doorways on the north side of the nave of St Mary Overie, Southwark, drawn before almost complete destruction in the early 19th century.

34. *Above right:* St Mary Spital in the mid-16th century, from the copperplate map. It still retained (though not for long afterwards) the spirit of suburban retreat.

32. *Opposite:* Reconstruction of Holy Trinity Priory, Aldgate, at its fullest monastic extent, by Richard Lea, from the ground-plan of 1592 by John Symonds. Such large, imposing communities were bound to influence both the shape and appearance of towns.

main periods of building throughout the medieval period. Little of the first church has survived; there have been many rebuildings, including one caused by the collapse of the nave roof in 1469. The only twelfth-century details to be seen today are two doorways to the cloister range, which lay to the north [33], a recess in the north wall of the nave and traces of one of the transept chapels. The church was destroyed by fire in 1212, and the priory's outstanding contribution to the medieval architecture of London is of the thirteenth century (p. 65).

The Augustinians participated, especially at St Bartholomew's, in social welfare; other hospitals sprang up around London in the twelfth century as further signs of pious devotion. Queen Matilda herself founded the leper hospital of St Giles in the Fields – then a remote place outside the city – as one of the first, perhaps the first, leper hospital in England, in or about 1117. Her namesake, queen to King Stephen, founded St Katharine's Hospital by the Tower for old folk in the late 1140s. St Mary Overie had its own hospital of St Thomas à Becket, founded within a few years of the saint's death at Canterbury in 1170; after a fire of 1213–15 it was moved by stages to its present site further east. A small hospital was founded by Becket's sister Agnes in about 1190 in the house in Cheapside where he was born; it was staffed originally by a small crusading order, the knights of St Thomas of Acre or Acon, but later by Augustinians. And in 1197 William Brown, a citizen, established the hospital of St Mary Spital outside Bishopsgate, astride the city boundary [34]. The early buildings of these hospitals have not been recorded.

During the twelfth century the outlying areas of the city must have been the scene of almost continual building activity. The catalogue of religious foundations of this period goes on to include those of nuns and the

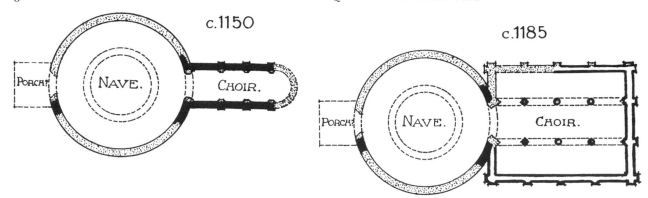

crusading orders. Fortunately substantial fragments of their buildings have survived as examples of important advances in architectural design. North-west of the city two priories were established by Jordan of Bricett, a Suffolk landowner with much sympathy for the crusading movement. His first was the Priory or Hospital of St John of Jerusalem in Clerkenwell, the first house of the Hospitallers in England. Like the other crusading orders, their church had a round nave [35], and a typically twelfth-century eastern choir. This was replaced by a larger three-aisled choir in 1185, subsequently burnt by Wat Tyler in 1381 and afterwards rebuilt. Beneath the ground, the crypts of the two twelfth-century phases survive, the earlier inside the later. From about 1140, at various places around the country, experiments in a revolutionary pointed style were being undertaken; and this shows in the differences between the two crypts. The earlier has a semi-circular vault and large, rectangular piers; the later is rib-vaulted, the arches rising to embryonic Gothic points in the tentative style seen at the same period in the arches to London Bridge (see 44), and the piers have become clustered columns. Presumably there was more of this very modern styling at the nunnery of St Mary Clerkenwell, which Bricett also founded north of the Hospitallers, but virtually nothing of this survives.

We are used to chronicling the history of architecture, and of common or 'vernacular' building, by reference to surviving examples; thus the development of Norman and Gothic architecture in this country is often treated as the history of such surviving buildings at Winchester, Durham, St Alban's and Canterbury cathedrals. One of the propositions of this book is that as we find out more about the buildings of medieval London, so the history of building and architecture is bound to change, if only at first by small degrees. London, by its position in the kingdom, its great wealth and cosmopolitan culture, may have led the way in architectural fashion more than is presently realised. Fortunately, at one further crusaders' foundation the buildings survive to underline this role in the medieval avant-garde, though restored in the last century and again after war damage: the church of the Templars, south of Fleet Street [36]. Imagine the elevation of the circular nave rolled out into a straight line, and the Temple church is a Gothic construction which may have been designed before the choir of Canterbury Cathedral of 1175. Its gracefully pointed arches are supported on piers of dark marble from Purbeck in Dorset, the first use in London of what was to become a very popular decorative manner. It is completely different in character from the heavy constructions of the previous century (compare 29, 31).

35. Plans showing the early development of the church of the priory of St John of Jerusalem, Clerkenwell.

36. *Opposite:* Circular nave of the Temple Church, consecrated in 1185. The shafts of the piers are of Purbeck marble; set into the floor are 13th-century effigies of knights, also of Purbeck.

To be up-to-date in style in large-scale building ventures was usually the prerogative of the king or the major religious houses, for they alone could afford them. Likewise, it was only the wealthier residents in towns, such as religious leaders, who had houses which could follow these fashions in building design and construction. The new generation of buildings, both religious and secular, were not only different in style but also in their basic materials of construction. The 150-year period after the Norman Conquest is remarkable for imports into London of vast quantities of stone for the first time since the departure of the Romans. The majority of houses and shops would be of timber, thus accentuating the occasional stone house or group of stone buildings in any street. The passage of time, changes in fashion or the accident of fire removed the majority of medieval buildings before the age of antiquarian interest, but the below-ground portions survived better, and thus we have tantalising records of a very few twelfth-century stone houses.

Two were recorded during demolition in the nineteenth century. In 1830, clearing operations for the approach to the new London Bridge railway station uncovered part of a twelfth-century town house, possibly built for the Earl de Warenne in Southwark and later occupied by the Prior of Lewes (the English mother-house of the Cluniac order, which held the nearby priory at Bermondsey). An undercroft 40 feet 3 inches by 16 feet 6 inches was divided into four bays by piers attached to the walls and barrel vaulting [37]. The piers had capitals showing five variants of the Norman scallop design. At one end were two windows; at the other end, from one corner, an arch led to a further building of at least two bays which is interpreted as the undercroft for a porch [38]. Exterior stairs would rise to the hall on the first floor, where the main doorway and a little walling survived. The doorway used Caen stone imported from Normandy, in the style of the new castles and churches.

Traces of a second Norman town house were discovered at Corbet Court, off Gracechurch Street, in 1870. Here, away from the street frontage, a square Norman undercroft had supported buildings for seven hundred years. The room was entered from a short porch or corridor with a small blind arcade on each side; circular columns with cushion capitals supported a barrel vault. The walls were of Kentish ragstone and plentiful Roman bricks (both materials probably from the underlying Roman forum), and Caen stone was used especially for the arcade. The position of windows on the north and south sides of the undercroft strongly suggests that, like the crypt of St Mary le Bow, the structure stood at or near twelfth-century ground level, though by the time of its discovery its original floor level lay eighteen feet below Corbet Court.

A first-floor hall on a vaulted undercroft, as indicated by these examples, was the usual type of stone dwelling for the person of position and wealth in the twelfth century, both in the countryside (as at Boothby Pagnell in Lincolnshire) and in towns, where such buildings have often been called Jews' Houses, as for example in Lincoln and Norwich. Certainly Jews often did build and occupy stone houses. The introduction of Jews to England, and to London, is traditionally dated to the arrival of William the Conqueror, and they probably came as an offshoot of the community at Rouen. Although at their greatest extent they may not have exceeded 2 per cent of the population even in large cities such as London or Norwich, they

37. Longitudinal section through the remains of the Norman town house of Earl de Warenne in Southwark, given to the Priory of Lewes. Above the vaulted ground floor can be seen the original doorway into the hall, edged with Caen stone.

38. The bay beneath the porch stair of the house of the Prior of Lewes. For the decoration compare 41.

were clearly a distinct richer element in society. In London the Jewry – it was as natural then as now for immigrant communities to stay together – was in the area still commemorated by the street name of Old Jewry (first mentioned as *Vicus Judaiorum* in 1128) and in several surrounding parishes. In the riots attending the coronation of Richard I in 1189 a lighted brand fell on a thatched roof in the Jewry and started a serious fire, indicating that the houses were closely packed together. Although there was some amicable financial dealing between the Jewish money-lenders and prominent citizens, the Jews' position was always uncomfortable. In 1215 the city walls are said to have been repaired with stone taken from Jews' broken houses, and the Jews were finally expelled from the country in 1290. In London one synagogue at the north end of Old Jewry became a chapel of the Franciscan Friars of Penitence, and later part of a house of the Black Prince.

In London, as in other towns, Jews were not the only people able to afford stone houses. The term 'stone house' is often used as a term of distinction in the twelfth- and thirteenth-century lists of properties belonging to religious institutions such as the nunnery at Clerkenwell. Before 1204, for instance, Master Roger, a canon of St Paul's, granted to the dean and chapter stone houses which he had bought from Herbert of Antioch, one in Honey Lane, and the other nearby in Milk Street. The latter was granted by the dean and chapter to William the joiner in about 1212. Any remains of these houses have been destroyed, but excavation a few yards to the north in Milk Street in 1977 gave a representative picture of life on

39. Stone house under excavation at Milk Street, 1977. The medieval and modern street lies to the right; the two small walls to the left may have supported an ancillary building such as a porch (compare 38 and 40).

several nearby properties. Near the southern end of the site an impressive stone building, provisionally dated to the twelfth or thirteenth century, was uncovered [39]. Only fragments of foundations and two small pieces of walling survived, since the tenement boundaries had been followed to the present and the medieval walls were punctuated by nineteenth-century concrete bases. The structure was only three-quarters of the size of the undercroft beneath the hall of the Prior of Lewes [40], with two small walls running roughly at right angles from the back wall to form an extra small block at the rear. The medieval foundations were of alternating layers of chalk and gravel, on a base of harder ragstone which was carried over the many rubbish pits of preceding generations by a thick bed of driven stakes. These had nearly all decayed and remained only as voids; the few which survived were of beech, split from trunks up to sixteen inches in diameter. The building, which is not securely dated, can be reconstructed as either a twelfth-century undercroft like that of the Prior of Lewes, or by analogy with the cellar still surviving beneath the Angel Hotel, Guildford, as a thirteenth century undercroft. The two spur-walls at the back may have supported a stair to a higher level; perhaps this undercroft was, like other thirteenth-century examples, half underground.

The disposition of stone houses through the streets of twelfth-century London will only be understood by much further archaeological and

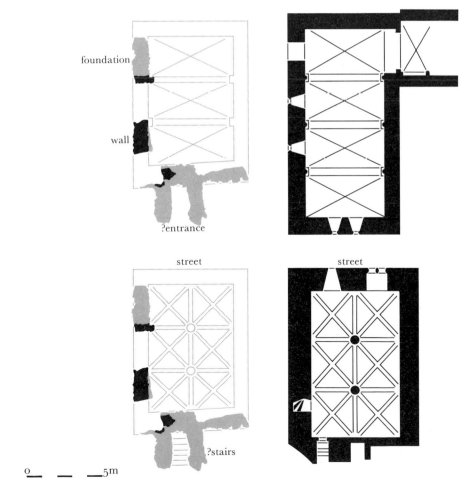

40. Parallels for the stone building at Milk Street: it can be reconstructed as a 12th-century undercroft like the house of the Prior of Lewes (*top right*), or as a 13th-century undercroft like that surviving below the Angel Inn, Guildford (*bottom right*).

documentary work. It is likely that they were occupied both by certain groups in London's medieval society who generally stayed in one place – for example the Jews, or the vintners with their vaults on the shore – and by merchants who wished to be near the market-places of the city such as Cheap (now Cheapside) and Gracechurch Street. By analogy with the larger churches and castles, we would expect similarity between the architecture (all of it Romanesque) of London's stone houses and those in other towns, both at home and abroad, where Romanesque was to be seen. Thus a London town house would seem familiar to the many merchants of Rouen bringing wine and fish, those of the Rhineland bringing hock and later claret, and those of Flanders with cloth.

The close similarity in proportions and decoration between small religious buildings and town houses of wealthier citizens in the early Middle Ages can still cause confusion. In more than one case secular undercrofts, rediscovered in the eighteenth and nineteenth centuries, were thought to be the lower parts of churches. Uncertainty still surrounds the origin of our final Norman building – perhaps the most remarkable survival of all, and certainly the least known.

The chapel of St James, situated on the city wall by Cripplegate, is first mentioned in 1189 when King Richard gave it to his chaplain, Warin. By 1253 it housed a hermit (as, from time to time, did some of the interval towers on the city wall) and was thereafter known as The Hermitage of St James. By 1299 it belonged to the monastery of Garendon, a Cistercian house in Leicestershire. At the Dissolution of the Monasteries the Hermitage was granted by the Crown to William Lambe, a rich clothworker, who bequeathed it to his company; it was surveyed for the company in 1612. The upper storeys must have been rebuilt after the Great Fire reached this point [143], but the undercroft remained substantially intact. Let a visitor of 1825 take up the story:

41. Interior of the undercroft of St James Hermitage, drawn by P. W. Justyne in 1855, before its removal to Mark Lane. The moulded stones of the ribs are now arranged differently, and the undercroft is smaller.

Descending a narrow flight of about ten or a dozen steps, we enter a low, vaulted chamber, 26 feet in length from east to west, and 20 feet in breadth. Nine short columns, six of which now remain, supported the groined roof of this apartment. The capitals of these columns are . . . of a form with any parallel examples of which I am unacquainted. The angles of these columns are elegantly ornamented with a leaf (on some placed upwards, on others inverted), or with a volute. Some of the intersecting ribs of stone, which spring from the columns, are adorned with mouldings, carved with a zig-zag or with a spiral ornament. . . . Thus an interior of much elegance was formed [41].

The undercroft is no longer at Monkwell Street, for it was moved across the city in 1872 by the Clothworkers' Company to a site near their hall. It was rebuilt on the site of the parish church of All Hallows Staining, Mark Lane, and access (by permission of the Company) is now gained via the church tower which still remains. The decayed but still beautiful decoration of the ribs and capitals can be dated to about 1140. But was it built as an undercroft for a chapel, or for a town house which subsequently became a chapel? Its situation virtually on the city wall (see 105), and therefore in the king's possession in 1189, perhaps suggests the former rather than the latter. Whatever the case, the undercroft remains as the most intimate and charming relic of the century of monumental building schemes.

The emergent city 1200-1300

3

England's economy prospered and expanded during the thirteenth century; trading communities proliferated, new towns were planted and the old were extended or substantially rebuilt, feeding on and regenerating wealth. During the century royal patronage of large buildings projects – most importantly for London at Westminster and the Tower – was at its most extensive, and the second half of the century saw another wave of religious building in London by the friars which was itself part of a nationwide increase in reconstruction programmes of major churches. The combination of new preaching methods introduced by the friars and the economic growth of towns resulted in a significant reorganisation and expansion of the parish church.

A thirteenth-century traveller approaching the city, from north or south, would first register the major stone buildings such as the Tower and monasteries, and a new, larger St Paul's which dominated the skyline [43, 147]. In the distance were fields and farms; for the moment the city was contained within its turreted wall, except where large houses were strung along the river bank towards royal Westminster. Entry to the city from the south was gained across one of the wonders of medieval England: London Bridge [44–5].

London's prime economic function, in all periods, has been as a place of trans-shipment of goods from land to river and sea. Its place in the centre of a radiating road system, inherited from the Roman occupation, was made viable only by a bridge over the Thames – a fact so well understood by the city fathers that they succeeded in preventing any other bridge being built within twenty miles of London until the eighteenth century, and then only submitted after a sustained campaign. The London Bridge which was to last, with many rebuildings and modifications, until 1831 was begun in 1176, when Peter, vicar of St Mary Colechurch (at the east end of Cheapside), formed the first of a series of guilds and fraternities which raised the money for a bridge as a pious, charitable work; bridges, like roads, became a suitable object of charitable donation or bequest. The bridge had nineteen arches and a drawbridge, and was 906 feet long. Recent work has dismissed the idea of a previous bridge just downstream – an idea widely held from the time of John Stow onwards, and based largely on a misreading of a Westminster charter relating to property on the north bank – and it now seems likely that the medieval bridge was on the same line as its Roman and late Saxon predecessor. Indeed, at water level among the foundations all three bridges may have been indistinguishable. Unfortunately, virtually nothing remains of the bridge in modern times, as most of the piers were removed by dredging in 1831.

On the bridge Peter de Colechurch seems to have founded a chapel in honour of St Thomas Becket, born a short distance away from Peter's church in Cheapside and martyred at Canterbury in 1170. Rebuilt in

42. Reconstructed section through the choir and crypt of St Paul's by Edmund Ferrey (1873).

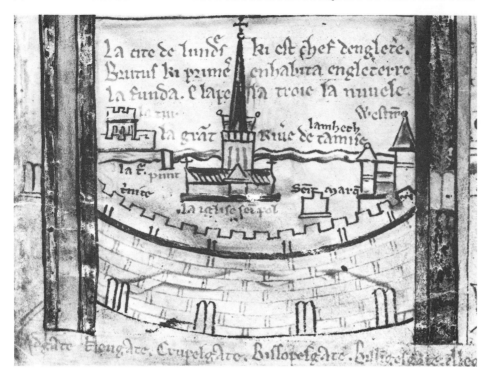

43. Detail from an itinerary to Rome by Matthew Paris, with a mid-13th-century view of London. The city is shown as a traveller arriving from the north would see it. Buildings identified include St Paul's, the Tower (*left*) and Westminster (*right*). Below are the names of the gates.

1384–97, the chapel is shown in later panoramas [44], as is the gatehouse of 1426 which guarded the drawbridge to allow shipping through to Queenhithe and the upper river. Other buildings on the bridge are implied in accounts of a fire in Southwark in 1212, three years after the completion of the main structure. By 1358 there were 138 shops on the bridge, the rents of which went towards the upkeep of the fabric. The city maintained a works department for this purpose, for the bridge was in constant need of maintenance. It kept large stocks of stone, timber and ironwork in a yard at the southern end of the bridge.

The works department of the bridge may have supplied materials for some of the many royal works then in progress. Henry III, who reigned from 1216 to 1272 – the equivalent of two generations – was a frantic builder. His major works on the rebuilding of the Tower, Westminster Abbey and repairs at Westminster Palace must have both revitalised and placed great demands upon the national and local building industries. Most of the master craftsmen, especially the masons, were specialists from Oxford, Colchester or other towns, but the labourers and the suppliers seem, from the surviving accounts, to have been locals. Building operations on the Abbey began in 1245, when the eastern part of the Confessor's church was demolished, and continued well after Henry's death in 1272. The chapter-house (see 46), south transept and cloister were all under way by 1250, together with a separate belfry (under the present Middlesex Guildhall). A sacristy 120 feet long was begun in 1250–1, and timber for the roofing of the western limb and transept ordered two years later. The choir was probably ready for the translation of the Confessor's body into a new shrine in 1269.

The pace of work, goaded by directives from the king, must have amazed contemporary onlookers. Detailed accounts of the workmen employed

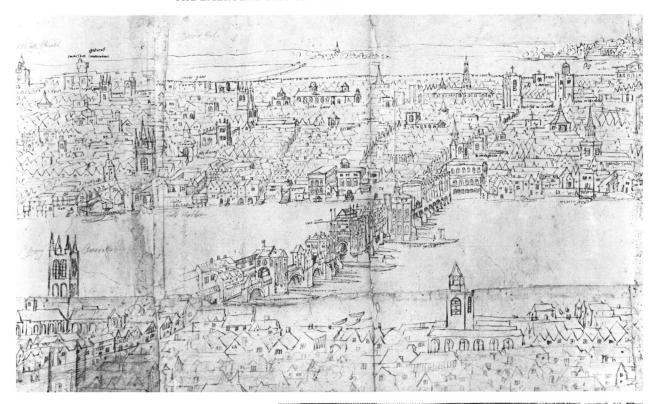

44. London Bridge, drawn by Wyngaerde in about 1540. The drawbridge and gates, St Thomas's Chapel (as rebuilt by Henry Yevele, 1384–97), and houses and shops on the bridge can all be seen.

45. An arch of the medieval London Bridge as it appeared in the Great Frost of 1814, drawn by J. T. Smith.

46. Floor-tiles from the chapter-house, Westminster Abbey, of mid-13th-century date. One authority has recently suggested that the widespread introduction of floor-tiles followed Henry III's marriage to Eleanor of Provence in 1236.

survive for 1253; from 1 February to 24 August there were over 300 men employed on the Abbey. For the week 23–9 June, in the high season, there were 433: 53 white cutters, 49 marblers, 28 layers, 33 carpenters, 15 polishers, 17 smiths, 14 glaziers, 4 plumbers and 220 labourers. During the autumn numbers declined, but there were still 109 workmen at the Abbey in the first week of December.

Many of the building materials would probably have come via London; some of the suppliers can be identified as being of the City. Richard of Eastcheap was the sole supplier of hurdles and withies used for scaffolding, ramps or covers. A certain Agnes supplied burnt lime; she is eventually identified as 'of London'. She also organised the carriage of 440 cart loads of sand to the work. Another fragmentary account for work on the church in 1265 mentions only Richard, who tendered a bill for $16\frac{3}{4}$ hundredweight of lime. Other local suppliers included Roger of the Tower for carved stones and Roger of Barking for two cartloads of charcoal.

A principal supplier of ironwork, especially nails, was Henry of Bridge, and it is clear that he, Richard of Eastcheap and Agnes were also engaged for repairs to the palace buildings in 1259 when the chimney in the king's chamber was dismantled and rebuilt, reinforced with iron, and the drains overhauled. Henry supplied $1\frac{1}{2}$ hundredweight of tough iron for the chimney, and throughout the summer of 1259 supplied nails of various sizes at a prodigious rate: 20,500 in June, 28,900 in September. He also supplied bowls, spades, and some of the shingles to be fixed by his nails. Richard of Eastcheap continued to supply hurdles and withies, but his place was taken by his widow at the end of May 1259; in the 1265 account Alice of Eastcheap supplied the hurdles, and this is probably Richard's wife. For the palace at the same time lead and iron were provided by Philip of Dowgate, and tin by Walter of Dowgate. The buildings which were

THE EMERGENT CITY 1200–1300

47. The east side of the House of Lords (*centre*), drawn in 1807 by J. T. Smith. Perhaps this was one of the buildings repaired in the mid-13th century, as described in royal building accounts.

repaired at this time [47] were mainly re-roofed in shingles, but 500 tiles had been bought from William of Smithfield in October 1259. He may have been from East Smithfield, by the Tower; excavation of the Tower moat in 1275–6 produced clay which was sold to the London tilers.

Henry was no less active in rebuilding the Tower, spending £9,683 on it between 1216 and 1272 and beginning its conversion into the great concentric fortress seen today [48]. Besides almost continuous repairs, two new towers (the Blundeville, later Wakefield Tower, and possibly the former Lanthorn Tower) were begun in the 1220s, using as their base the Roman riverside wall which formed the south side of the inner bailey. The inner curtain wall was extended to the east, adding about an acre to its area, with new towers to match, in about 1238–9. The western inner curtain wall and its towers were built around the same time. In 1240 a gateway, probably that giving access to Great Tower Street, fell down and the Coldharbour Gate seems to have replaced it. A kitchen was built in 1230 and the hall extensively repaired about the same time. Recent excavations in the inner bailey, designed to uncover the Roman riverside wall, incidentally revealed foundations of the hall; they were of alternate layers of ragstone with occasional flint and gravel, the standard foundation technique from Saxon times until the later thirteenth century. The White Tower and the chapel of St Peter within the Tower were redecorated and finely adorned with images in glass and stone or wood. An unusual addition to the service buildings was a building 40 by 20 feet for an elephant, a present to the king in 1253. The animal survived only three years; the site of its house and of its eventual grave are equally unknown.

Henry's son Edward I (1272–1301) continued building at the Tower between 1275 and 1285. His works include the completion of the western wall between the Devereux and Bell towers, the digging of the present moat (in which citizens went swimming on pain of death) and construction of two entrances on the south side: moving the main landward entrance from

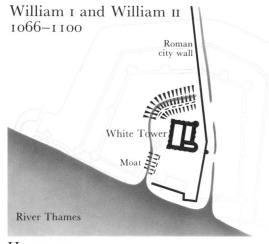

William I and William II
1066–1100

Roman city wall

White Tower

Moat

River Thames

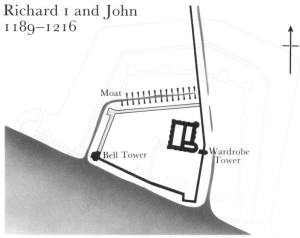

Richard I and John
1189–1216

Moat

Bell Tower

Wardrobe Tower

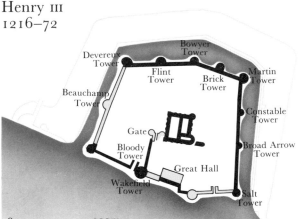

Henry III
1216–72

Bowyer Tower

Devereux Tower

Flint Tower

Brick Tower

Martin Tower

Beauchamp Tower

Constable Tower

Gate

Broad Arrow Tower

Bloody Tower

Great Hall

Wakefield Tower

Salt Tower

0   100m

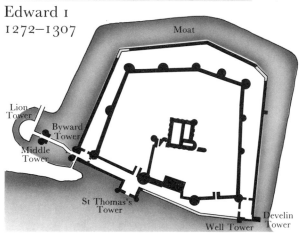

Edward I
1272–1307

Moat

Lion Tower

Byward Tower

Middle Tower

St Thomas's Tower

Develin Tower

Well Tower

Tower Street to Thames Street in 1280–1, and building a new watergate, now known as St Thomas's Tower or Traitors' Gate, which was finished by 1279. This had a stimulating effect upon the topography of the waterfront area immediately to the west; the earliest quays excavated next to the present Custom House in 1974 were of the early fourteenth century.

Such monumental works were accompanied by improvements in lighting, sanitation and luxurious furnishings which were imitated by the lesser magnate and nobleman, lay or ecclesiastic, in his castle and lodge. Henry's additions were mainly to provide more chambers, wardrobes and privies for personal use; his taste for glazed windows and tiled floors provided work for local industries which later catered to wider markets. In London the later thirteenth and early fourteenth centuries saw the building of many town houses for members of the court and especially for provincial bishops, abbots and priors who needed a London base. The palace of the Archbishop of Canterbury lay across the river from Westminster at Lambeth; of this period only the chapel and its crypt (c.1225–45) survive. It is an important example of the 'lancet' or transitional period in its windows, but the double doorway by which it is entered was as modern as the similar entrance to the chapter-house at Westminster Abbey. Along the Strand bishops and priors established their houses, forming a superior suburb between the two cities. To the north-west of the City, the Bishop of

48. Plan of the Tower of London, showing the main medieval building periods as the Norman nucleus grew into the great fortress seen today.

49. Ely Place, Holborn, 1776. This view from the back of the principal buildings demonstrates the layout of a 13th-century mansion: the hall (*left*) with a public courtyard on the other side; the private cloisters (*centre*) and the private chapel (*right*), now St Etheldreda's, Ely Place.

Ely, John de Kirkeby, acquired properties over a large area north of Holborn and on it built a town house for his successors [49]. A large courtyard led to a hall (probably built in 1286–90) measuring 72 by 32 feet, and 30 feet high. Beyond the hall was a cloistered quadrangle, a chapel (finished in 1290), and extensive gardens including vineyards. The chapel survives today as St Etheldreda's, Ely Place. This imposing group of buildings lay on the hill to the south-west of Smithfield and Bartholomew Fair, and would have been constantly in view of the traders there as well as being visible from across the river to the south.

At St Bartholomew's Priory and other large religious houses, also, the thirteenth century saw several notable extensions and rebuilding programmes. Work of this period can be inferred at St Martin-le-Grand and Holy Trinity Priory. At St Bartholomew's the nave was completed about 1225, and the present archway entrance to the churchyard is all that remains of an Early English west front [50]. Lively Romanesque decoration (see 33) was giving way to simplicity and severe reticence. This is best demonstrated by comparing the Temple church's richly decorated west doorway of about 1185 with its new choir of 1240. Here are tall, grey-green Purbeck marble columns and a high, pointed vault; we are in an aisled hall, dignified and restrained. The same effect is found in the Lady Chapel or retro-choir of St Mary Overie (Southwark Cathedral), built in *c.* 1213–35. With its square east end, St Mary Overie is an illustration of the peculiarly English way of rebuilding a Norman church in the thirteenth century, in contrast to the French Gothic fashion of several sprouting chapels which was employed shortly afterwards by the king at Westminster Abbey.

The square east end at Southwark is useful because it gives an impression of the similar feature at the greatest church of all, St Paul's. The tower of the cathedral was rebuilt by 1221, and the choir extended in two phases in 1240 and 1255 [51]; a wide bay and slight differences in the column and triforium details mark the point of division. At the east end, a dazzling rose window formed the focus of the cavernous vista of the

50. South-west doorway of St Bartholomew's priory church, West Smithfield. In the 13th century the west end of the nave faced onto the market space of Smithfield. The nave was demolished in the 16th century, after the Dissolution.

choir [42]; below, the former parish church of St Faith was absorbed into the body of the church and housed in a four-aisled crypt. In 1326 the bones of St Erkenwald, the church's own saint and early bishop, were translated to a new shrine behind the altar, in a position matching that of Edward the Confessor's shrine at Westminster Abbey [51], and with the same intention of attracting pilgrims. Nearby, in the north aisle of the new choir, the remains of two Saxon kings, Sebba and Ethelred (the 'Unready'), saved from the fire of 1087, were rehoused in recesses in the wall. Apart from the western portico to be added by Inigo Jones, the cathedral had now achieved its largest extent, and it is worth trying to visualise it: 596 feet long – 66 feet longer than Winchester Cathedral, which is the longest surviving medieval cathedral in Britain; a tower of 260 feet and a timber and lead spire of a further 208 feet, rising nearly 50 feet higher than that of Salisbury Cathedral. Taking advantage of its site on the summit of the western hill, St Paul's would have dominated a view of the city from every point of the compass [107].

The thirteenth-century traveller, casting his eye over the city, might well first remark on the new building works at the Tower, St Paul's and the larger churches. His next impressions would be of the tightly containing effect of the Roman walls, marking off the relatively built-up area from the fields, and the city from its countryside. The only notable suburb was that to the west along the Strand.

The city wall, John Stow later calculated, was 2 miles 608 feet long. Apart from an extension in the south-west corner caused by the arrival of

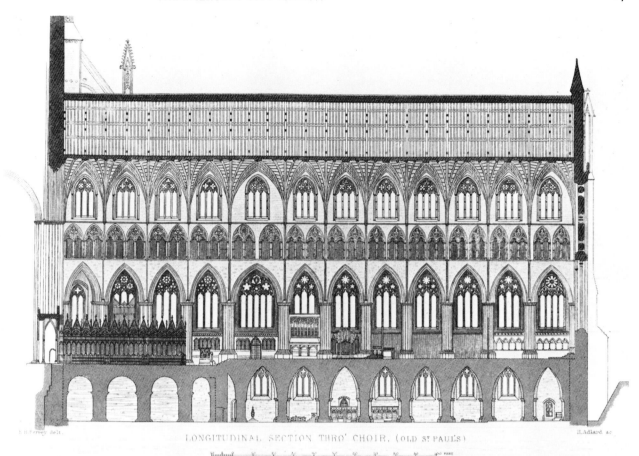

LONGITUDINAL SECTION THRO' CHOIR. (OLD ST PAUL'S)

51. Reconstructed section through the choir and crypts of St Paul's by Edmund Ferrey. The join between the new two stages of 13th-century work and the presumed Norman crypt are both shown. Behind the High Altar (*centre*) stood the shrine of St Erkenwald (compare 28).

the Blackfriars in 1275, it was based on the Roman wall of the early third century. Although the earlier phases of the Tower were contained within the south-eastern angle of the wall, later circuits of the castle broke through and pushed eastwards across the wall's line, so that the Tower Postern, on the north side of the Tower moat, marked the eastern limit of the city defences. From there the wall stretched north- and westwards in a great arc punctuated by six (later seven) major gates and a number of other posterns for pedestrian traffic.

The characteristic Roman construction of squared ragstone with bonding courses of red building tiles would have been visible above ground along many stretches of the wall in the medieval period (see 8). The walls must have been kept in good repair in Saxon times, for they were formidable enough to discourage William from a protracted siege in 1066. In John's reign concern about the defences as a whole led to the taking of stone from Jews' houses for repair work and gifts of money from the king. Murage, a tax on merchandise levied principally at the gates, was allowed in 1233 and sporadically thereafter when necessary; as the name implies, the proceeds were spent on wall repairs. The tax was predictably unpopular with merchants, who complained that it drove trade to other towns.

The medieval work can be seen in surviving pieces of wall at Tower Hill [8], Cooper's Row and St Alphege's churchyard, London Wall; at the first a section 110 feet long and 35 feet high is preserved. The upper medieval part contains round-headed embrasures, possibly of the twelfth century, and traces of a stair to the walkway. In the fragment at St Alphege traces of a rebuilding of the thirteenth century have been identified on the north face, but as with all fragments of the city wall, there has been much modern restoration.

London's principal gates are known for the most part only in their late medieval and early modern forms, as shown in later illustrations [52, 104]. Like other medieval cities, London was also defended by bastions, or towers, at intervals along the wall. The eastern series of bastions, from the site of the Tower to the headwaters of the Walbrook, are probably late Roman in date; perhaps there were eighteen, though not necessarily all were still in use in the Middle Ages. The western series were until recently a group of a further ten, numbered B12, which is at the north-west corner of the city, now preserved in the Barbican development, to B21, immediately north of Ludgate; but a further bastion, now numbered 11A, was found in 1965 between Cripplegate and B12 [53]. Except for one bastion, this group are all hollow, and likely to be medieval; Norman and Early English carved stones were used in the building of B16 (on the east side of King Edward Street), and twelfth- or thirteenth-century pottery was found below Bastion 11A itself. Perhaps they date from several periods, but a possible date for some is 1257, when Henry III 'caused the wall of this Citie, which was sore decayed and destitute of towers, to be repaired in more seemly wise than before'.

52. Bishopsgate and the adjoining city wall, from the copperplate map. The gates and bastions resembled some of those surviving at York and Canterbury.

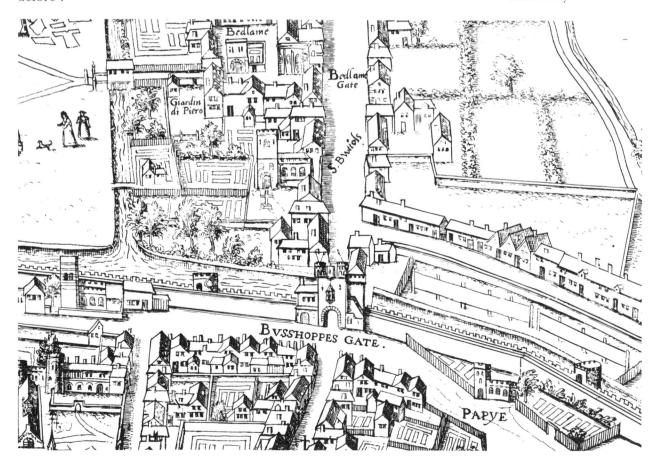

53. Reconstructed foundation of Bastion 11A, discovered in the blitzed cellars of the Barbican in 1965; it overlooked the adjacent suburban church of St Giles Cripplegate.

The gates were often let for non-military purposes, or had other functions: two permanent prisons were to be found at Ludgate and Newgate. The rooms over each gate were occasionally let as dwelling houses to city officials or other trustworthy people on condition that the fabric was kept in good condition and the premises vacated in time of emergency. In this way Cripplegate was leased to Thomas de Kent, serjeant to the mayor, in 1307; Geoffrey Chaucer himself lived above Aldgate for fourteen years from 1374, and while there probably wrote *Troilus and Criseyde*. In addition the bastions or *tourelles* were often let. In 1235 Henry III, for instance, made a life grant to Alexander Swereford, treasurer of St Paul's, of the use of the turret north of Ludgate (B21), enabling him to erect in the turret such buildings as he pleased, to have full use of it in time of peace for the storage of goods, and to enjoy free entry and exit on both sides of the turret within the wall; presumably it adjoined Swereford's house or garden. In time of war when 'it may be needful to munition the city wall with arms and men, the turret and even the buildings in it shall be exposed to receive the munitions of the city like the other turrets in the wall' – perhaps some towers had been built from the murage grant of 1233. In 1305 and 1314 there are references to tourelles near Bishopsgate which strongly suggest that they were occupied by the chaplains of adjoining churches [52]. From the thirteenth century at least two and perhaps as many as four of the bastions were regularly inhabited by anchorites or hermits. The best known of these was Simon the Ankar (Anchorite), who occupied Bastion 11 alongside the church of All Hallows on the Wall, London Wall. We know from bishops' regulations that he would have had a squint or window into the chancel of the church to see the consecration of the Holy Sacrament; but it is not clear how the men of the ward patrolling the wall, or citizens out for an evening stroll along the parapet, made their way between the tower and the church. Map-views and plans of the sixteenth century show that the bastions stood one storey higher than the wall, and the room below was furnished with arrowslits.

The advances in stone fortification of the time were helped by improved techniques of siege-craft, and the development of weapons such as the cross-bow, trebuchet, mine and Greek fire made it more desirable to keep one's enemy at a distance. In the reign of John castle ditches were dug deeper and wider; and at this time the ditch or moat surrounding the city of London was recut on a large scale. Whenever the defences are examined archaeologically, the early medieval ditch is seen to obliterate almost totally traces of the Roman and any Saxon ditches. The width of the ditch was about 80–90 feet; pathways along the outer edge became extramural streets such as Houndsditch and Old Bailey.

There is usually a relationship in medieval towns between the circuit of the walls and the siting of the houses of the mendicant orders or friars, who began to arrive in England during the thirteenth century. Their mission to the urban population meant that they established themselves, whenever possible, inside the walls, but usually only just inside, where large tracts of open space were still available. In London, although peripheral land within the walls was comparatively undeveloped, it was still occupied by houses, streets and two redundant castles.

The Dominican (Black) friars settled in Holborn in 1221, but first on a permanent site within the city were the Franciscan (Grey) friars, who had a chapel near Newgate in 1239, later expanded into the choir of the great church, 296 feet long, 83 feet wide and 64 feet high, finished by 1337. Its columns and pavements were of marble; twenty great beams were provided from the Earl of Gloucester's forest at Tonbridge for the roof, and 36 large windows were glazed by individual donors. Queen Margaret herself was buried by the altar, now beneath the widened King Edward Street. The long list of nobility who chose to be buried here reads like a medieval *Who's Who*; the friaries quickly attracted pious offerings and bequests previously granted to established monasteries.

The Whitefriars (Carmelites) founded their house south of Fleet Street in 1241, and the Augustinian (Austin) friars began building their church at Broad Street in 1253, but known remains of these houses are of a later period. The most important friary in London, both historically and topographically, was that arranged for the Blackfriars by the Archbishop of Canterbury in 1275 [54]. He acquired the sites of the slighted Castle Baynard and Montfichet Tower south-west of St Paul's. By order of the king, the existing city wall between Ludgate and the river was pulled down and the stone given to the friars, the wall afterwards being built down to and along the Fleet valley, to enclose the priory [56]. The church was started in 1279, and completed in 1288; it must have occupied the same site as any remaining buildings on the motte of Baynard's Castle. The airy spaciousness of a friary church, specially designed for improved preaching, can be appreciated by visiting the surviving Blackfriars church at Norwich, now used as a concert hall; the London Blackfriars [54, 55], later to be used as meeting-places for the Privy Council and Parliament, is described in an anonymous fifteenth-century poem. Friaries in the capital, for all their

54. Plan of the friary of the Dominicans (Blackfriars), reconstructed by A. W. Clapham. The whole complex would have been terraced into the hillside, with the large church forming the apex.

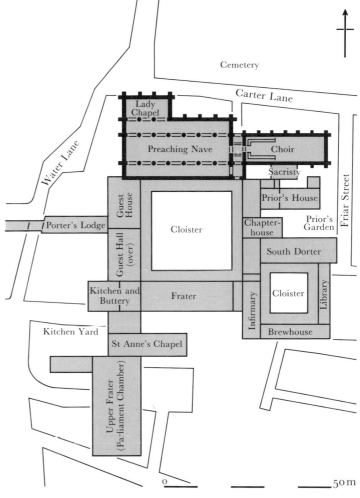

Cemetery

Carter Lane

Water Lane

Friar Street

Lady Chapel

Preaching Nave

Choir

Sacristy

Prior's House

Prior's Garden

Guest House

Cloister

Chapter-house

Porter's Lodge

Guest Hall (over)

South Dorter

Kitchen and Buttery

Frater

Infirmary

Cloister

Library

Brewhouse

Kitchen Yard

St Anne's Chapel

Upper Frater (Parliament Chamber)

0   50 m

55. Arch of the undercroft below the South Dorter of the Blackfriars, probably of late 13th-century date, drawn in watercolour by Philip Norman shortly before 1900. Several other traces of this medieval building were uncovered during building works at the time.

professed poverty, were bound to attract royal and noble support. The author clearly thought the friars had by then gone too far:

. . . I gat me forth to look at the Church,
And found it well and wonderfully built,
With arches on each side, embellished and carven
With crockets at their angles and knots of gold.
The wide windows all wrought with numberless writings
Shining with shapely shields to make a display,
With merchants' marks all figured between,
To the number of more than twice two and twenty . . .
Tombs upon tabernacles raised up aloft
Railed in with iron, with many an effigy
In armour, of alabaster, seemingly clad;
Laid upon marble in divers manners
Were knights now clothed in their martial dress –
All, it seemed, saints who were sacred on earth! –
And lovely carved ladies lay by their sides
In many gay garments that were beaten gold . . .
Then came I to the Cloister and gazed about
How it was pillared and painted and carved so well,
All roofed with lead low on the stones
And paved with painted tiles, one after another,
With conduits of clean tin, closed all about,
Washing basins wrought of shining latten . . .
Then was the Chapter House wrought like a great church,
Carven and roofed and curiously constructed,
With a beautiful ceiling set up aloft,
Like a Parliament-house all painted about.
Then fared I to the Frater, and found there again
A hall for a great king, to hold his household,
With broad tables and benches beautifully furnished,
And windows of glass . . .
And yet these builders will beg a bag full of wheat
Of a poor man that may, for once, pay
Half his rent in a year and half be behind.

At Blackfriars, no doubt, ordinary houses had to be removed when the precinct was created and two lanes were rebuilt to go round, and not through, the friary; recent archaeological work near Newgate has confirmed that the Greyfriars laid out their gardens, east of their great church, over the sites of houses in Stinking Lane (now King Edward Street). In 1319 the Crossed or Crutched Friars, the latest arrivals, negotiated with Holy Trinity Priory to obtain several properties in order to lay out their church and cemetery south of the street today bearing their name. The Whitefriars, south of Fleet Street, could employ a different solution to the problem of space; they reclaimed a large tract of land at the expense of the river.

During the thirteenth century, also, the complete array of 107 parish churches in London (see map, pp. viii–ix) are mentioned in documents. Even if there had not been a Great Fire in 1666, only a handful of details of their appearance in the thirteenth century would have survived seven hundred years of change in style, wear and tear or commercial pressures. Work of this period survives only in a vault below St Olave Hart Street, and above ground at the combined Benedictine nunnery and parish church

56. Square interval tower or bastion on the extension to the city wall, built to enclose the Blackfriars precinct in the late 13th century; drawn by J. T. Smith in 1792.

of St Helen's, Bishopsgate (see 57). Much of the main church walls, and some of the restored windows of the south transept, are of this period. In the south wall of the nave, partial outlines of round-headed windows and a door can be picked out; if these are, as they seem, of the twelfth century, they represent the south wall of the parish church to which the nunnery was attached.

The thirteenth century was a time of ecclesiastical change; possibly under the influence of the great friary churches, parish churches contained their expanding urban congregations by adding aisles to both nave and chancel. Altars multiplied, and glass began to reach even the smallest churches; it is reasonable to assume that the richer London churches would have had some stained glass, comprising small medallions showing single figures or holy incidents, and the first heraldic devices in windows by the end of the century. Monumental sculpture became an important industry, some of its practitioners living by St Paul's. A group of Purbeck marble

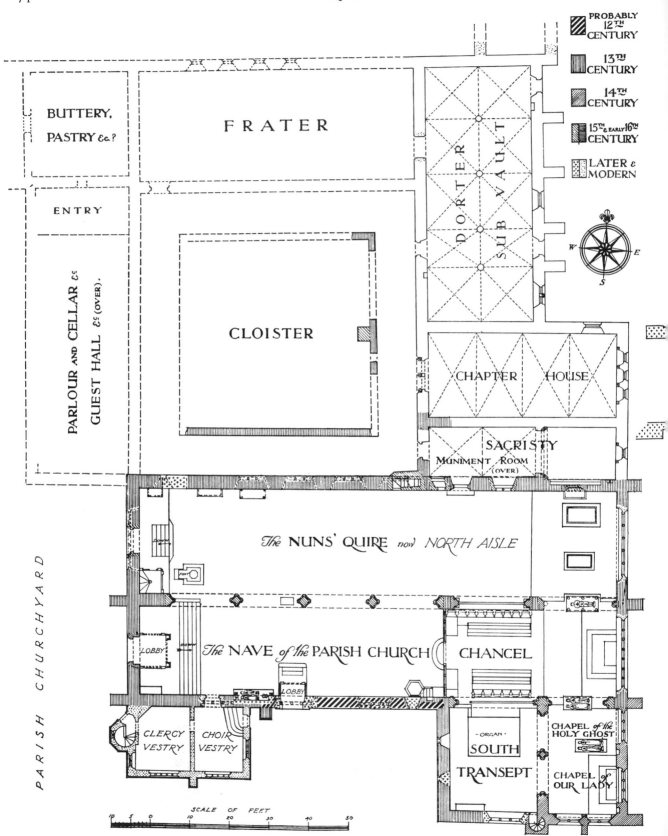

PROBABLY
12TH
CENTURY

13TH
CENTURY

14TH
CENTURY

15TH & EARLY 16TH
CENTURY

LATER &
MODERN

BUTTERY,
PASTRY &c?

ENTRY

PARLOUR AND CELLAR &c
GUEST HALL &c (OVER).

FRATER

DORTER

SUB VAULT

CLOISTER

CHAPTER HOUSE

SACRISTY
MUNIMENT ROOM
(OVER)

The NUNS' QUIRE *now* NORTH AISLE

FONT

PARISH CHURCHYARD

LOBBY

The NAVE *of the* PARISH CHURCH   CHANCEL

LOBBY

CLERGY
VESTRY

CHOIR
VESTRY

ORGAN

SOUTH

TRANSEPT

CHAPEL *of the*
HOLY GHOST

CHAPEL *of*
OUR LADY

SCALE OF FEET
10 5 0   10   20   30   40   50

a

b

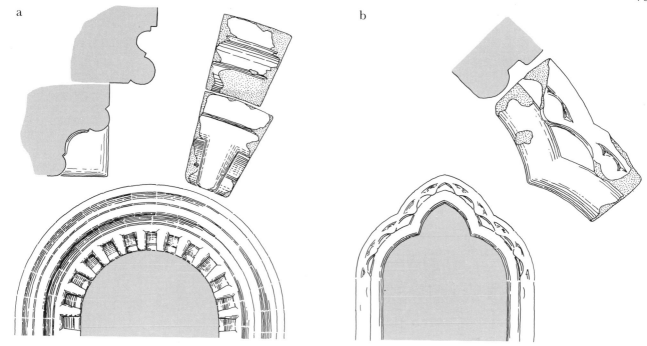

58. *Above:* Moulded stones from a 17th-century context on a site in Harp Lane:
a) 12th-century arch mouldings, probably from a door.
b) Fragment of a late 12th- or early 13th-century trefoil arch probably forming a door or recess.
These stones possibly come from the adjacent church of St Dunstan in the East.

57. *Opposite:* Plan of the nunnery of St Helen's, Bishopsgate (1929), with outline of some of the conventual buildings (now destroyed). The nunnery was attached to an existing parish church. The south wall of this 12th-century (and possibly earlier) parish church still forms the south wall of the nave.

effigies of knights remains in the Temple Church, and a wooden effigy of a knight at St Mary Overie (Southwark Cathedral). Some evidence of these developments in church construction and decoration may remain in the ground, to be found when the site of a church is excavated [58].

Wandering through the streets, the visitor would notice the hand of civic authority in the construction and appearance of ordinary dwellings. Thatched roofs were banned; stone walls were by regulation three feet wide and windows overlooking a neighbour's property were sixteen feet from the ground. A gradual replacement of timber buildings by others of stone during the late twelfth and thirteenth centuries has now been noticed by archaeologists in towns such as Winchester, Bristol, Oxford, Stamford and Southampton. It is also likely that in London this process of improvement was hurried by several serious fires which are known to have badly damaged the city, especially in 1132 and 1136. The first surviving building and fire regulations were probably issued between 1192–3 and 1212 by London's first mayor, Henry Fitzailwin. A further set of regulations was drawn up by Fitzailwin after another serious fire in 1212.

The rules cover dimensions of walls, provision of gutters, arrangements for building upper storeys and for the siting of privies. Stone walls on property boundaries were to be three feet wide and usually constructed jointly by the neighbours, each giving half the land and bearing half the cost, to a height of sixteen feet. Alternatively one party donated the land and the other party built on it, the donor receiving half-ownership (and therefore building rights) of the wall. It was also possible, if desired, to build two walls back to back along the boundary. If arches (usually taken to mean recesses) were required, each neighbour could excavate to a depth of a foot, leaving a foot between them. Gutters were to draw water on to the land of the owner whose buildings they served, unless water could be directed on to the highway. If a person had vacant land on which he wished to build, but a neighbour's house had a gutter which spilled water on to his land, the person could take down the neighbour's gutter during rebuilding but had to make provision for it in the new construction.

Cesspits ('necessary chambers') were either of stone or timber; a privy of stone had to be $2\frac{1}{2}$ feet from the boundary, a wooden cesspit $3\frac{1}{2}$ feet (sometimes in subsequent cases called '$3\frac{1}{2}$ feet of earth'). Since in a 3-foot wide party wall the boundary would run down the middle, this meant that the edge of the pit in stone could be as close as one foot from the interior face of the wall. This was clearly the usual practice, together with the use of wall-chutes from upper chambers. The very few twelfth- and early thirteenth-century stone buildings so far recorded in London have not produced evidence of intramural chutes and stone cesspits, but examples are known outside London, for example, in undercrofts of merchants' houses in Southampton. Many of the timber-lined pits which riddle house plots in the twelfth and thirteenth centuries must have been cesspits of some kind, possibly outside buildings in some cases.

Rules about roofing were formalised further after the fire of 1212. Reeds, straw, rushes or stubble were banned and roofs were to be covered with tiles, shingles or boards. Buildings roofed with reeds or rushes were to be plastered over within eight days, and wooden buildings in Cheap which endangered their stone neighbours were to be removed. By this time roof-tiles are appearing in archaeological deposits, indicating that some fire-conscious citizens, probably those already with stone houses, were ordering new tiled roofs. A similar date is found for the introduction of roof-tiles in Southampton and Canterbury.

Two glimpses of the checking of unlawful building occur in judges' reports (*Eyres*) for 1244–6 and 1276. The earlier shows the concern of the king's representatives about encroachments or *purprestures* into the streets (which were still deemed to be in royal possession), by cellar steps up on to the highway, and the narrowing of streets by building pentices or porches, and of rooms called solars with jetties or overhangs into the street. These complaints are especially vigorous in the later Eyre of 1276, and although it is nowhere certain that buildings of more than two storeys are being indicted, we can presume from other documentary evidence that three-storey houses were becoming common in London streets by the end of the century.

Thirteenth-century timber buildings in London have of course long since disappeared. Their appearance above ground must be reconstructed by analogy with surviving buildings in the surrounding counties, especially Essex and Kent (Middlesex having long ago succumbed to urban development). The aisled halls of the Saxon and Norman tradition can be presumed in London: the largest must have been the twelfth-century Guildhall, itself small by comparison with William Rufus's great hall at Westminster. Examples of domestic aisled halls are still found at Fyfield Hall in Essex (perhaps just before 1300), or Chennels Brook Farm, near Horsham in Sussex (late thirteenth century). At the former the arcades between the posts have slightly pointed curving braces, in imitation of stone arches. In such halls and their contemporaries, the great aisled barns, the feature which has usually undergone least change over the centuries is the roof, and thus the science of dating medieval buildings concerns itself with the intricacies of jointing and roof design.

The dating of timber buildings by the carpentry joints has been developed over the last fifteen years, notably in Essex. The argument is that carpentry joints were refined and developed over long periods, and individual joints, such as lap or a mortise-and-tenon, developed separately and achieved their most advanced forms at separate dates. The thesis is not universally accepted and is internally inconsistent at times, but many of the basic ideas and propositions hold true. The only example of thirteenth-century carpentry in London so far studied in detail is the floor of the Bishop of Ely's chapel, now St Etheldreda's [49], and its supports in the crypt below, dating to 1290. The joists of the chapel floor are lodged in the crypt walls, which are up to 8 feet thick. Six aptly-termed Samson posts and a seventh respond in the west wall support bolsters and then a bridging joist which runs the length of the crypt. The scarf joint used to form its timbers into a continuous run is of a splayed type known only in the reign of Edward I (1271–1307). The timber posts now sit on stone bases, probably inserted during the restoration of 1872–3 when the floor level was reduced by $2\frac{1}{2}$ feet.

On archaeological sites, only the lower parts of walls survive [39, 76]. Later cellars have cut down to below medieval floor level in the majority of cases, and only deeper foundations, wells and cesspits can be recorded, in damaged, truncated state. Nevertheless, some vaults have been found along the waterfront, where deposits are deeper. It is known that in the twelfth and thirteenth centuries London was a leading centre of the wine trade, and merchants from Bordeaux and Rouen hired cellars on the shore; the area of their specialisation is still known as the Vintry, part of Upper Thames Street. Between Billingsgate and the bridge lay another area of trans-shipment for goods. Excavation at New Fresh Wharf showed that the wharves were expanded, and stone cellars erected, to meet the needs of commercial growth at exactly this time [59]. The rapid turnover of buildings along the waterfront, which was constantly changing its character and shape, means that we have few details of their appearance. Fortunately, this can be supplied from instances away from the waterfront,

59. Twelfth- and thirteenth-century properties with buildings (A to E) along the waterfront between Billingsgate and the Bridge, excavated at New Fresh Wharf in 1974–8. The thin lines indicate medieval property boundaries; the thick lines represent excavated walls. Unfortunately documents are largely silent as to who their owners were during this period.

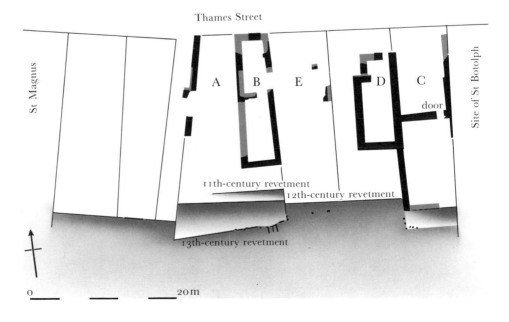

where several undercrofts of merchants' houses of the late thirteenth
century were recorded in the nineteenth century. In style they resembled
the storage and ancillary rooms below the principal rooms of monastic
buildings [55], and may have often had the same functions. In addition,
some may have been for the display of merchandise; others were taverns.
One of the most notable was destroyed for the westward extension of
Cannon Street in 1852. Gerard's Hall, Basing Lane [60], belonged to the
Gisors, a rich wine-importing family; their new hall is recorded in 1290,
and the undercroft probably supported the hall. When, despite antiquarian
outcries, the road level of the new Cannon Street could not be raised two
feet to go over the medieval structure, the stones of the undercroft were
carefully numbered and removed to Crystal Palace for re-erection; but,
enthusiasm having waned, they were eventually ground up to make the
concrete of the prehistoric monsters on display there. I have looked in vain
for a late thirteenth-century moulding poking out from behind the ear, or
tail, of an iguanodon.

As the city's administration grew more refined and sophisticated attention was turned from regulations concerning buildings to the state of the

60. Undercroft of *c.* 1290
of Gerard's (Gisors)
Hall, Basing Lane,
demolished for the
extension of Cannon
Street in 1852. These
cellars were used for
storage (in this case,
probably wine),
wholesale trading and
sometimes as taverns.
Watercolour by C.
Wichelo, dated 1810.

streets, the water supply and to general hygiene. The city's major achievement was the creation of a civic water supply, though, as in other medieval cities, the provision of fresh water was promoted by the efforts of the monastic houses to have a high standard of plumbing. In the 1230s the newly-arrived Greyfriars brought their own water supply from outside the city. In 1237 the city bought land containing wells or springs at Tyburn, and brought it via lead pipes to a great conduit in Cheap. The management of this public service was typical of many which were to follow. A warden or marshal, often a neighbour of the conduit, was in charge of its upkeep; the revenues, levied from certain foreign merchants and, after 1312, the brewers and fishmongers who used it, were supervised by a committee under an alderman.

A more rigorous policy towards public health followed in the years between 1270 and the end of the century. Although many houses had indoor privies, a major problem was the disposal of normal everyday waste, especially that discarded by butchers, tanners and other tradesmen. The habit of keeping pigs in the street was tolerated as a natural remedy. In 1297, however, the city ordered that pig-sties in the streets should be speedily removed, and no swine should be found in the streets, on pain of forfeiture of the beasts; any fines would go towards the upkeep of the walls and gates. This order took some time to be totally effective, for we find two men being fined in 1337–8 for feeding their pigs on trade refuse in Gracechurch Street. Four men of each ward were appointed as 'scavengers', whose responsibilities were to keep the streets of their ward clean and the pavements in good repair, using men called 'rakers'; the expenses were levied on the citizens of each ward. Tolls were also periodically imposed on carts passing through the gates in aid of local repairs to the highway. The number of city officials concerned with the well-ordering of the city also gradually increased; particularly important were the small staff of masons and carpenters who advised the mayor and aldermen in cases of *Assize of Nuisance*, which dealt with court cases arising from the existing building regulations. Others supervised the markets, or the small ward prisons or compters. By the early fourteenth century the number of civic officials had grown to about four times what it was in the mid-thirteenth. By developing more efficient and far-reaching organs of civic control, London was learning how to cope with the problem of growth.

The London of Yevele and Chaucer 4
1300-1400

The opening decades of the fourteenth century were a short period of spectacular growth for London's economy. In the 1290s, London gradually caught up with, and by 1306 had overtaken, her great rival Boston in the export of wool; by 1334 London's exports were double those of Boston. After a war with the French in 1324–7, Londoners took control of the valuable wine trade, ousting foreign interests. In 1334, as measured by taxation, London was five times richer than Bristol, her nearest competitor, with York third. In the 1350s Londoners took over merchant banking in the city from the prominent Italians who had been ruined by Edward III's campaigns. The prominent new buildings of these years – if we were to take a snap-shot, for instance, of the townscape around 1330 – are in the mainstream of the architectural style of the day, Decorated Gothic. This can be seen in the houses of the upper clergy, hospitals and churches and would, if we had examples, probably be visible in the houses of London's more prominent citizens. At the same time, new works at Westminster and St Paul's contained the seeds of a new style.

Several buildings, though new, carried on the traditions of the previous century. The Bishop of Winchester had a large town house built next to the priory of St Mary Overie in Southwark; the hall, probably one of the largest of its type, was 79 feet long [62, 71]. The contemporary great hall of the Archbishop of Canterbury at Lambeth has not survived, but there is a smaller hall of this date at the palace, now called the Guard Room [70]. The halls of the wealthiest citizens were comparable to smaller halls such as the Guard Room. The house of John Yakeslee, tent-maker to the king, in Threadneedle Street, may still form the core of Merchant Taylors' Hall [96]. Sir John Pultney, mayor in 1336, had a mansion in Pountney Lane (the name corrupted from his own) called the Manor of the Rose, which is probably the house he was allowed to crenellate (fortify, a special privilege granted by the king) in 1341. A battlemented tower forming part of the mansion was still visible in 1550 (see 83), and a fourteenth-century undercroft was recorded in 1894. The house may well have resembled Pultney's country house, Penshurst Place, in Kent.

There is little evidence at present for the supposition, reasonable though it is, that these houses were in the vanguard of architectural fashion. More evidence comes from buildings less pressurised by changes of later centuries, the churches and hospitals. Piecemeal work and alterations continued at many monastic houses and friaries: new chapels were added at the east ends of St Mary Overie [146], and St Bartholomew's Priory (c.1330), which survives, restored. The last of the hospital institutions to be founded by individual piety was one for the blind, by William de Elsinge, a mercer, in 1329. It lay near the north wall of the city, by St Alphege's church; at the Dissolution the parish church moved into its foreclosed choir, helping to preserve the walls of the choir and a crossing tower which

61. South cloister of Westminster Abbey, 1349–62. The main builder, John Palterton, was possibly following a design of William Ramsey, since there are close parallels with Ramsey's cloister at St Paul's (1336). Yevele, who assumed control of the king's works in 1360, probably finished it.

T   H

Winchester house

62. The Bishop of Winchester's house in Southwark, drawn by Hollar in 1647. The surviving gable with its rose window (*c.* 1330) formed the western, further end of the great hall (see 74).

still survives as an eloquent ruin at London Wall. The Decorated Gothic style, prevalent from about 1290 to about 1350, can be traced in the replacement of lancet windows (as at St Helen's) by wider windows of more panels (lights) and with more elaborate tracery. We can only presume that this filtered through to secular patrons.

It is said that Pultney, despite his country retreat at Penshurst, died of plague in 1348–9. The Black Death reached London in November 1348, and raged for over a year. Its effects on the city are curiously difficult to discover. Certainly many died – the true figure evades computation, but it is very unlikely to be the 50,000 guessed at by John Stow (perhaps 30 to 40 per cent of the city's population of about 30,000 – itself a guess). The city would have been depopulated by flight into the country and abroad, as well as by the epidemic. One result was a rapid inflation in building costs, especially for labour, and presumably a shortage of craftsmen and transport facilities. The interruption was no doubt serious, but building work went on, and new projects were even started: the south cloister of Westminster Abbey dates from 1349–62, and in 1354 Humphrey Bohun, Earl of Hereford and Essex and possibly a grandson of the founder a century before, financed the rebuilding of the great church of the Austin Friars in Broad Street [63]. The large windows, destroyed in the Second World War, were however slightly old-fashioned when compared to a building which had been standing at St Paul's since 1336, twelve years before the Plague: William Ramsey's chapter-house.

Around the beginning of the fourteenth century Edward I had encouraged a Court style in his buildings, which combined French influences and native innovations. Most notably for London, this included the royal chapel of St Stephen attached to Westminster Hall (still the old structure of William Rufus), built in 1292–7 and resumed in 1320– *c.*1350. The crypt survives, greatly restored, as the chapel of St Mary in the Houses of Parliament. The upper chapel was destroyed in the nineteenth century, but antiquaries recorded its painting, stained glass and stonework [64]. A tall, aisleless building, it had large windows divided into long vertical lights, the rectilnear design continued by panels of tracery over the window arches, and a prominent horizontal cornice at roof level. It was a building to

64. *Right:* St Stephen's Chapel, Westminster, before the fire of 1834 had died out, by J. Taylor. Few illustrations of the whole building survive, though there are many of the paintings and glass [3].

63. *Right:* West end of the church of Austin Friars, Broad Street (1354–60), in a watercolour of the late 18th century. The western half of the church survived up to the Second World War. The windows are fine examples of the Curvilinear style, twenty years after Perpendicular ideas are introduced at St Paul's chapter-house across the city.

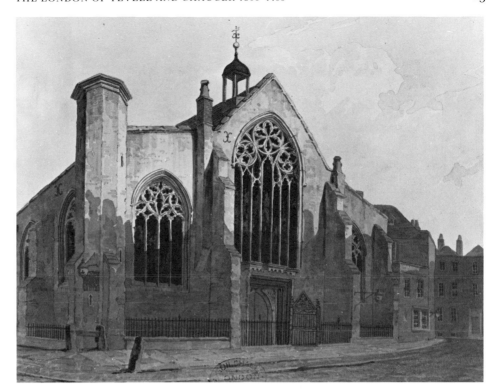

influence generations of masons, especially when war with France promoted separatist notions in architecture. The king's masons and carpenters,
by 1330 acquiring a national reputation, went their own way. Through
them the style we call Perpendicular spread to major buildings in other
parts of the country: to Gloucester and Ely Cathedrals (then prominent
monastic houses), for instance. Gloucester Cathedral, remodelled in stages
from 1331, stands as the earliest surviving Perpendicular building. It is in
the Court style brought to the west country; and it must stand for the two
lost buildings in London which preceded it, St Stephen's chapel and St
Paul's chapter-house. William Ramsey worked in a subordinate capacity at
St Stephen's, and in 1332–6 executed his own commission, the St Paul's
chapter-house. The single surviving representation of it by Hollar [65]
shows how features of the new style were shared with St Stephen's: large,
high windows, traceried or blind panels and tracery designs based on the
hexagon.

If precise knowledge of Ramsey's innovations is just beyond our reach
due to the fragmentary records of his buildings, the half-century after the
Black Death is dominated by the work of another man whose work is well
known: Henry Yevele. Perhaps he came from the family home in Staffordshire in the years immediately following the Plague, for he is known in
London by 1353, and was by then an accredited mason. Yevele was
possibly introduced to royal building projects by John Tyryngton, the
mason in charge of building the Cistercian monastery of St Mary Graces,

65. William Ramsey's
chapter-house and
cloisters, St Paul's
(1336), in a print by
Hollar of 1656. The
octagonal chapter-house
stood on an undercroft,
and was entered from the
upper floor of the two-
storeyed cloister.

DOMVS CAPITVLARIS S. PAVLI
Meridie Prospectus.

founded in 1349 at East Smithfield on the site of one of the supplementary graveyards for plague victims. Tyryngton had worked for the Black Prince at his palace at Kennington, a village south of the river, in 1351, and possibly he arranged for Yevele to direct further rebuilding at the palace in 1359–61. By 1360 Yevele became the king's designer of masonry, especially at Westminster and the Tower. Yevele and his colleagues thereafter dominated architectural design in England for the next forty years.

Essentially conservative in his treatment of detail, Yevele developed or adapted existing features – the less acute (four-centred) arch, the square frame above a door, and tracery in Perpendicular style. Given the leadership and authority of the King's Masons, Perpendicular became the standard style for all polite building. A succession of surviving buildings in London and Westminster can be attributed to Yevele himself. He possibly took over the building of the west cloister of Westminster Abbey in 1362; he certainly designed the vault in the Bloody Tower at the Tower of London in the same year. At the same time he was building a house for the Abbot of Westminster in its own courtyard adjoining the west end of the abbey (now the Dean's house), though it was not finished until 1385 [71]. In 1372 he laid out the cloister of another new religious house, like St Mary Graces founded first as a chapel on a mass grave, to the north-west of the city: a Charterhouse or monastery of the Carthusian order. Here individual cells were arranged around a large square [116]; some of the doorways survive, one encapsulated in decaying state in a modern development entered from Aldersgate Street. The great oak doors today facing Charterhouse Square, each composed of five panels with traceried heads divided by a rail, have been attributed to the original fourteenth-century building, though the gatehouse is of the fifteenth century and the boundary wall of chequerwork panels may date from 1405, when it was ordered that 'a strong wall should be built south of the church, and women should not be allowed within it'. In the 1380s Yevele was working in Canterbury on the city's west gate and possibly on the cathedral nave, and at Bodiam Castle (begun in 1385) and Arundel; in 1378 his sphere of influence had been officially extended to cover the whole country. In London he found time to design a south aisle for the parish church of St Dunstan in the East in 1381, and rebuild the chapel of St Thomas on London Bridge in 1384 [44]. He owned property nearby in Thames Street, and was eventually buried in St Magnus's church in 1400. At his death two major projects were in progress: the rebuilding of the nave and west end of Westminster Abbey [84], and of Westminster Hall [66, 68].

The roof of the Hall, by Hugh Herland, covers nearly half an acre and weighs 660 tons. Since building accounts survive, even this great structure can be brought, at least figuratively, down to earth. Wood came from Hampshire and Hertfordshire; it was prefabricated at a place called 'the Frame' at Farnham, then conveyed overland to Ham in Surrey for transport by river. The angels carrying shields depicting the king's arms, who still stare down with rather haughty expressions, were done by taskwork at prices between 15s and 26s 8d each; the differences in price are not explained. The roof took up to two years to put in place, for a prodigious amount of scaffolding and cranes would be required. Fortified by a little metal bracing in modern times, Herland's creation remains the masterpiece of medieval English carpentry. It is not the first, but is

certainly the largest, hammerbeam roof, though it also relies on collar arches entwined with the hammerbeam structure. There is nothing like it in the world, and probably never was; and therefore, paradoxically, it stands almost outside our story as a climax, after which the roofs of later royal halls, such as Eltham Palace or Hampton Court, are lesser achievements.

Both Yevele and Herland owned property in Thames Street in the city of London, within three-quarters of a mile of each other, and both may have lived there. The appearance of the kind of houses they and their neighbours would have occupied, and many of the problems of living in a great medieval city, can be brought to light from documentary and archaeological evidence. Court cases and deeds combine with scattered remnants of buildings in the ground to provide a picture of how houses were composed, the functions of their various parts and the gradual development of amenities.

By 1300, there was a wide range of ways in which buildings could be laid out around a property. We can distinguish, however, three main arrangements which formed the basis of most of the variations. Larger houses would have a courtyard, entered through a range of buildings which fronted on to the street [100]. At the back of this courtyard, the principal building of the complex – the hall – would face the visitor, its doorway or screens passage opposite the entrance to the court [67]. Such a spacious layout was only possible on large and wide properties; but thinner, medium-sized plots could still have a narrow yard behind the street-range with the hall forming one side of it. This second type is the one most commonly found in town properties in surviving English medieval towns. The third, smallest arrangement was for the smallest properties, only one

66. North front of Westminster Hall (1394–1402) by Henry Yevele, drawn by J. T. Smith in its early 19th-century surroundings. Note its similarity to the west end of the nearby Abbey [84].

67. *Above:* A courtyard
house – the town house of
the Bishop of Bath in the
Strand, from a print by
Hollar of 1646 when it
was known as Arundel
House. The medieval
hall (*right*) still formed
the nucleus of the
complex. Between the
hall and kitchens, the
service rooms are timber-
framed, partly over an
undercroft.

68. *Right:* Interior of
Westminster Hall,
showing the roof by
Hugh Herland. The floor
was originally somewhat
lower.

or two rooms in extent, which fronted the streets and thus often occupied the fringes of larger complexes. Here a single building filled the narrow property, its gable end to the street; behind, in the better examples, lay a small yard with a kitchen, but the majority of these smallest houses had no adjacent private open space.

A medium-sized house would have several rooms. A typical arrangement is given in a lease of 1384 for a property known as Pakeman's Wharf in Thames Street, just downstream of Billingsgate, which specified that the tenant should rebuild the property. A range of buildings along the street was to be three storeys high, the individual storeys measuring 12, 10 and 7 feet in height; behind, towards the river, would be a hall 40 feet by 23 feet, a parlour, kitchen and buttery, all on cellars 7 feet high, expressly for the storage of merchandise. The wharf was to be enlarged and faced with stone.

The street-ranges of medium and larger houses, where the property might be thirty or forty feet wide, very often included shops. These could include one of the owner, but were often let separately as lock-ups [130]. Since management of property was a significant source of wealth for many of the richer citizens, a man might own shops scattered through several streets, none of which were part of his dwelling house. In the majority of streets, shops would have only one upper storey – a solar – over the ground floor. Such two-storey units, either one or two rooms deep, could be built in ranges or rows, such as the two rows, of five and six shops, built for the Prior of Lewes to connect with his gatehouse in Southwark in 1373, modelled on the 'long Rente' of Adam Fraunceys at the east end of the Austin Friars' church in Broad Street. A fifteenth-century example of such a row can still be seen in Tewkesbury. Sometimes, in addition, part of a street was taken over by a specialised craft; thus we hear of Stockfish-monger Row in Thames Street, Bowyer Row (the former name for Ludgate Hill) or Budge Row (budge was the skin of a young goat). Alternatively, an alley down a private property might be turned into a small shopping precinct, as is evident when in 1332 Simon Frank bequeathed to his daughter Alice his whole lane, containing about twenty shops on either side.

From the early fourteenth century, and increasingly thereafter, a wide-spread type and size of 'ordinary' house can be suggested from archaeological and documentary sources. This had two rooms in plan, one behind the other, with its gable to the street; the front room was usually a shop. It is likely that from 1300 many such houses were three storeys high (or two storeys with garrets), especially in major streets [79]. Evidence for the number of storeys and upper chambers comes chiefly from plans and descriptions of around 1600, such as the Treswell surveys, and we cannot be certain that the buildings remained unchanged since they were first built [69]. This house-form is so far associated with the trades of middling status, such as fishmongers or clothworkers.

The social centre of the well-to-do household was the hall; but it was required less by tradesmen than by those with large households, and so the smallest units often had only a shop and a kitchen. On larger properties, particularly those with a courtyard, space allowed a hall of timber or sometimes of stone, a lofty room on the ground floor with a fine roof and no chambers above it. The 'high table' would often be emphasised by a raised

69. Axonometric reconstruction of houses in Abchurch Lane as surveyed by Ralph Treswell, 1612. These are probably the houses built by Simon Basse, draper, shortly before 1390. All five are variants of the two-room plan, with separate kitchens.
C   cellar
K   kitchen
Sd shed
Sh shop
W   warehouse
Y   yard

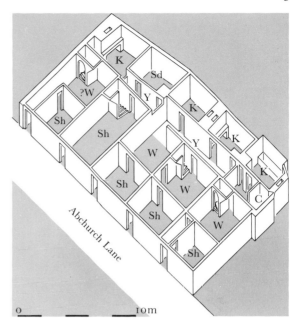

step or dais, and by side-lighting from windows larger than those along the walls of the hall (see 7). The grandest stone halls were raised on undercrofts, as in the cases of the monastic domestic ranges, Norman town houses, the Guildhall or Gerard's Hall; but these must have been comparatively rare. The Saxon and Norman building tradition had handed down another form, a large, aisled hall, which stood directly on the ground with its roof supported on two rows of wooden pillars. The name *Stapled Hall*, first recorded in 1283 and in 1333 attached to the houses in Holborn which survive in sixteenth-century form as Staple Inn [4], may refer to a house or hall with pillars (Old English, *stapel* = post). It is probable that this form was quickly superseded in London, where more chambers on several floors were required. In London streets, where space was at a premium, the hall moved upstairs over the shop, often into the room nearest the street. This was specified in a building contract of 1310 for a house and shop at the west end of Cheapside, and a will dated 1328 mentions a hall 'erected on a stage over the street' – probably a reference to a first-floor jetty – in Friday Street. The functions of 'hall' and 'solar' probably overlapped when there was only one chamber over a shop.

The solar (from French *sol*, 'floor', and *solive*, 'beam') was a private room on an upper floor and, for many households, remained the only withdrawing room or bedchamber. It was the place a man might be carried to, having been wounded, to receive the last rites and die, as in a case reported in 1324; two years previously a man had retired to his solar to hang himself with his own shirt from a beam. The solar could also be used as a workplace; in 1300, in Cheapside near Milk Street, a man was shearing cloths in a solar when a piece of wood fastened to the outside of the room, used for drying saddles, fell on a passerby and killed him. The solar would have its own door and window, for we hear in 1300–1 that Adam le Coteler tried to quieten down revellers in a brothel in Fleet Street, but they pursued him to his house and 'broke the door of his hall and entered. Adam resisted them and then took refuge in his solar, closing the door on himself, but

70. The Guard Room, Lambeth Palace; a first-floor hall of the early 14th century, where the Archbishop may have housed his men-at-arms. The quality of workmanship in timber at this time could easily equal that in stone.

Credo and the others broke down that door also. Seeing that he was likely to be killed, Adam climbed out of the window and so escaped'.

Less happy was the fate of John Toly who, one night in 1325–6, stood naked at the window of a solar thirty feet high to relieve himself into the street and fell out, killing himself on the pavement. The building of solars on their jetties into the street was a widespread problem, to judge from the Eyre of 1246: 'a solar built to the great nuisance of passers-by' is a common criticism. The older ground-floor halls might be added to, as in 1308 when a skinner planned to build two storeys at one end of his hall, containing a larder and a chamber with a chimney on the ground floor and a solar above.

One reason for such additions was a desire for greater privacy. Towards the end of the fourteenth century there are the first mentions of the *interloquitorium*, or parlour (both meaning 'place of conversation'), in the larger houses (see 71). This was a reception room, for conversation and entertainment, separate from the hall but usually not a bedchamber, and usually on the ground floor. Here might be chairs, or one of the family chests. Many larger houses would have had several separate bedchambers, or the garrets might have been used, especially where the buildings were of three storeys. Newel staircases of stone or timber to upper floors were known in larger houses but ladders, sometimes with a rope for a rail, led to the smaller solars; several fatal slippings from them are recorded.

In the fourteenth century, as far as the meagre evidence goes, kitchens were frequently separate buildings (see 69), for fear of fire; the kitchen contained the largest, and sometimes the only, hearth in the house. During the century there was an increasing trend to provide chimneys to heat other chambers and this encouraged a wider range of possible positions for the kitchen, since the chimney-stack for a kitchen could also service chambers above it. By 1400 the kitchen had commonly joined the hall on the first floor of the house, above the shop, so that a compact living and working unit was created: shop and warehouse on the ground floor, hall, kitchen and service rooms (often only cupboards) on the first floor, and two bedrooms or garrets on the second floor.

It has been said that the functions of the rooms in the medieval house were not particularly specialised, and certainly rooms were quickly adapted for many different purposes. In 1377, for instance, Thomas Yonge and Alice his wife, who lived on the south side of Watling Street, complained that their neighbour Geoffrey Chadenesfeld and others built a forge of earth and timber in the close (alley) of their tenement. The

71. The Dean's House, Westminster Abbey, finished 1385. It shows the usual arrangement of parlour at the head of the hall, both of which were, on this occasion, in stone.

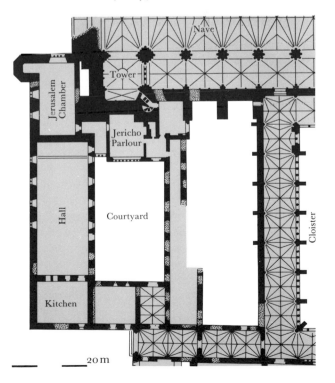

72. Reconstruction of a medieval kitchen in the Museum of London. Most of the activities which took place within it can be reconstructed by archaeological means. Fashions in pottery and other utensils may be subject to the same regional and European stimuli as development in building style.

chimney was not built of plaster and stone as the custom of the City required, and was twelve feet lower than it should be; the din of armourers at work in the forge shook the party walls and the smoke penetrated the plaintiffs' hall and chambers. The defendants (eager to defeat the prosecution on a technicality) replied that their tenant had in fact set up his anvil in the kitchen, and adapted the chimney with mortar and clay. Sadly, the judgement in the case is not recorded.

The furniture and decoration of rooms in the houses of merchants and tradesmen were at times simple, but could have symbolic significance. Furniture, even more than the size and character of the house, spoke of the owner's *estate*; certain pieces of furniture, such as the now humble chair and cupboard, were adjuncts of ceremony and played an important part in the sustaining of dignity within the social structure of the household. Although some furniture in the medieval period was built in, most was movable; and thus the lord, whether churchman or knight, could take much of his household paraphernalia with him, as a travelling statement of his position in society.

What we know as a cupboard was then called an *aumbry* or *armoire*, and could be free-standing or built into an alcove. A free-standing example still survives in the Muniment (archive) Room of Westminster Abbey, but its simplicity of construction has meant that dates given for it vary between 1380 and a hundred years later. An inventory of 1485 for a house in Botolph Lane mentions 'almaryes' in the Summer Parlour and the kitchen. Special armoires are known for plate and coin, or as wardrobes for clothing, textiles and armour. They could also be found in the pantry or buttery, and at least one fitted with vats was found in the storehouse of a fishmonger in 1373.

Buffet, *dresser* or *cupboard* were three overlapping terms for furniture used for displaying and storing plate in the hall, or storing plate and utensils in the kitchen. The hall form, very often called simply *cupboard*, was a stepped structure with open shelves on which pewter or silver was shown as on a modern Welsh dresser. Its natural position alongside high table came to give it an air of dignity; from at least 1503 to stand by the cupboard was part of the ceremonial of those ordained to be serjeants-at-law at Middle Temple.

Chairs were also originally symbols of authority; kings were crowned in a chair of state, and they and bishops had thrones from which they dispensed judgement. In ordinary houses the head of the household might have a chair, while others sat on benches; even in halls of any consequence, such as company halls, chairs were reserved for high table. Window seats were no doubt common in buildings with thick stone walls; one survives at the fifteenth-century Guildhall. Tables were mainly of boards laid on trestles (as remaining at Penshurst Place in Kent), but from the late fifteenth century fixed or *dormant* tables are known; folding and later extendable tables were also to be found. In the hall, parlour or bedroom would be the family chest. This was considered both furniture and luggage; generally it had feet if its main purpose was as furniture, but none if, like the popular 'ship's chest', it was to travel.

Four-poster beds are known in France from shortly after 1300, but were not common in England until about 1500 [73]. Canopies suspended from the head of the bed were the norm, at least in well-to-do houses. The embroidered textiles of the hangings could be lavish or imaginative, with hunting dogs, dolphins or dragons. The richest beds had conical canopies of velvet, silk or cloth of gold. Truckle beds for travelling, or for servants, were stowed beneath the main beds. The common man slept on a mattress of straw, which could lead to fatal accidents if candles were left alight while sleeping.

Though civic buildings and larger houses could have ornate glazed windows [74], the earliest reference to glazing in private houses is in a deed of 1263–4; more frequently unglazed windows were barred with iron or wood, and most windows had shutters. The glass was translucent rather than transparent; in 1341 a skinner was told to repair the broken glass in his windows because they overlooked a neighbour's garden. By law, windows along property boundaries were not allowed to be less than sixteen feet from the ground; to have them lower was considered an invasion of privacy, and was often bitterly contested. Even the parson of St Stephen Walbrook was stopped from making an opening in the south wall of his church where it touched private property.

A popular feature of larger houses was the bay window [7, 96]. This had originated in the *oriel*, a bay window forming a porch at the head of an exterior stair, and had been adapted for the high-table end of the hall,

75. *Left:* Bronze door-knocker of the 15th century in the shape of a monkey's head from Thames Street (the ring is now missing). Similar door-knockers in the form of lions' heads survive on the doors of Charterhouse and St Andrew Undershaft, both also of the 15th century.

73. *Far left:* A medieval bed with a celour, from a manuscript in the Louvre. Though the details may be stylised here, it is clear that beds, like chairs, were places of some dignity.

74. *Left:* The rose window of 1330–40 at the Bishop of Winchester's house, Southwark. Twelve feet in diameter, it was originally glazed, and would have filtered the light from the setting sun into the hall. Compare the rose window in the east end of St Paul's, finished thirty years earlier [42].

looking either into the courtyard or the private garden on the other side. The stone arch of a late fourteenth-century example can be seen at Merchant Taylors' Hall, discovered during repairs in 1913 [78]. A contract to build the Peter and Paul tavern in Paternoster Row in 1342 specified that the hall and bedroom, here both on the second floor because the tavern occupied the ground and first floors, were both to have bay windows, no doubt of timber. In timber-framed buildings the frames of both windows and doors would be part of the larger structure, the doors hung on elaborate ironwork hinges; an iron or bronze door-knocker faced the outside world [75].

Window shutters, glass and doors were frequently removed by departing tenants, but even tiled floors and panelling were not safe. In 1473, for instance, the Goldsmiths' Company found that a distinguished tenant, the mercer and alderman John Lambard, had departed with twenty-seven window-shutters, eight panes of glass from the parlour and all the ironwork of the windows there and in the hall, iron bars in the kitchen and over the shop counter, the great pewter laver kept by the hall for handwashing and the panelling of the private chapel. Other cases report that axes were used to remove fittings. On the other hand, the Corporation ruled in 1445 that if fittings installed by a tenant were fixed with nails, or wood, or mortar, or if plants had thrown roots or branches around them, they should not be removed at the end of a tenancy, but remain with the landlord.

During the fourteenth century there was a gradual improvement in the amenities available to most households, especially in sanitation and heating. Although wood was the principal domestic fuel, the more widespread building of chimneys in houses coincided with an increasing exploitation of coal. Coal had been worked in Britain in Roman times, but was only rediscovered towards the end of the twelfth century. By now it was being exported and, in the thirteenth century, with the expansion of mining, it was used more widely in forging, evaporation of brine, burning of lime, brewing and baking. In the early Middle Ages a fireplace was merely reinforced by a stone or daub wall behind and above it, called a *reredos*; above would be a chimney of lath and plaster. From the twelfth century stone fireplaces were present in noble houses or castles, such as the fireplace of about 1230–40, with its pyramidal stone hood, which survives in the Salt Tower at the Tower of London. The skinner rebuilding his hall in 1308 added a chamber with a chimney, of unknown materials; and at the Peter and Paul in 1342 two chimneys were to be built, one at each end of the cellar, carried up in stone to the first floor in the gable walls. During the fourteenth century tiles and flat bricks were being imported from Flanders; and thus in 1370, when rebuilding an L-shaped row of shops forming the corner between what is now Godliman Street and Knightrider Street, the property managers of St Paul's could demand a chimney for each of the eighteen shops, arranged in eight pairs with two single chimneys for the ends. The fireplaces, $5\frac{1}{2}$ feet wide, to be of stone and 'Tylesherd' (stacked roof-tile fragments, such as archaeologists constantly find in buildings dating from the early thirteenth century), the flues of Flanders tile, and the chimneys were to project about one foot above the roof. Clay chimney pots could be bought, as early as 1278, from Ralph de Crocker-lane, south of Fleet Street at Whitefriars; presumably he also made roof-tiles, and perhaps pottery.

As heating facilities improved, so houses also received better arrangements for sewage and drains, and for the provision of fresh water. Timber
cesspits are known from earliest times, but in the fourteenth century they
were commonly built of stone [76]. Privies were frequently the subject of
litigation, where sewage leaked into a neighbour's property – frequently his
cellar. It was natural for a cesspit to be near a party wall, for it was usually
served by a chute in the wall, lined with boards, called a *pipe*. Convenience
and the small size of many central properties dictated that privies were
often inside buildings rather than outside, and often the privy was situated
in or off the solar or withdrawing room. Sometimes a cesspit was actually
astride the boundary and was shared by two neighbours. In the 1370
contract for the St Paul's shops, the privies matched the chimney-stacks:
ten stone pits were to be dug, eight of them double privies, 10 by 11 feet and
10 feet deep. A house mentioned in 1360 had a latrine with two pipes to
separate rooms and was no doubt not unique.

Along the waterfront, privies could empty directly into the river; but in
1314 the ingenious Alice Wade was brought to court when she connected
the privy in her solar, via a wooden pipe, with the drain which took rain
water to clean the Queenhithe public latrines. The drain ran under several
other houses before reaching the common privy, and the neighbours were
'greatly inconvenienced by the stench'. Rainwater drains, sometimes from
cisterns, often ran through houses, especially through the kitchen. Gutters
at roof level led rainwater to the street, where they ended in spouts
throwing the water away from the building, or led back on to one's own
land; these were clearly valley drains of lead or timber (and possibly, from
recent discoveries, of shaped tiles), and there seem to have been virtually
no down-pipes except in special cases (as to the White Tower, to avoid
staining the rendering). Litigation about gutters was understandably

76. Lower part of a stone
privy of a house in
Basing Lane opposite
Gerard's Hall, excavated
at Watling Court in
1978. These privies were
emptied at intervals of
several years by breaking
open the masonry
around the top. Many
houses had private
sanitary arrangements
by 1350.

fierce, when most houses were built of timber, lath and daub and thus were extremely susceptible to damp and penetration by water.

In 1237 the city brought piped water to Cheapside, and in 1378 extended the service to a conduit in Cornhill. In 1350 various houses appear to be charged a water rate, indicating they had tapped into the public supply; but water was usually carried from the public conduits by waterbearers. Some houses had rainwater cisterns; many also had wells, either in a courtyard or alley, or dug within a cellar or kitchen. Some wells were built of superimposed casks, but these quickly decayed, and stone-lined wells became standard.

Medieval properties in towns were usually long and narrow, so that a side alley was necessary to give separate access to buildings behind the street-range. These alleys can still often be seen today in small towns where the old property boundaries have been preserved. In the waterfront areas of ports such as London most riverside properties had an alley at one side to give access between street and wharf [79]. Often these alleys originated as private thoroughfares, but need for water – not only for drinking, but also for laundering, or industries such as dyeing or brewing – gradually gave them a public status through time and custom. In 1343 several such alleys were regarded as public, and one was ordered to be paved because of this. Lanes were usually wide enough for a cart to reach the wharf; one of the buildings excavated at New Fresh Wharf in 1974 was known as *Le Brodegate* by 1349, and the excavated alley was 2.06 m (7 feet) wide. The surfaces of the alley under the street-range (which would have sailed over at the first floor) were of mortar and oyster shells – often used in quantity when well-draining foundation layers were required – but cobbled to the south where the alley was out in the open air. The lanes were occasionally the source of litigation between neighbours, and in 1346 William Trig was accused of blocking Fissyngwharf Lane (later called Trig Lane) to the west of his tenement with wooden stalls, wood and other things so that access formerly allowed to all citizens conveying their goods and merchandise to and from the river by horse and cart was denied. In this case the defendant could prove that the lane, though common, had never been wide enough for use by carts, which could not turn in it.

Much of the land inside the city walls at this time would have been open space; gardens were widespread, often large and well cared for. In 1304, for instance, a court case mentions a herb-garden in the middle of town, next to what is now the Bank road junction. Dovecotes are frequently mentioned, as are fruit trees and vines. Even in the city, the loss of agricultural produce was a serious matter. In 1363 Margery de Honylane, prioress of St Helen's nunnery in Bishopsgate, successfully prosecuted a neighbour, Thomas Hore, a smith, over lack of repairs to the wall between their two gardens, through which 'strange men and animals enter her garden and trample down the grass and other things growing there, and carry off the fruit', besides the more usual crime of interfering with her privacy. Poultry and farm animals were kept for fresh dairy produce and meat; cows often knocked down fences, presumably when grazing.

Although some yellow brick and Flanders tile appeared here and there, the texture of the London of Chaucer would have been predominantly of timber and stone. The main building wood was oak, *Quercus petraea*, which produces tall straight timbers. Accounts of the building corporation which serviced the Bridge and its portfolio of investment properties show oaks brought from Croydon, Carshalton and Beddington; much was brought down the river from Kingston, Weybridge and Datchet, or up-river from Thurnock and north Kent. Other oaks came from Lewisham and Coddington. The best oak, from the older middle of the trunk, was called 'heart of oak' and could be specified by the fastidious client. The second main timber to be used was elm, which has a tendency to warp, but is most suitable for underwater conditions such as piles or drains. It was used above ground for sheds and roofing, and with ash for shelving or dressers; the sources of elm for London were also the surrounding villages and countryside. Boards could be of oak [77] or elm, but were commonly of deal; oak and deal were imported from the Baltic under the term Eastland boards.

Very little medieval woodwork now remains in London, though well-preserved examples have been found recently in waterfront excavations and other instances occur in the area outside the destruction zone of the Great Fire. Elsewhere in the country, the portion of a medieval building which survives least altered is most often the roof, and it is therefore no surprise that the three largest surviving examples of medieval carpentry in London are the roofs of St Etheldreda's (c.1290), the Guard Room, Lambeth (early fourteenth century) and Barnard's Inn, Holborn (early fifteenth century). The last [86] is the city's earliest surviving fragment of a medieval town house, built by the Dean of Lincoln and bequeathed by him to become one of the Inns or colleges of lawyers. Its timber roof, complete with what is probably the original louvre, stands on walls of stone.

The quarrying and use of building stone was one of the most important industries of both the medieval and Tudor periods, in England and abroad. It employed a significant portion of the population; the men at the top of their profession, the master masons and carpenters, were highly regarded in ecclesiastical, court and social circles. Their achievements must be understood in terms of the materials they had to hand.

Today a wide range of igneous, metamorphic and sedimentary rocks are used in the City, most as facing slabs over concrete and steel. A slightly different range of stones, usually not merely decorative, can be seen in the buildings and works of previous centuries, particularly the railway age. The range of rocks used in medieval London, however, was much more limited, largely because of the high cost of transport. The creamy chalk from Beer near Seaton in Devon, much used in medieval churches in the south-west, could be brought to London for St Stephen's chapel, where sixty-eight stones 'de Bere' were bought of William Hamele of Weymouth for £11; but in 1350 Bere stone cost 6s 8d a ton, whereas a whole boatload of local chalk could be had for 7s 6d. Stones from regional and foreign quarries were used on prestigious buildings: Wheatley stone from the Oxford area is found in some medieval London churches, and St Stephen's also received York (i.e. Yorkshire) sandstone from Pontefract. Portland and Bere stones were used at Westminster, the Tower and for London Bridge. Caen stone from Normandy continued in favour, being used at St Stephen's for the quoins, mullions and sills of the windows. Particularly popular, for the shafts of pillars and occasionally floors, was the hard grey-green limestone from Purbeck, composed of small freshwater mussel and snail shells, which takes a high polish. This was used in thirteenth-

77. Section through a 12th-century oak board, reused in a waterfront construction at Seal House, Upper Thames Street (excavated 1974). The vessels forming annual rings of growth can be clearly seen; the direction of growth is upwards. Analysis of the relative widths of the rings (dendrochronology) can produce the felling date of the timber, and therefore the approximate date of use.

century churches (e.g. Salisbury Cathedral) all over southern England; related 'marbles' were quarried in the Weald. It was going out of fashion in the fourteenth century, though used occasionally later [87]; one authority has suggested that the dark vertical emphasis of Purbeck shafts did not agree with the new ideas blossoming as Perpendicular architecture.

The main stones used in the making of medieval London were, however, from more local sources: ragstone, chalk, and flint. Kentish ragstone continued to be used, but the greater flow came from quarries around Reigate in Surrey. The stone here was softer, with less glauconite, but hardened on drying. It was much used for carving – especially for the moulded stones which formed piers and arches in churches – and for the simple chamfered blocks forming window and door surrounds. Kentish stone was favoured for rough locations, such as the river wall at the Tower, probably another of Yevele's works, in 1389. Chalk from quarries around London was generally soft, and could not be exposed to frost; its main use was inside ragstone exteriors, or in foundations for walls, wells or cesspits [76, 78]. In the fourteenth century it was about one-third to a half of the price of rag. Ninety-six shiploads of chalk and flint were required for a wall at the Tower in 1283; often chalk and flint (a silica nodule occurring within the chalk) were used together for rubble walling, roughly plastered on one or both sides. Towards 1300 flints are broken in half, or knapped, and laid in regular courses, and in the first half of the fourteenth century London enjoyed the contemporary fashion of chequerwork walls, in which flints were carefully composed into black squares to alternate with a paler stone; rag or a pale limestone when exterior, or chalk when inside [80]. In the

78. A 14th-century stone foundation arch beneath the north wall of Merchant Taylors' Hall, exposed during building works in 1912. The dark earth under the arch is the accumulated deposits of previous centuries which made deep foundations necessary for stone buildings; the technique of using arches first appears about 1290.

middle of the fourteenth century, judging from repairs to the city wall and buildings such as the Lady Chapel at St Bartholomew's (1337), flints were arranged in bands about a foot in height; and at least one house was known in 1399 as *Le Flynt Halle*, presumably from its external decoration.

Buildings built predominantly of stone must, however, have always been in the minority. Even the city authorities were not immune to considerations of cost: there is a hint, for example, that although Ludgate might present a formidable stone façade to the outside world, its back was timber-framed, like the surviving Walmgate Bar in York. Churches and other public buildings such as the first Custom House (1382) were built in stone and enlarged by spasmodic individual donations. In the fourteenth century such bequests or gifts to churches resulted in the building of aisles or, more often, chapels, as can be seen still at St Helen's, Bishopsgate [57]. In ordinary houses the foundations and cellar walls were probably carried up in stone to at least first-floor level along party walls – no longer three feet thick, but somewhat thinner – with timber framing above; and timber would form the front and rear elevation from the ground upwards [79], by analogy with medieval houses in other towns.

Around the riverfront area the fourteenth century must have been one of the periods of greatest change and development, as hundreds of properties along the whole mile of Thames Street pushed out into the river in fits and starts. Excavations at Custom House, Seal House (now the extension to Fishmongers' Hall) and especially Trig Lane (to be part of the site of the new City of London Boys' School near Blackfriars) have uncovered twelfth- and thirteenth-century revetments in good condition; they formed the riverside ends of properties south of Thames Street. At Trig Lane the area excavated in 1974–6 allowed examination of the process of land reclamation from the late thirteenth century to 1480. Detailed investigation of several properties has also prompted some suggestions about the medieval uses of timber and stone.

Trig Lane can be traced in documents back to 1256, and in 1291 is referred to as 'the lane by which the Fishwharf is approached'. From the excavation of a site immediately west of the lane we know that by this time a front-braced revetment had been erected at the south end of the plot, 45 m (47$\frac{1}{2}$ feet) from Thames Street (which is now represented only by a short length next to the church tower of St Mary Somerset). Traces of buildings north of the wharf were also recorded, and the revetment was repaired at least twice. By about 1350 the frontage had been extended and redesigned, and with it a building on deep chalk foundations reused the former revetment as piling, leaving 3 m (9$\frac{3}{4}$ feet) of space to the new edge [81]. Timbers in the foreshore indicate a private river stair or access route. In about 1365 the new linc was continued to the west in stave-wall construction; twenty-eight incised marks on the timbers probably related to the method of assembly. Twenty years later, the property nearest Trig Lane advanced a further 6 m (19$\frac{1}{2}$ feet) into the river with a similar but more ambitious structure [82] which incorporated a small tank (possibly a *vivarium* for live fish) at its riverwards corner. During the fifteenth century parts of the revetments were rebuilt and heightened; the original builders apparently knew well where the tidal ebb and flow would weaken the timbers, and had designed the revetments for easy replacement of decayed parts. The property was owned by the fishmonger Trig family between

79. *Right:* Reconstruction of two houses at New Fresh Wharf from excavations of 1974. Building H (*foreground*) is of the 14th century, Building J of the 16th; both share the two-room plan. Behind the main house the alley acted as light-well to thinner buildings along the narrow plot. For the cellar behind Building J see 6.

80. *Bottom right:* Flint and chalk chequerwork in the cellar of a tradesman's house of the 14th century, at New Fresh Wharf, Lower Thames Street. The fashion was still evident in the eastern crypt of Guildhall, a century later (compare 79).

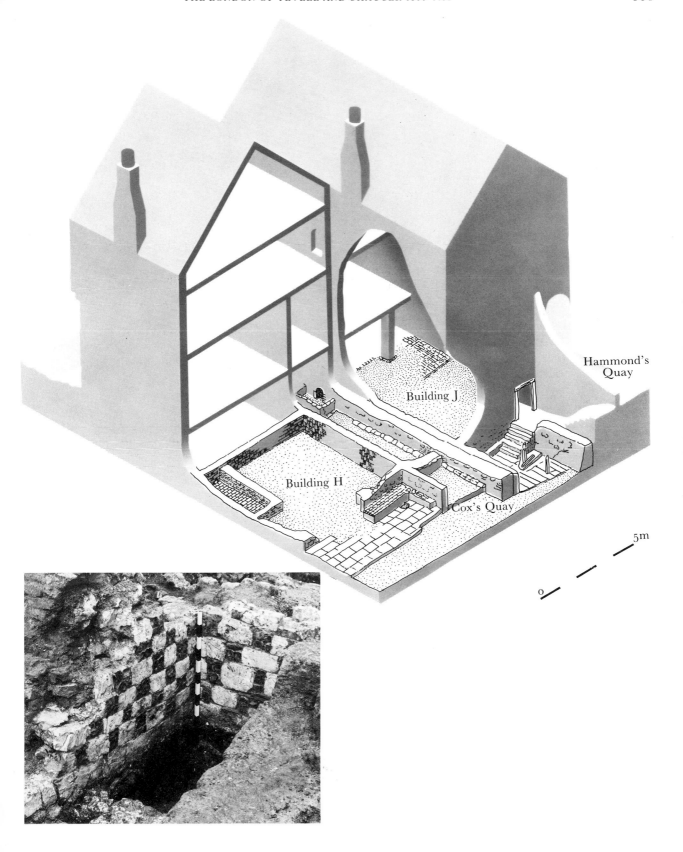

Building J

Hammond's Quay

Building H

Cox's Quay

5m

0

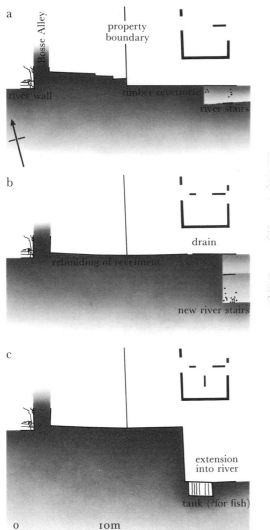

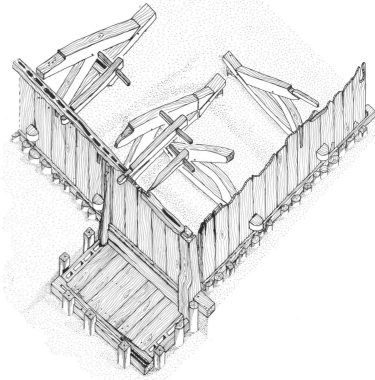

81. *Left:* Stages in medieval land reclamation, from excavations west of Trig Lane (which forms the right-hand side of the drawing) in 1974–6:
a) *c.* 1330–50
b) *c.* 1365
c) *c.* 1385.

82. *Above:* The timber revetment of *c.* 1385 at Trig Lane, with a tank, possibly for fish, at the river's edge. The working surface of the quay would be the top of organic rubbish tipped around the internal braces. Buildings on the property lay to the top left (north).

1367/90 and 1420, and it is possible that these modifications to revetments and buildings can be attributed to them.

Across Bosse Alley to the west another property had been given a stone revetment wall as early as 1330 (see 81). The area between Bosse Alley and Trig Lane, by this time split into three properties, was reunited when it passed into the hands of the Armourers' Company shortly before 1481. The Company then also built a revetment wall of ragstone with chalk infilling behind, which virtually marked the end of property extension into the river at this point. In the main, extensions to the properties were to replace wooden revetments which decayed, a repair often best achieved by erecting a new revetment a small distance to the south on the foreshore. Thus the growth of individual properties out into the river may be less a result of commercial pressure, or need for extra space, than the simpler needs of constantly rebuilding the artificial end of the property; a process which stopped – again, with exceptions – once a durable stone wall could be afforded. Presumably the increasing use of stone for this purpose in the fourteenth and fifteenth centuries – a reasonable inference from the number of stone river walls now being recorded from development sites along the waterfront – was a product not only of increased resources but also of the greater availability of stone for this comparatively humble purpose.

Riverside properties were not only being built out into the river, but by necessity had to be built higher. Where shipping docked at the approved entry points of Queenhithe, the Steelyard, Billingsgate and the Custom House, such rebuilding was probably partly in response to developments in the size of ships. In 1300 a sea-going vessel of 200 tons was exceptional, but by 1330 the average size was between 250 and 300 tons. The replacement of the medieval cog by ships of larger burden was the death of many small ports of eastern England; but they were also hard hit by the silting of rivers and estuaries. Here London also suffered; it has even been suggested that the lifetime of a quay wall or revetment can be roughly measured in the depth of silt which accumulated against it before being buried in the next reclamation deposit. The sea level was rising in relation to the land, a process which had really begun after the last Ice Age, and is continuing today. When the tide was out, ships were grounded on the foreshore; at Billingsgate they paid 'strandage', which was assessed according to the size of vessel. In a coroners' inquest of 1336 the record is at pains to point out that a ship called the St Marie Cogge, lying at St Laurence Wharf in the parish of St Dunstan in the East, was not moving (i.e. beached) when a drunken sailor decided to ascend the mast by rope and fell to his death on the way down. High tide, on the other hand, could flood the quays and riverside alleys. In 1338 Richard, son of a cornmonger, was drowned at the nearby *Tykenedleswharfe* in the parish of St Mary at Hill when he chose to walk on the wharf, 'the Thames being full and flooding it', and fell in; in 1367 a wall of a house in Desebourne Lane, by Queenhithe, had to be broken down to aid the passage of flood-water out to the river. A heightening of the nearby Trig Lane revetment took place at about this time.

Among the riverside houses and workplaces of ironmongers, chandlers, fishmongers, dyers and brewers were occasional larger houses, such as Pultney's second mansion called Coldharbour, its site now beneath Mondial House (see 83). The house immediately to the east, which belonged for a time to Edward III's mistress Alice Perrers, later took over the name of its neighbour and so confused many modern historians, who thought both houses were the same. Two of these larger tenements, which emulated courtyard houses elsewhere in the city by occupying wider properties, were bequeathed to rising groups of traders who used the waterfront to form their craft or livery halls: those of the Vintners and the Fishmongers. Both halls, rebuilt many times, still occupy their fourteenth-century sites in Thames Street.

Waterfront traffic revolved around four nodal points on the waterfront, which have already been mentioned: Queenhithe and the Steelyard (now beneath Cannon Street railway station) above the bridge, and Billingsgate and the Custom House below. What is known of the first three is mostly of the fifteenth and sixteenth centuries; but it is appropriate to conclude this chapter by describing the excavation of the Custom House, the workplace of Geoffrey Chaucer.

By 1370 Chaucer was a respected royal servant, paying many visits on the king's business to the Continent, including the cities of Florence and

Genoa; two great cities which he no doubt compared to his native London. In 1374 he rented the house or rooms above Aldgate from the corporation, and lived there until 1388. In 1374 also he was made Comptroller of Customs and Subsidy of Wools, Skins and Hides in the port of London, though he continued to be employed on embassies. He must have been intimately concerned with the decision of John Churchman, a merchant, to build a Custom House at the seaward end of the waterfront in 1382 'to serve for tronage, or weighing of wools'. Tax on the export of wool was a valuable source of income for successive kings, and it is hardly surprising that the site lay under the watchful eye of royal officials in the Tower. Excavations of 1973 uncovered Churchman's original building and an extension, presumably the small chamber for a latrine and a chamber over the counting-house known to be added a year later in 1383. Between the two buildings was a timber latrine drain running south to the river; the excavators were proud to claim that Chaucer himself probably used it.

Chaucer would have known Henry Yevele, for they were both highly-placed civil servants. In 1387 Chaucer could have looked across the river from the counting-house and seen that Yevele was building two watermills which he and others had just bought on the southern bank of the river, near other mills belonging to Battle Abbey; by a nice coincidence these mills were to be bought in 1439 by Sir John Fastolf, the prototype of Shakespeare's Falstaff. And in 1389 Chaucer was appointed Clerk of the King's Works, the post previously held by the old Master Mason.

Both men died in 1400; Yevele on 21 August and Chaucer on 25 October. Many must have mourned the passing of the architect, for all around they saw his fine buildings and creations, from Westminster Hall to his own tombstone in St Magnus's. Many others would celebrate the memory of Chaucer as his works became more widely known after his death. Yevele and his colleagues contributed to the development of the city by founding a style in building that would not be superseded until the sixteenth century. From this city emerged Chaucer's characters on their pilgrimage, and it is in buildings such as we have described that his stories are set.

83. *Above:* Part of the London waterfront, from a panorama of *c.* 1550. It shows the second Coldharbour on the waterfront (*centre*) and, behind, the tower of All Hallows the Great. On the extreme right is the tower of Pultney's mansion in Pountney Lane.

84. *Right:* The west end of Westminster Abbey in a print by Hollar of 1647. Although the design was originally Yevele's, only the porch was completed in his lifetime; the window was not glazed until 1506–12. Compare the porch with that of Croxton's Guildhall [87].

Stability and consolidation 1400-1500

5

Although the fifteenth century produced many great buildings of high quality throughout the land, the country's political history was rent by faction and warfare, its economy burdened with debt. Many towns, for a multitude of reasons not yet fully understood, were suffering (especially in the second half of the century) from decay and impoverishment. There may be signs of this in London, but they have largely still to be found. The Guildhall and the market of Leadenhall are products of the first half and middle of the century, enhanced and largely funded by charitable bequests of major figures such as Richard Whittington and Simon Eyre. Lower down the scale of buildings, townspeople endowed and extended parish churches or later bequeathed property to their own trading organisations or crafts. Though, as at York, there are few exceptional buildings of the second half of the century, London still produced nearly thirty livery company halls and the high and magnificent hall of Sir John Crosby, which was to be matched only by royal palaces.

It was the proximity of the major royal palace at Westminster, and the associated machinery of government, which prompted a second wave of development in the city's western suburb to overlie and enmesh with the existing group of prominent town houses for bishops and others attending parliament described in chapter four. One of the professions now appealing to the sons of wealthy citizens was the law, and the final settling of the royal Chancellor's household in what came to be called Chancery Lane, in fairly open country north of the Strand, was a natural magnet for students of the law who were soon organised into groups based upon prominent town houses or Inns. The earliest recorded seems to be David's or Thavy's Inn, on the south side of Holborn by St Andrew's church, in the late fourteenth century. On the north side of the street nearby, Furnival's Inn was established at about the same time, and Staple Inn shortly afterwards. The last of the Holborn Inns was probably formed by Lionel Bernard or Barnard in the 1430s, in a house next to Staple Inn which we have already seen [86]. No doubt the influx of crowds of rowdy young men also helped the proliferation of taverns in the western suburb for which it was shortly notorious. To the west and south of the Holborn Inns lay the more established and sober Inns of Court, to which the Inns of Chancery were eventually subordinated: Lincoln's Inn, Gray's Inn, and the Temple, whose origins also lie in the fourteenth century, but whose surviving buildings are substantially of a later period (pp. 137, 151-4).

Other signs of prosperity were not peculiar to London. The major towns of eastern England built their finest Guildhalls in the first half of the fifteenth century; if the level of activity in building construction is related to economic fortunes, then things cannot have been so bad in Norwich (where the Guildhall was finished by 1411), King's Lynn (1433) or York (1449). In the case of London there was more than merchants' pride to consider:

85. The eastern wing of Leadenhall during demolition, drawn by Smith in 1812. In the foreground, remains of the chapel (1466), with carefully arranged samples of the mouldings from it. Similar blank arcading is found in the Guildhall porch.

86. Interior of Barnard's Inn hall, of about 1400; watercolour of c. 1875 by J. P. Emslie.

the king had just finished building Westminster Hall. The Guildhall had stood on part of its present site from at least the late thirteenth century, and possibly from the second quarter of the twelfth. It is likely that about 1270–90 the rising fortunes of the city promoted the building of a new guildhall, probably with aisles, on a stone undercroft which survives in part as the western crypt of the present Guildhall. In 1411, less than ten years after the completion of Yevele's Westminster Hall, John Croxton, evidently a disciple of Henry Yevele, was engaged as Master Mason to design and build a further replacement by the City.

Given the fixed points of the existing west end of the building and the need for a public entrance from a Guildhall Yard much narrower than it is today, Croxton chose to incorporate most of the old undercroft and extend the building, providing it with an eastern undercroft [88]. The two crypts, having survived the Great Fire of 1666 and another in 1940, both of which badly damaged the hall above, have recently been restored and are open to the public. The porch, its façade rebuilt in the eighteenth century, still has its original medieval two-bay roof with bosses and blank arcading on the walls; similar blank arcading originally screened the interior walls of the great hall. The pattern of arcading, with each panel ending in a cinquefoil (five-leafed) head, was repeated by larger screens of tracery above, through which the outer windows could be seen; the effect was like that of the galleries around the choir at Gloucester Cathedral. At each end was a great window, not only in proud imitation of Westminster Hall (see 87), but larger than those at Norwich and King's Lynn.

In the same year that the rebuilding of the Guildhall was begun, the City received the site of the Leadenhall, a large house which had formed the core of the city estate of the twelfth-century dynasty of the sheriff Gervase of Cornhill. The site had been used as a market for poultry since before 1321; in 1377 the sale of cheese there was regulated. Fresh from his labours at Guildhall, John Croxton was diverted to build a 'garner' at the Leadenhall in 1442. Either building was already in hand, or not much was

87. *Above:*
Reconstruction of the
medieval Guildhall by
Terry Ball. For the
statues on the façade of
the porch which
symbolised Law,
Learning, and other civic
virtues, see 93. Next to
the porch was the
Guildhall chapel.

88. *Right:* The eastern
crypt of Guildhall, *c.*
1430, photographed
about 1897.

required, for the new building was given a lead roof only one year later, and in 1444 land was bought to make an entrance to Leadenhall Street. The garner or storehouses formed a quadrant; the two sides which survived to be drawn by nineteenth-century antiquaries [85] were of two floors on a ground storey which was at least in part on an open arcade. From the east range the market people could enter a chapel built at the cost of Simon Eyre, draper and mayor in 1445, lit by large windows with cinquefoiled heads reminiscent of the newly-finished Guildhall. A Fraternity of Priests was founded in the chapel in 1466 to service the market.

St Benet Sherehog

The building of granaries at Leadenhall was necessary because the city, as it grew larger, relied ever more precariously upon food supplies, especially of corn, from a wide area of supply. When the English harvest failed, corn had to be sought in the Baltic. The finance for the building, as for that of Guildhall and many civic works, came from the private purses of richer citizens, often when they were in office as mayor, but privately financed nevertheless. To allocate a proportion of one's assembled fortune was both a civic duty and a gesture of the piety which would ensure eventual salvation in heaven. In the twelfth and early thirteenth centuries it was the fashion to create or endow the monastic houses or hospitals; in the late thirteenth century the civic leader Henry Waleys, besides contributing to the nave of Greyfriars, turned to more practical works in establishing the Tun, a lock-up for 'nightwalkers' in Cornhill, and setting up a covered market for fishmongers and butchers at the Stocks (commemorated by the Blue Plaque on the north face of the Mansion House). Improvements in the city, or the rebuilding of public buildings such as Guildhall, often relied on the stimulus of individual bequests. John Churchman, a pepperer who lived periodically in both London and Norwich, built the Custom House in 1382 to help the regulation of international trade; Thomas Falconer, a mercer, built a postern in the city wall at Moorgate in 1415 to enable the citizens to escape into the open air of Moorfields. The executors of Richard Whittington, a few years later, spread their generosity over several projects.

St Martin Vintry

St Andrew Undershaft

St Bartholomew Exchange

The real Dick Whittington was a man of even greater stature than his legend. Born not into poverty but into a well-off family, he rose to be what has been called a 'merchant prince' by trading in the risky but profitable North and Mediterranean seas. He supported three successive English kings with loans, and left a fortune equivalent to the wealth of a medium-sized kingdom. During his lifetime he performed several works of public benefit: the first was the rebuilding of his local church, St Michael Paternoster Royal, in 1409, possibly to provide a place for his own tomb and for the burial of his wife. Two years later he contributed most of the funds needed to build and equip a library at the Greyfriars; he also added a refuge for unmarried mothers to St Thomas's Hospital in Southwark. At his death in 1423 he bequeathed the bulk of his fortune to various charitable uses. His executors rebuilt Newgate jail, in which prisoners had been dying from the corrupted atmosphere, contributed to the building of Guildhall and of its library, and built a south gate at St Bartholomew's Hospital. They also carried out his wishes in establishing a College of Priests and an almshouse between St Michael's and Whittington's own house in College Hill. Each poor inmate was to have a place of his own, a cell or little house with a chimney; there was probably to be also a parlour

St Helen's Bishopgate

St Antholin

St John the Baptist
(Cloak Lane)

St Dunstan in the East

St Benet Gracechurch

St Gabriel Fenchurch

St Magnus

89. Selection of churches
from the copperplate
map of *c*. 1559.

or hall for communal meals, and the almsmen were buried in the yard or entry alongside the church. Some details of the buildings, and several burials, were recorded at 19–20 College Hill during recent redevelopment.

The most curious, but in spirit most medieval, product of Whittington's charity was the building of 'Whittington's Longhouse', a public privy of imposing size over the Thames at the south end of Frier or Greenwich Lane in the Vintry near the mouth of the Walbrook. The latrine comprised two rows of sixty-four seats, one for men and the other for women. The seats overhung a gulley which was flushed by each tide, and built above were five rooms for pensioners of the parish of St Martin Vintry. Centuries later the offices of the Public Cleansing Department now cover the site.

During the fourteenth century, however, the charity of the aldermannic class had turned chiefly in the direction of their local parish churches and craft halls. Townspeople everywhere were being generous to their churches on an unprecedented scale, either by extensions to the fabric, donating vestments or relics, or establishing priests to chant soul-masses for themselves or their families. Naturally the more prominent citizens could afford to be remembered in spectacular fashion. John Lovekyn, for instance, was a childless fishmonger who died in 1368, having founded a chapel in his home town of Kingston-upon-Thames and also having rebuilt the fishmongers' church in London, St Michael Crooked Lane (now covered by the north approach to London Bridge), in four stages between 1348 and 1366. He was buried in the choir, under a tomb with images of himself and his wife in alabaster. Nearby, that other famous fishmonger, William Walworth (who slew Wat Tyler) was buried in the Fishmongers' chapel. The brass inscription on Lovekyn's tomb, removed by Protestant reformers in the 1540s, was turned over and used for another tomb at Walkerne in Hertfordshire, where the original inscription was found on the hidden side in 1870. Many other parish churches received bequests or donations for extensions or embellishments; John Barnes, mercer and mayor in 1371, was a great builder at St Thomas Apostle (now covered by Queen Street), as his arms in the windows and stonework testified to John Stow. John Hinde, a draper, rebuilt St Swithin London Stone, where he was buried beneath windows glazed with his shield of silver and azure, a silver lion *passant* or with the right paw defiantly raised. Nearby, St Antholin's in Budge Row was the guild-church of the grocers and the recipient of several donations for the building of chapels; in the churchyard was a well which William de Hanhampstede, pepperer, thought worthy of his bequest in 1348 (see 89).

Although much information about the appearance of these parish churches is forthcoming from their own records, the absence in the majority of cases of a plan of the church in the medieval period means that the details are incidental and cannot be placed in their context. It is as though we possess one or two items of furniture for a doll's house, but we do not yet have the house to put them in. This may improve as study increases of the later map-views and panoramas of the city. These views of London – principally those by Wyngaerde in *c*. 1550 [83], Hollar in 1647 [97, 147] and the 'copperplate map' of *c*. 1558–9 [52, 89] – show many of the churches, particularly those in waterfront areas, in their late medieval form. By comparing the representations of the churches with evidence from documentary and archaeological sources, some general comments about the development of London's parish churches may be attempted. The following outline is based upon study of the sixty-six churches in the eastern half of the city which are shown in the copperplate map; fortunately, only half of this area was devastated by the Great Fire of 1666 [143] and thus details of many churches, and in some few cases the churches themselves, survived into the age of more detailed recording.

The evidence for the enlargement of churches by the addition of aisles during the thirteenth and fourteenth centuries is at present very fragmentary. Several churches had one or both aisles added in the thirteenth century, and in 1381 St Dunstan in the East could employ Henry Yevele as designer for a south aisle. When St Ethelburga's [90] was rebuilt in 1390–1400, space allowed only one aisle to the south; but it seems probable that the great majority of London's churches comprised a nave and two aisles by 1450, and many had two aisles fifty years earlier.

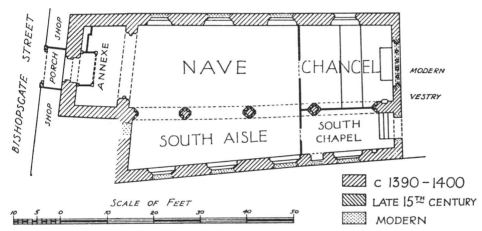

90. Plan of St Ethelburga's, Bishopsgate, in 1929, before the removal of the shops built against its west end in the 16th century.

Very little information about the body of the church is forthcoming from the copperplate map, since the artist does not seem to have been as interested in that as he was, by comparison, in the towers. Some churches are shown with lead roofs; in one case (St Martin Vintry) this is confirmed by documentary evidence. Several churches had their roofs rebuilt during the fifteenth century, endowed by parishioners or churchwardens who had their arms carved in the roof timbers. Towards the end of the fifteenth century are found bequests for battlements, which also figure widely on the churches shown in 1559.

Several of the more prominent churches, such as St Antholin, Budge Row, and St Michael Cornhill, are known to have had chapels, almost all dedicated to St Mary, before the Plague. In the decades which followed there was a spate of chapel dedications to a host of saints. Two fourteenth-century chapels still survive at St Helen's, Bishopsgate [57], but otherwise little is known of their form. In many churches a side aisle might be composed of one or more chapels, separated by wooden screens and with separate doors, as at St Mary at Hill; occasionally a chapel might be entered from the choir itself. The building of chapels, or the larger generosity which built a whole aisle, continued throughout the fifteenth century. The latest for which a specific building date is known was the chapel attached to the south side of St Bartholomew Exchange built in 1509 by Sir William Cappell, mayor in 1503 [89].

The chief value of the copperplate drawing, from the point of view of the church, is the attention given to towers, though they are in simplified form, perhaps even reduced in height. As might be expected in the sixteenth-century city, a large proportion are Perpendicular in style. The largest group are of the type called Kentish, though the distribution is found throughout the Home Counties, especially in north Kent, Middlesex, north Surrey and south Essex. Their characteristics are an embattled parapet, an external round or polygonal stair-turret at one corner, rising a little above the parapet, and buttresses stopping below the top-stage at a well-marked string course. The type was built from the late fourteenth century to the Reformation; possibly one of the earliest may have been that of Maidstone collegiate church in 1395–8, attributed to Henry Yevele. An example dated to 1440–1 still survives at All Saints, Fulham [92]. Variants of the type, all unfortunately undated, can be seen on the copperplate [89]. A more elaborate tower of this age occurs in the larger city churches; in it the corner buttresses are carried up into small spires at the corner. There are also a small number of spires. The timber spire of St Ethelburga's, now removed, is shown in an engraving of 1736 [91]; the spires of St Lawrence Pountney and St Dunstan in the East were notable landmarks from the south. On the panoramas some older, Romanesque towers may be identified in between the newer rebuildings [97].

91. St Ethelburga's Church in 1736, still surrounded by pre-Fire buildings; by West and Thoms.

92. *Left:* All Saints, Fulham. All but the tower is a competent Victorian rebuilding in medieval style. The Kentish tower (1440–1) shows how many London parish churches must have appeared.

Whenever the ground-floor stage of the towers can be seen in the copperplate, the main entrance to the church is very often through the tower. The doorway occasionally has a porch; in one case it came from a dissolved priory. The tower was usually the most upstanding part of the fabric facing Sir Christopher Wren in 1666, and it is not surprising that in several instances he retained the tower, and its entrance into the church.

The first thing the medieval visitor would see on entering many of the churches would be the rood: statues in wood of the Crucifixion, flanked by SS Mary and John, over a screen. The beam of the rood spanned the division between nave and choir, and was continued over at least one side aisle to the rood stair which rose in an external turret, entered from the aisle [123]. The church, from about 1350, would have pews, though men and women, even when married, sat in different parts of the church. Hardly any pre-Fire stained glass has survived; a series of shields-of-arms of the contributors to the major rebuilding of St Andrew Undershaft, which still stands in Leadenhall Street, are now in the vaults of the nearby Baltic Exchange, having been removed for safe keeping in the Second World War. Some late fifteenth-century fragments remain, restored at St Helen's. Also in this church are brasses, including some from the demolished church of St Martin Outwich; but the best collection of brasses can be found at All Hallows Barking. One major loss (due to the Reformation) is that of the hundreds of statues and painted images which, especially when lit by flickering candles, must have dazzled and uplifted the medieval parishioner. The side altars in chapels were often adorned with a statue or image of the saint to whom they were dedicated. At St Mary at Hill there was a *Pietà* (Our Lady of Pity); presumably this was not unique.

Many parish churches also housed holy relics. The bones of St Erkenwald were St Paul's greatest tourist attraction; some parish churches assembled collections of holy relics, perhaps in part as souvenirs of

93. *Below:* Medieval
figures which survived
the Reformation, drawn
by John Carter in 1783:
left St Basil, and Roger
Russell and his wife
Anne, from the window
in the hall owned by the
Fraternity of the Trinity,
Aldersgate Street; *right*
stone statues of Law and
Learning, Discipline,
Justice, Fortitude and
Temperance from the
façade of the Guildhall
porch. The last four were
found in a Welsh garden
in 1972 and are now in
the Museum of London.

pilgrimages abroad. A poor church such as All Hallows on the Wall would report in 1500–1 that it possessed only one relic, a bone of St David; but a remarkable list of relics survives for St Margaret Bridge (next to the site of the Monument) in 1472. From the life and times of Christ were preserved part of the manger and crib, part of the Sepulchre, and two parts of the clothing of the Virgin Mary; there was also part of the vestment of St Mary Magdalene, as well as a piece of the stone where she did penance. The most precious item, encased in a silver cross, was part of the holy cross itself. The early church was represented by part of the cross of St Peter, and of the cross of St Andrew, along with some of his bones, and some clothing of St Matthew; nor were more recent saints forgotten, for there were also bones of St Hugh (of Lincoln), some flesh of St Wulfstan, clothing of Edward the Confessor and a tooth of St Brigid. Even the city's own saint, Thomas of Canterbury, had donated a lock of his hair.

In the confined spaces of the city the parish church was often the centre of neighbourhood life. It would be used as a meeting-place by the ward authorities, debating policing or military matters, and occasionally the mayor and aldermen would meet in a church to discuss a local case of *Assize of Nuisance*. When All Hallows on the Wall had fallen into ruin and decay, the church applied for a licence to hold a stage play to help with the funding. During the fourteenth century many parishes founded fraternities based on the church and dedicated to a particular saint. Some fraternities were dedicated to a good and holy life; many emphasised benevolent social activities, helping out members when they were ill, or in prison, or providing the accoutrements, such as an embroidered pall and candles, for a decent funeral. The popular fraternity of Holy Trinity, founded in St Botolph Aldersgate in 1377, owned property in the neighbourhood; it may have met in a first-floor hall in Aldersgate Street [94].

On the whole parish fraternities were patronised more by citizens of middle rank than by merchants and the more prominent trades. For the richer crafts, the guild was a similar association, but with the intention of pooling strength to attain common commercial objectives and increase rewards; it was for the protection of a craft monopoly as well as for the undoubted social benefits. In 1422 the Clerk of the Brewers' Company made a list of the crafts in London: it totalled 111 names. Although the Brewers had a hall of their own by this date, on the site of the present hall in Aldermanbury Square, it was a luxury enjoyed by very few other companies; one of the purposes of the Clerk's list may have been to look forward to a sizeable income from hiring the hall. Twenty years earlier there were probably not more than five or six livery companies with halls of their own; the other crafts mainly used local hostelries or the houses of prominent members for their meetings. In the reign of Richard III a hundred years later, there were at least twenty-eight halls, and more were being built; John Stow mentions forty-six in 1598. The process of acquiring a hall was almost always the same: a prominent member of the craft would bequeath his house – nearly always a courtyard house, with a large hall suitable for the ceremonies or convivial meetings of the craft – to a group of trustees, often other members of the guild. The company would then adapt and expand the buildings, but not alter their general arrangement. It was therefore natural that when in the later fifteenth and sixteenth centuries the finances of the richer companies enabled them to rebuild their halls or

94. Trinity Hall, Aldersgate Street; a first-floor hall built, from the style of its roof, towards the end of the 15th century, with a later fire-place. The Fraternity of the Holy Trinity owned this property, the Falcon on the Hoop brewery, from 1431; this hall is unlikely to be a rebuilding to form part of the brewery, but the Fraternity's records never mention using it as an assembly hall. In 1612 the Farriers' Company leased it for their hall.

acquire totally new sites, they followed the existing form of hall, parlour and associated buildings which derived ultimately from the domestic models of the fourteenth century. The need for a central hall for feasting, working meetings and ceremony helped to prolong the natural life of the large, open-roofed hall as a building form. The halls of the Inns of Court of Elizabeth's reign – Gray's Inn, Middle Temple and Staple Inn, for instance – were up-to-date in decorative detail, but in form resembled halls of two hundred years before. The medieval open hall became old-fashioned only in the seventeenth century.

Companies which are known to have had halls by 1400 include the Cordwainers, Merchant Taylors, Goldsmiths, Saddlers and perhaps the Skinners. Nineteen goldsmiths acting for the company bought a house in Foster Lane, on the site of the present Goldsmiths' Hall, in 1339. Extensive building works followed, and in 1362–3 the company's 'Common place' is described as containing a hall, kitchen, pantry, buttery and two chambers with the hall; the frame of timber for it cost £25. Similar refurbishing and extension was carried out by the Merchant Taylors, at their new premises in Threadneedle Street and fortunately much of the medieval work survives, though considerably altered by the ravages of a direct hit from enemy bombing in the Second World War and piecemeal adjacent development [95]. The house had belonged to John Yakesley, the king's tent-maker; the tailors acquired the site in 1349, at the height of the plague. The natural conservatism of the new owners does not help to sort out the building dates of the surviving portions; possibly the hall itself dates originally from the private mansion, though it has been suggested that the house was pulled down, or that it lay to the south-east by Cornhill, where there was a great gate. Building works of 1910–13 revealed arched chalk foundations [78] under the north wall of the hall which are only datable roughly to the fourteenth century. Certainly the hall must have been in its present position by about 1375, the date of a surviving undercroft below the screens end; originally projecting one bay further into the yard to the north, it supported the company's chapel. Since works later than the late fourteenth century must be those of the company, we can also suggest the Merchant Taylors added a 'buffet' for displaying plate with a vault of stone tracery as later at nearby Crosby Place, and an oriel looking south into the garden [96].

To the south-east of the hall lies the great kitchen, a square stone building first mentioned in 1388, and rebuilt in its present form in 1425–33. As it neared completion, men of the company went to inspect the roof of the kitchen at Kennington Palace, presumably because their roof was to be similar. It rose in an octagonal pyramid and was topped by a gilded vane. It had a stone well in one corner, and the fireplaces, later rebuilt, are probably in their medieval positions. The north wall, facing the hall, is occupied by an impressive trio of arched openings; but they lead nowhere in particular, forming the side of a passage. If, as some have argued, the kitchen is a relic of the Yakesley mansion, then they might have led originally to the former hall.

The company halls were social centres where the crafts exercised their self-discipline – the goldsmiths had a set of stocks in their hall for unruly apprentices – and where they prayed to their patron saints. A silver-gilt statue of St Dunstan looked down on the goldsmiths, a carved and painted image of St John in a tabernacle on the Merchant Taylors. In the hall the craft also entertained themselves, their wives and their guests; sometimes even royalty. The visit of James I to dine with the Merchant Taylors in 1607 is said to have been the occasion of the composition, in his honour, of a song called *God Save the King*, now the first verse of the national anthem. The halls were often let out, as the Brewers' Clerk foresaw, to lesser companies who still had no hall of their own, or to brethren and even 'strangers' for weddings. The Pewterers' new hall of 1498 in Lime Street was hired out principally to the ward of Langbourne for ward meetings.

At first the parlour, the withdrawing room inherited from the large private house, was a retiring room for the wardens of the craft, but later the livery – the senior membership of the guild – would dine there, separate from the fellowship in the main hall, in the same way that the lord of the house, it was being noticed, began to dine apart in large households. The younger element, the yeomanry, had developed into a recognised but subordinate branch of most of the companies by the end of the fifteenth century. They sometimes dined apart, as did the members' wives, who had a separate chamber at the larger halls such as the Drapers' and Clothworkers'.

A company hall was also an estate office, for during the fifteenth century prominent tradesmen began to mistrust the administration of charity by the church and turned to their growing guild organisations as trustees of charitable bequests. These often took the form of property, which could be rented either to members of the company, including the infirm or members' widows, or to strangers to provide income for the guild. Several companies, such as the Drapers, Brewers and Taylors, had almshouses by the hall; these would be occupied by retired members of the company, and, incidentally, the hall was thus provided with cleaners and part-time gardeners.

The company garden was an important feature of many a hall, a quiet retreat for its members away from the bustle of the market streets. Thanks to the survival of wardens' accounts we can reconstruct the appearance of several company gardens in the fifteenth and sixteenth centuries. The hall of the Carpenters' Company in London Wall, for instance, had two gardens, the main one and a second garden in the courtyard of the hall. The larger garden was surrounded by a wall of lath and earth, with diagonal supports or *spores*. The principal plant was a large vine, which had a frame made for it in 1491, and was frequently cut and bound. There had been much work in both gardens over the previous year: box trees were planted in the courtyard, and herbs set in knots, which were raised square beds divided into quarters and each laid out in a geometrical pattern; rosemary, thyme and hyssop were bought as seed. The garden was manured with dung and soil brought in from outside. The purchase of rails, stakes and bindings suggests that as in other medieval gardens there were trellises, walks and trained plants. More detailed lists of seeds bought for the garden occur in 1565 and 1568: beets, bugloss, camomile, chicory, clary (*Salvia sclarea* or 'clear-eye', considered good for the eyes), endive (used as a salad), gilly-flowers, hyssop, langue-de-boeuf, lavender, lettuce, marigolds, parsley, rosemary, sage, sorrel, spinach, stock, sweet marjoram and thyme. By this later date the garden had a 'great arbour' covered with roses, and a pear tree with a bench beneath it. Medieval and Tudor gardeners concentrated on sweet-smelling or aromatic plants, to provide a haven of beauty by counteracting the many offensive smells of the street.

The company halls were expressions of the fortunes of trading groups within the city, but they did not have to take much account of the requirements of trade or industry in their design. The trading installations along the waterfront, on the other hand, incorporated features made necessary by their loading and unloading functions. Apart from the Custom House of 1382, which was replaced in Elizabeth's reign, the three other major waterfront institutions largely achieved their final form in the fifteenth century. These were the Steelyard, Billingsgate and Queenhithe.

German trade links with London had been strong before the Norman Conquest, but the house of Cologne merchants, the basis of the later Steelyard, is first heard of in 1170; by 1235 they had a guildhall of their own

95. Merchant Taylors'
Hall from the garden, in
1930, before war damage
destroyed the
(modernised) medieval
windows. The top of the
arch of the oriel to the
garden can just be seen
(*on the left*) above the
19th-century cloister.

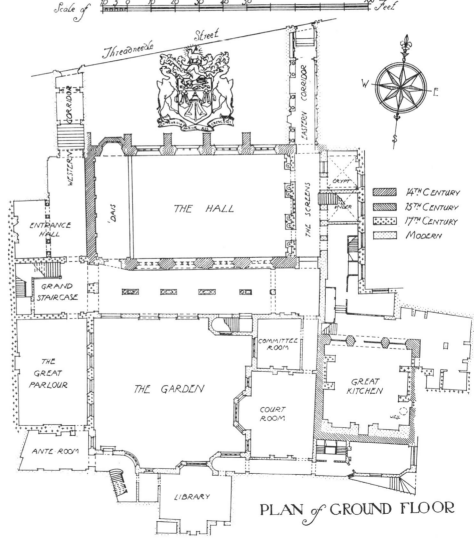

96. Plan of Merchant
Taylors' Hall,
Threadneedle Street, in
1929. In the medieval
period a courtyard lay to
the north of the hall;
nearby along the street
was a courtyard of
almshouses built in 1414.
The undercroft on the
east side, now only two
bays long, was originally
at least three and
perhaps four bays long,
projecting into the court;
it may be a relic of the
14th-century mansion
which preceded the
company hall.
Restoration after war
damage has altered some
details.

in Windgoose Lane, one of many leading from Thames Street to the river. At this time, as nearby waterfront excavations have shown, the reclaimed shoreline was only half the present distance south of Thames Street, and the hall, probably the oldest part of the complex, lay up by the main street. The complex of buildings forming the Steelyard is shown in sixteenth and seventeenth-century panoramas [97], and was surveyed immediately before the Great Fire by Hollar. Study of the surviving documentary evidence by German scholars has shown that the greatest extent of the Steelyard was reached by 1475, and several of the buildings shown in Hollar's drawing of 1647 may well date from about this time.

97. The Steelyard and its surroundings, drawn by Hollar in 1647. The tower, and the row of shacks to its left (which should be a crane) are both mistakes, probably arising from working up sketches by using previous panoramas. The large stair below the 'tower', however, is correct; it belonged to the Clothworkers' Company, who moored their barge there – hence the ornate posts, like traditional mooring posts on modern jetties in Venice.

South of the hall was a tower (unfortunately shown in the wrong place by Hollar), and then a garden, known for its vines; the garden wall, recorded in a watercolour of 1853 just before the imposition of the Cannon Street railway viaduct on the whole site, was of a chequerwork design similar to the Charterhouse wall. The complex included a council chamber, warehouses and houses of the merchants, a Rhenish wine tavern (the merchants were allowed to sell their imports), and a crane (misdrawn by Hollar, but identifiable in earlier drawings). The most distinctive building in the Steelyard is the Hanse Master's house in the south-west corner, on the riverfront. A gallery roofed in two sections sits on a high river wall; through a round-headed archway in the wall Windgoose Lane reaches a 'bridge', or river stairs on the foreshore, around which the watermen's boats are congregating like taxis outside a modern railway station.

In several ways the London Steelyard resembled the Steelyard at King's Lynn, which can still be visited. There two parallel rows of warehouses run to the wharf on either side of a narrow courtyard, possibly originally closed off from the river by a further range. The side ranges are probably fifteenth-century in date; one, built of timber, is in two storeys, the other, in brick, is in three storeys. The first resembles shops in the town of the same period, and to the viewer from outside both kinds of buildings may have looked very alike, in London as in Lynn.

Parallels with buildings of King's Lynn appear again as we turn to Billingsgate. At Lynn a large merchant's house on the river, known as Hampton Court, has a waterfront range; it was built in the fifteenth century, with an open ground floor and arched openings to enable merchandise to be unloaded easily. A long building, placed on the western, upstream side of the Billingsgate dock, is shown in one of the earliest views of medieval London, an illuminated miniature of about 1500 in the British Library [98]. The building consists of a range of two or three storeys, built of timber and possibly in part of stone, over a vault three bays wide, which may also have been of stone; the south end of this building is shown by Wyngaerde in his drawing of about 1540 [99]. Such a major building would be the result of unusual munificence; and the donor may have been Sir Thomas Haseley, who bequeathed £1,000 from his lands to extend Billingsgate in 1449.

Although Wyngaerde shows two ships pressed tightly within the confined space of the dock, there was a wide area to the north called the *Romeland* ('open space'), equivalent to the northern half of the nineteenth-century fish market, at the head of the medieval inlet. An open area was clearly the centre of such places; a *Romeland* was to be found at Queenhithe (where it was used for illicit rubbish-tipping) and Dowgate, where the Walbrook flowed into the Thames alongside the Steelyard. Another *Romeland* existed just inside Aldgate, and the name is also used for a street outside the abbey gate in St Alban's.

Queenhithe and Billingsgate were the two main landing-places for goods throughout the medieval period. Although there was a certain amount of overlap in their functions, Queenhithe handled down-river traffic, and Billingsgate the international sea-going ships. Each had its own connection with an inland market: Queenhithe with Old Fish Street (now surviving only at the east end of St Nicholas Cole Abbey church, on the north side of Queen Victoria Street) and Cheapside; Billingsgate with Eastcheap. Regulations of 1463 divided cargoes, especially of foodstuffs, between the two places. Corn and foreign fish could only be landed at Queenhithe, the latter intended for sale in Old Fish Street. Granaries for the corn are recorded in the north-east corner of Queenhithe by 1307, and two granaries with garrets in 1310; presumably they resembled those later at the Steelyard. Bakers, brewers and others bought corn there, and rates for porterage were worked out. Little else is known of the development of the medieval buildings. Wyngaerde shows the dock in his panorama as an open wharf on three sides, surrounded by high buildings, with a stair down to the foreshore on the east.

The panorama of 1616 drawn by Visscher – alas, not on the spot, but far away in his Flemish workshop, from drawings by others – suggests that the western ranges of both Queenhithe and the Steelyard (the latter facing not on to a dock, but on to the wharf, with its crane) were open arcades on the ground floor, like those at Billingsgate and the western range added at the

98. View of the London waterfront with the Tower in the foreground, from the poems of Charles, Duke of Orleans, *c.* 1500. The arcaded building shown behind the tower is probably that at Billingsgate (compare 99).

99. Billingsgate and the neighbouring wharves, from Wyngaerde's panorama of *c.* 1540.

Custom House. This arrangement must have borne some relation to the way large ships loaded and unloaded their cargoes. The colonnades also appear to be on the upstream sides only, facing incoming shipping. They would function like open market halls in other medieval towns, such as that at Thaxted in Essex: temporary storage areas for bales or crates, and space for the examination of goods.

We have almost arrived at the London of Shakespeare's time; and these are certainly the buildings in which he set some of his characters. He would have known the mansion in Bishopsgate built by Sir John Crosby, in 1466, known as Crosby Place, for Shakespeare was himself a resident in the same parish of St Helen's in 1598. Crosby Place itself is alluded to three times in *Richard III*, as it was here that the Duke of Gloucester stayed while making his plans to engineer the offer of the Crown from the citizens of London.

Crosby, the son of a wealthy fishmonger, became a freeman of the Grocers' Company in 1452–4 and traded in silks from a warehouse in Coneyhope Lane, next to the company hall off Poultry. Before 1466 he leased a large house in Bishopsgate Street from the Prioress of St Helen's nunnery, whose churchyard it adjoined. A previous owner had been Cataneo Pinelli, a distinguished Italian merchant. Crosby evidently wished to add apartments worthy of his status to an already large mansion; he retained one wing of the former house to form the southern range of a courtyard entered via a passage under six tenements which fronted on to the street [100]. The principal buildings stretched north to the priory close, to which there was a side entrance, and some distance to the south, as indicated by vaults found in the early nineteenth century. A second, inner court lay to the rear of the main buildings to the east, and is now represented by Crosby Square; to the south of this were extensive gardens.

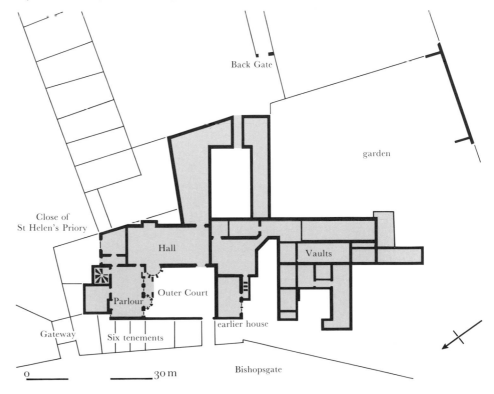

100. Plan of Crosby Place, Bishopsgate, from studies associated with its removal in the early 20th century and recent archaeological excavations.

Since it was outside the area of the Great Fire, the hall of Crosby Place survived until 1907, when it was carefully removed to Chelsea to form part of the hostel of the British Federation of University Women [101]. A stone doorway from the house went even further, to the dairy of Fawley Court, Buckinghamshire; the ceiling of the great parlour, removed in 1825, was bought by Cottingham's Museum in the Waterloo Road, sold on the break-up of the museum in 1850 as 'Lot 291. A highly enriched panelled ceiling of oak with its corbels, spandrils, pendant, &c, painted and gilt' and then disappeared. From these surviving fragments and records we can reconstruct much of the house which John Stow, a hundred years after its building, called the highest in the city in its own time.

The visitor entering the main court from Bishopsgate would see three sides of the court raised on undercrofts; that of the southern range retained from Pinelli's house. Ahead was the hall facing him and the parlour block to his left on new vaults of brick, lit by small windows low down. As at Merchant Taylors' Hall, the main entrance to the hall lay straight ahead, a screens passage with a gallery above. The original aspect of the entrance is not known, for a cartway was driven through this primary access long before the age of antiquarian interest (see 7), but the original joists of the gallery were found to form its ceiling when the hall was dismantled. Within the screens would be doorways to the hall, a lofty room with high windows to allow for tapestries on the walls, a large side fireplace, and probably a central hearth in addition. The roof, really a false ceiling, was divided into thirty-two compartments with twenty-seven ornamented pendants, no doubt originally also painted and gilt. At the dais end (no dais was ever detected, so perhaps it was of wood) a bay window with a stone vault incorporating Crosby's crest looked out into the main court. At this corner a doorway led to the two-storeyed parlour block, built like the hall in stone and with its own semi-octagonal bay window rising through both storeys.

The house was clearly exceptional, the mansion of a merchant who was knighted by Edward IV for his services to the Yorkist cause; no wonder that subsequent occupants of the house included the future Richard III, the lord mayor of 1516, Sir Thomas More and visiting ambassadors. More than any other recorded building, Crosby Place symbolises the political and diplomatic aspirations of prominent London merchants, who wished to build houses in which diplomacy, entertainment and display could all be politely combined. John Crosby and his first wife Agnes lie nearby in the chapel of the Holy Ghost in the south transept of St Helen's church [57], though their effigies are perched so high that both interference and sympathetic examination are equally difficult. He is in plate armour, with a collar of roses and suns showing his allegiance to Edward IV; his feet lie on a griffin, whereas his wife has two small dogs at her feet. On the sides of the defaced tomb are shields-of-arms: at the west end they are of the Grocers' Company, and in the middle of each long side are the Crosby arms. The arms of Agnes, of the Grocers, and Crosby's merchant mark are also preserved in the city's only collection of medieval stained glass, now restored and on show in the windows of the chapel.

It was but a short step from the house of a merchant prince to that of a real monarch, as comparison between the hall of Crosby Place and that of Eltham Palace, built in 1479 by Edward IV himself, will show. This rural

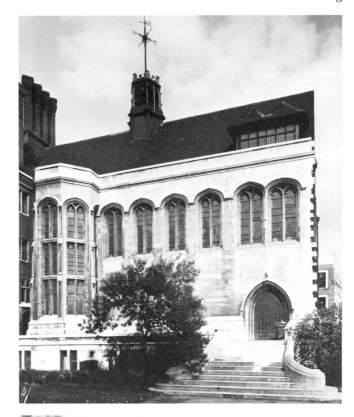

101. Crosby Hall, rebuilt in Chelsea. The entrance door is a modern reconstruction (compare 7).

102. Eltham Palace Hall: the main entrance and façade of the hall, photographed in 1923 before restoration of the 1930s (compare 7 and 101).

residence to the south-east of London was in essence a moated manor, approached over a fifteenth-century stone bridge which still links the hall with what was formerly a larger outer courtyard, the Green Court, outside the moat. The hall [102], later complemented by royal apartments by Henry VII and a chapel by Henry VIII, occupies a central place on the site, dividing the space into the public court on one side and private areas on the other just as larger halls had done for centuries. Matching doors in the two square oriels led to the royal apartments. The resemblance to Crosby Hall is such that it has been suggested that Thomas Jurdan, the King's Mason, who is presumed to have designed Eltham Palace hall, may have also been the architect of Crosby Place. The mouldings and vaults over the oriels are very similar.

On the other hand, the roofs of the two halls are very different. That of Crosby Hall is hard to assess because its design is unique among recorded examples. The roof at Eltham, presumably the work of the King's Carpenter Edmund Graveley, a former warden of the Carpenters' Company, is an imitation of a hammerbeam roof. The structure of the hammerbeams, which are meant to take the thrust of the roof's weight, hangs instead on the framework provided by stout principal rafters linked near their apex by a cross-timber or collar. It is a structural hybrid which reveals an occasional lack of confidence and ability even at the level of royal building.

Whether or not they had the same architect, Crosby Hall and Eltham Palace hall shared a significant new building material. Although the walls of both halls were faced with fine ashlar stone, brick was also incorporated – to a much greater extent in the walls at Eltham, while Crosby Hall was built on a brick undercroft. Brick was rarely used in quantity before the mid-fifteenth century, but it had been around for generations. Imported Flemish bricks – over 101,000 – had been used in 1283 for the curtain wall of the Tower, where they can be still seen today. Yellow bricks have also been recovered from part of the city wall around the Blackfriars precinct, built at about the same time. The experience of English workmen in using brick in the harbour works at Calais may have promoted its wider use in England during the fourteenth century; the first major public work in brick was probably Hull's town wall, with its interval towers, in the second half of the century. Locally manufactured yellow bricks are found at Eltham in the early fourteenth century, and in other manor houses or palaces, such as that at Kennington, about 1350, possibly from a kiln made for the purpose at Vauxhall. The account books of the Bridgemaster of London Bridge show purchases of brick and tile from a works at Deptford between 1404 and 1421; the establishment was on Bridge property, and engaged craftsmen from Holland. It included a small dock and, later, cottages for the immigrant workers.

The rebuilding of the palace at Sheen by Henry V in 1414 seems to have been the first extensive use of brick in a royal palace. Thereafter, no doubt, it became a fashionable as well as increasingly cheaper alternative to stone, partly because the centres of production – the kilns – could be set up closer to London than stone quarries. Richard Buckland, treasurer of the king's works at Calais, was accused of stealing 20,000 of the king's bricks to repair a place of his in London; the new hall of the Drapers' Company used 12,000 bricks in 1425. Two million bricks were made for the construction of

Eton College by 1451. Brickmakers are known in four of the suburban eastern parishes of London by the late fifteenth century, and no doubt brick was being supplied to the capital for decades before that. It could be combined with stone, or used for chimneys; in 1425 the house at Moor Park, Rickmansworth, was crenellated with stone and brick, and a stone wall at the Tower given a crest (battlement) of brick in 1440. Brick was much used for garden and courtyard walls, undercrofts (as recently discovered beneath 8 Philpot Lane and Crosby Hall) and in 1480 Richard Morley, a tallow chandler, requested – probably through a wish to be thought progressive rather than for reasons of economy – that he should be buried in the Austin Friars' church in a tomb of brick. By this time brick had largely replaced stone as the main material for buildings of any size; bishops' palaces, such as that of the Bishop of Ely at Hatfield (1480), now part of Hatfield House, served as precedent for the brick palaces of Wolsey and Henry VIII. The gatehouse of the Archbishop of Canterbury at Lambeth Palace (1490), called Morton's Tower after its builder [103], and the gateway and courts of Lincoln's Inn (1518; see 113) show the further spread of brick for building.

103. John Morton, Archbishop of Canterbury from 1486, was the holder of many state offices and was deeply involved in Henry VII's administration. He had this gatehouse built for his palace at Lambeth in 1490–5, using brick (including diaper patterns) with stone dressings.

104. *Left:* North façade of Cripplegate, built in 1490–1, in a line engraving of *c.* 1750.

105. *Below:* Ralph Jocelyn's rebuilding of the City wall and parapet, in the section of wall along the churchyard of St Giles Cripplegate, drawn by Smith in 1793. This section of wall is now preserved in outline only [53]. Behind, the buildings include Lambe's Chapel (*right*), originally the Hermitage of St James (see illustration on p. x).

But to follow these buildings further is to find ourselves in the sixteenth century, a long way from the beginning of this chapter and Croxton's Guildhall. To pass from 'medieval' to the 'Tudor' period of the next chapter is not to cross any firm boundary. It is, however, significant that one of the last great building works of the fifteenth century in London was the last large-scale rebuilding of the wall of the 'medieval' city. In 1471 Kentish rebels attacked the city and were repulsed at Aldgate. This must have caused concern about the state of the city's defences, for in 1477 Mayor Ralph Jocelin ordered, and mostly financed himself, some substantial repairs. Moorgate was enlarged from a postern into a proper gate, the ditch was dug out, and brickearth in Moorfields quarried to make bricks. The company of Skinners repaired the wall between Aldgate and Bishopsgate, the mayor and his company, the Drapers, the stretch between Bishopsgate and Moorgate; other companies and the executors of Sir John Crosby continued as far as Cripplegate, and the Goldsmiths repaired the section nearest their hall, from Cripplegate to Aldersgate. Traces of the rebuilding of the wall have been found at a number of places. The parapet of the wall was rebuilt in brick with a diaper pattern of darker bricks [105]; this can still be seen in the preserved section of wall in St Alphege churchyard. In addition, on at least three sections, low brick arches were built against the back of the wall, perhaps to give strength against bombardment by cannon, or to carry some superstructure such as a widened walkway. Cripplegate itself was rebuilt in 1491 through a bequest of Edmund Shaa, a goldsmith who was mayor in 1483. Although we do not know the construction materials, it is possible that the gate, like the contemporary Morton's Tower, was built of brick [104]. Thus the city was provided with patched-up defences, which became increasingly irrelevant as suburbs expanded in the following century.

The greatest change of the fifteenth century was therefore not in architectural style, which remained Perpendicular throughout, but in the materials of construction: the widespread introduction of brick. By 1500 there were not only many brick walls to be seen, but brick was being used in arches – to form undercroft vaults or take the load over windows and doorways, and in 1477 to form support arches behind the city wall. Already façades and new buildings were being constructed of brick, especially by religious bodies and leaders of the church. When the nave roof of St Mary Overie in Southwark collapsed in 1469, for instance, the upper part of the west end of the church was rebuilt in brick with an octagonal stair-turret, in contrast to the remaining stonework below. Given further fashionable approval by Henry VII and his son Henry VIII in their palaces, brick was to take the place of stone in every structural context. In the construction of Henry VIII's palace at Bridewell the foundation arch, long built of stone, was to be formed in brick.

London in the 16th century

6

What do people know about the sixteenth-century monarchs of England and their buildings? That Henry VII built a chapel at Westminster Abbey, and Henry VIII built a palace at Hampton Court and dissolved the monasteries? What is known of Edward VI and Mary, who, according to those who were good at remembering lists at school, came between Henry and Elizabeth? Edward seems memorable only for his many grammar schools, and Mary for something called the Counter-Reformation and for being Bloody. There are, by contrast, thousands of ordinary buildings we think of as 'Elizabethan' – small black-and-white timber-framed houses, shops and cafés, and some grand, if a little fairy-tale, country houses.

Although much building history cannot be compartmentalised into the reigns of individual monarchs, the sixteenth century was a period in which certain significant changes in attitudes to buildings were initiated by royal policy. In addition, the sixteenth century, much more than the previous one, was a period of radical and serious political and social upheaval in this country. Some changes reflected others abroad, some were home-grown. Much of the evidence for these changes remains above ground, even in London, and other forms of record are fuller than ever before. In particular, there survive panoramas of the city viewed from the south [83, 97, 107].

To give an account of this lively period we must be selective in description of the most important trends for buildings in the city of London itself; and thus the unique, overpowering splendour of Henry VII's chapel (1503–c.1512) at Westminster Abbey, like the nearby Westminster Hall, stands almost outside our narrative. Though the innovative design of its windows was to be fashionable again eighty years later, the standard of decoration, use of foreign artists and its purpose (though Henry VII intended it to be a new Lady Chapel, his successor completed it as a royal chantry chapel or mausoleum for his parents) set it apart from the mainstream of events.

The most important consequence for the history of buildings in the sixteenth century is that Henry did, indeed, dissolve the monasteries between 1536 and 1540. The effects were not instantaneous, but when an influx of both English and foreign immigrants into towns caught up with the large amounts of suddenly-available land, the larger towns found their composition changing in a process which lasted in London to the end of the century. Some of the leading buildings of the towns – the large monastery churches – disappeared or were turned, if they were lucky, into parish churches. The wholesale disposal of religious houses resulted in the proliferation of new, large and rather bizarre town houses for the wealthy, hacked out of monastic carcases. In the countryside we see them everywhere as the superior residence known as The Grange, The Priory or The Abbey; we should transport them in our mind to the city of London, for this

106. Interior of Middle Temple Hall, 1562–70. The ornate screen, in the new classical taste, is of 1566.

was the immediate fate of every monastic house whose foundation was described in chapter three.

If in the previous century England and its Perpendicular architecture had been rather insular, the sixteenth century is characterised by ever-increasing contact with the Continent. Henry brought Italian craftsmen to adorn his palaces and to create a style worthy of a Renaissance prince – but this did not reach the buildings of the ordinary man until later in the century when the Flemish version of Renaissance motifs flooded the country in the minds and hands of political refugees from the Low Countries. Many Englishmen with capital had grown rich, or at least improved their circumstances, from the acquisition of land when it was cheap in the reigns of Henry and Edward, and the management of it as landlords in the reigns of Mary and Elizabeth when it became expensive, especially in the metropolis. They could afford good houses with the up-to-date fashions in woodwork or plaster, with suites of rooms, well-lit by an excess of glazed windows [127, 137].

Around this central theme – the vanishing of the religious landlords and the appearance of their successors – the other developments of the century are minor; but it is interesting to compare the most impressive group of surviving buildings, the Inns of the legal profession, with Henry's brick palaces, for they were contemporary variants of the courtyard building, with similar functions and problems. A college is rather like a large, almost unmanageable royal household; Cardinal Wolsey, who began building Hampton Court, also began Cardinal College, now Christ Church, Oxford's largest university college, and parallels may be drawn between the two. We should start by describing the two Tudor royal palaces built within the City itself, both of which have only recently been rediscovered: Baynard's Castle and Bridewell.

Baynard's Castle, the large riverside house which took its name from its locality in the ward and district of the Norman castle destroyed in 1275, was rebuilt after a fire in 1428 by the Duke of Gloucester, uncle of Henry VI. Here the Crown was offered to both Edward IV in 1461 and Richard III in 1483. Henry VII, despite much rebuilding at his palaces of Greenwich and Richmond, made Baynard's Castle his principal London residence, and in 1501 set about transforming it so as to be, in Stow's words, 'not embattled, or strongly fortified castle-like, but far more beautiful and commodious for the entertainment of any prince of great estate' [108]. Here the king stayed during the marriage of his elder son Arthur to Katherine of Aragon, whose second marriage to the younger son Henry was to help precipitate the break with the Church of Rome. Excavations of 1972, prior to the realignment of Thames Street and again in 1974–5 and 1981 have pieced together the outline of Henry VII's palace. The previous house had enjoyed its own stone wharf and dock to the west; this was now filled in and the adjacent area made into a walled garden. On the riverfront two octagonal towers formed the corners of a range faced with five smaller projections at intervals between; four were also semi-octagonal, the fifth squared up to form a watergate which communicated with the courtyard within. Panoramas of the sixteenth and seventeenth century suggest octagonal towers at the northern corners, but their sites have not been found. A gate through the northern range allowed access from the section of Thames Street which is now obliterated by Baynard House; the line of

107. The City of London from the south; a woodcut panorama. The 'burning of St Paul's' took place in 1561, when lightning hit the spire; afterwards it was taken down and not replaced. Larger shipping is contained downstream of the Bridge, whose drawbridge ceased to function after 1500.

108. Plan of Baynard's Castle and nearby Trig Lane, from excavations of 1972–6.

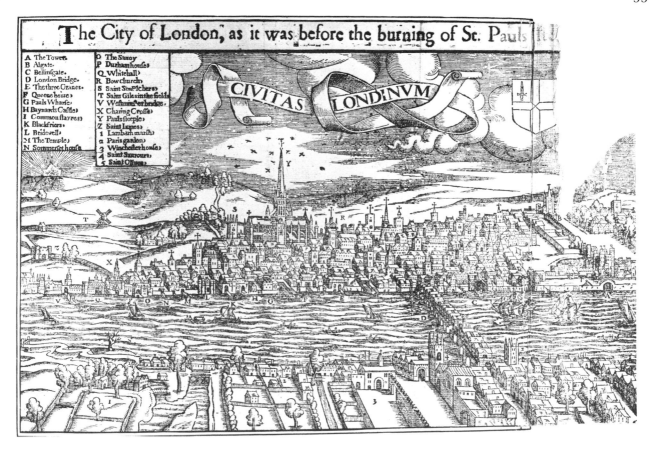

The City of London, as it was before the burning of St. Pauls

CIVITAS LONDINVM

A The Tower.
B Algate.
C Belinsgate.
D London Bridge.
E The three Cranes.
F Queens house.
G Pauls Wharfe.
H Baynards Castle.
I Common stayres.
K Blackfriers.
L Bridewell.
M The Temple.
N Sommerset house.
O The Savoy.
P Durham house.
Q Whitehall.
R Bow church.
S Saint Sim Pchers.
T Saint Giles in the fields.
V Westminster bridge.
X Charing Crosse.
Y Pauls steeple.
Z Saint James.
1 Lambarh marsh.
2 Paris garden.
3 Winchester house.
4 Saint Saviours.
5 Saint Olaues.

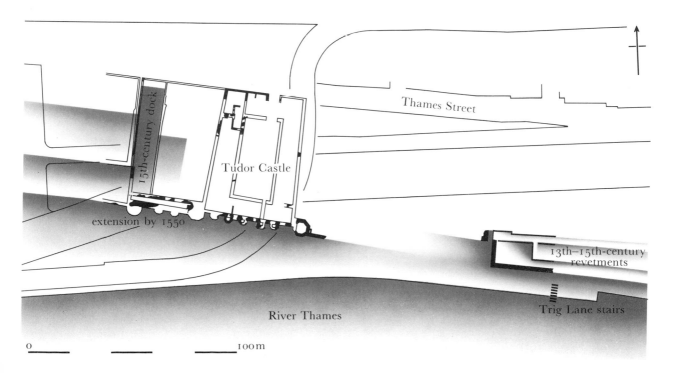

Thames Street

15th-century dock

Tudor Castle

extension by 1550

13th–15th-century revetments

Trig Lane stairs

River Thames

0 ———— 100 m

the street can be seen very briefly on the south side of Wren's St Benet's church. It is hoped that the outline of the riverfront of the castle may be marked out in the playground, adjacent to the motorway, of the future City of London Boys' School.

Henry VIII gave Baynard's Castle to Katherine of Aragon in 1509, and it remained with her until their divorce. The king's apartments at the Tower and at Westminster had both been destroyed by fire early in his reign, and Henry was therefore looking for a site on which to build a palace more fit for a European prince. Bridewell Palace was built between 1515 and about 1523. Though positioned in the middle of the built-up area south of Fleet Street in a busy suburb, its site was of a suitable size because the palace buildings were raised largely on reclaimed land at the confluence of the Fleet and the Thames. Even so there were problems of restricted access which affected the design.

The palace was laid out around two main courtyards [111]. On the south side of the northern, principal courtyard lay the great hall, now beneath Bridewell Place. In 1978 redevelopment allowed two areas of the palace to be investigated. In Bridewell Place excavations recovered remains from the eastern and southern ranges of the principal courtyard. These were of brick, and matched the plans precisely. In the south-east corner, where these two ranges met, the foundations for a polygonal stair-turret with a spiral staircase were uncovered; this turret is shown in a drawing of 1803 during demolition [109]. A second stair-turret, at the

109. The south-east corner of the principal courtyard of Bridewell Palace during final demolition in 1803, when it was part of Bridewell Hospital. Though rebuilt after the fire of 1666, the original stair-turret survived. Plans of 1791 show that the southern range on the extreme right hid, in rebuilt form, the hall of the Tudor palace, which occupied the first and second floors shown here.

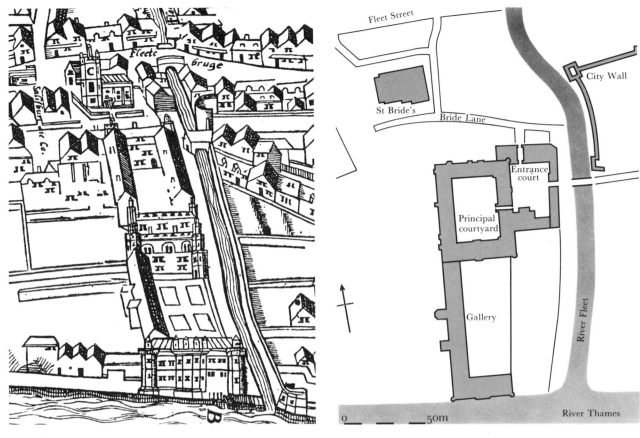

110. *Above left:*
Bridewell Palace, from
the 'Agas' woodcut
panorama, based on the
lost copperplate sheets of
c. 1559.

111. *Above right:* Plan of
Bridewell Palace, in
its Tudor surroundings.

outer, south-east corner of the range, survived, complete with its Reigate stone dressing. In all, six of these 'vyces' were specified in the building estimate. Several of the main walls were built up from brick arches springing from deep chalk piles, which were necessary to provide stability on the marshy land.

The problems of erecting a substantial brick building close to both the Thames and the Fleet must have been more acute at the extreme south of the site, and there is a reference to the raising of the foundations of a long gallery 'into the Temmes' at an early stage in the building programme. Parts of the foundations of the long gallery were recorded in 1978 in Tudor Street, to the south of Bridewell Place. A modern polygonal stairwell on the west side of the site appeared to preserve the outline of an earlier stair; its position suggested it was the northern of two projections shown on the west wall of the gallery in the sixteenth-century views [110]. In general these foundations were somewhat less impressive than those recorded in the principal ranges; where arches were employed they were often skimpier and shallower. No doubt this was partly because at certain points relatively firm gravel surfaces underlay them, but there is reason to suppose that, unlike the rest of the building, the gallery, the only part of the palace to be completely destroyed by the fire of 1666, was built largely of timber. None of the internal floor surfaces of the palace rooms survived, since modern cellars had been cut down to below Tudor floor level, though part of the principal courtyard surface, made of bricks set on edge, was found alongside Bridewell Place.

A third, outer courtyard lay between the principal courtyard and the bank of the Fleet. There was clear evidence from the excavations that the original form of the east side of the inner court had been subsequently modified indicating that its construction was at least well advanced before the outer court was designed, or perhaps even envisaged: the line of flow of drains beneath the east range of the main court was cut off by the building of the new court. It is likely, from documentary evidence, that work on the palace may have ceased from 1519 to 1521, when land fronting on to Bride Lane to the north was acquired from Westminster Abbey. It therefore seems likely that the outer court, with access through Bride Lane to Fleet Street and the two cities of London and Westminster by land, was an afterthought in a palace which in the original scheme was only approachable by river. The new court had a further innovation; it led to a grand staircase, possibly the earliest stair designed for state occasions in England.

Whereas the foundations, at least, of Baynard's Castle were of stone, both Bridewell Palace and, later, the palace of Hampton Court, were built almost totally of brick. This was not merely Henry's wish to be thoroughly modern. As we have seen, brick was becoming plentiful and cheap by the last quarter of the previous century. The Archbishop of Canterbury said to the scholar Erasmus of his new palace at Otford in Kent, which was in use by 1518: 'Stones are heavy carriage, as I know to my cost when I want them for building purposes'. Brick did not bring with it heavy transport costs, especially when brickearth could be dug locally and bricks made in a kiln on the site of the future building, as happened at Hampton Court and Lincoln's Inn. It has been suggested that English bishops, rebuilding their many rural palaces, were the pacemakers in the use of bricks for the twenty or thirty years before they came into general use about 1500. Of the twelve palaces of the Bishop of London, Fulham Palace remains closest to London for comparison with royal houses [112].

The best surviving parallels for several design and constructional features of Henry VIII's Bridewell can, however, be found just half a mile to

112. Fulham Palace: the courtyard, c. 1510–20. The porch leads to the screens passage of the hall (*left*). This arrangement must have been common in larger London houses of courtyard plan.

the north-west of the palace, at Lincoln's Inn. Though the society of Lincoln's Inn did not obtain the freehold of their property until 1580, they appear to have become dissatisfied by the late fifteenth century with the house of the Bishop of Chichester, which may still have been in its thirteenth-century form; a stone doorway of this date has been placed to one side in their hall, now itself called the Old Hall, of 1489–92. The structure is raised, as at Crosby Hall of twenty years earlier, on an undercroft of brick; here, however, the walls are also of brick. The hall was originally four bays long, with rectangular oriel bays on both sides at the northern dais end; the original entrance remains on the west, indicating that the hall was best approached from the Westminster side through the walks and gardens of Lincoln's Inn Fields. The roof is of solid fifteenth-century style, with arched braces, collar-beams and wind-braces with carved spiky points or cusps, though they are bent into the s-shape then becoming fashionable in exposed timber-work. The third and fourth oriels at the south end are additions of 1623, perhaps to give more light, for adjacent buildings did not allow windows in the end walls as at Guildhall or Westminster Hall.

Old Buildings, the court to the east, and its gatehouse to Chancery Lane, were built shortly after, by 1520. The gatehouse, finished in 1518, is a smaller version of Archbishop Morton's gateway at Lambeth Palace, with blue diapering enlivening the inside as it once did also the outside [113]. Over the archway, on the front, are the arms of Henry de Lacy, Earl of Lincoln on the left (a lion rampant), the Tudor arms in the middle, and those of Sir Thomas Lovell, a contemporary member of the Inn, on the right (the design includes three squirrels). The two leaves of the gate, hung on massive iron strap-hinges, are original; in the southern leaf, as at Oxford and Cambridge colleges, is a small wicket door for pedestrians and enquiries after dark. High up inside the carriageway of the gate is brick toothing for a vault, unfortunately never constructed. The buildings of Old Square to the south of the gatehouse were built at the same time, but have since been rebuilt; they do however have polygonal stair-turrets at the corners, as at Bridewell. Through the delicate passage by the hall, dating from 1583, which connects the two courts, the smaller continuation of Old Square is reached, and here the brickwork, of 1530, is better preserved. The stair-turrets have some original windows, and the stairs are of oak treads around octagonal or circular oak newel posts, as they must have been in Henry VIII's palaces.

The opening years of the sixteenth century, not yet clouded by the violent fate about to descend upon them, were also the time of extension, redecoration and rebuilding for several religious houses in London [114, 115]. At the priory of St John in Clerkenwell, Prior Docwra built the south gate in 1504, mainly of brick but faced with stone, which still survives. At St Bartholomew's Prior Bolton built an oriel window in the south aisle of the choir, which was reached from his adjacent house; below the window is a rebus of his name: a bolt and a tun, or barrel (rebus = 'things', representing a name in objects). St Mary's Priory in Southwark received, from the ever-friendly Bishop of Winchester, a reredos or screen of stone statues to place behind the altar in 1520. The most interesting new building of this period which survives is the lay brothers' court or Wash-House Court at the Charterhouse (1500–35; see 116). The east range is of stone,

113. Gate of Lincoln's Inn, Chancery Lane (1519), in an engraving published in 1800, when the diapering (since restored) was intact. Compare with 103.

but the other three sides are of brick in two storeys, with stone window dressings. Both faces of the west range have diapering in black brick, and on the outside are the initials I.H., probably for John Houghton, the last prior, who led a stalwart band of Carthusians to a martyr's death in 1535 for opposition to Henry VIII's religious changes; one of his arms was nailed to the priory gate.

The Dissolution of the Monasteries had many causes, some of the moment, some the boiling over of tendencies and feelings a long time in brewing. There was at the time a widely-held view that the monasteries were out-of-date, stifling and degenerate institutions, and men like Thomas Cromwell in charge of the programme of confiscation were quick to make propaganda out of these charges. Two hundred years after the Dissolution such a view was still current; the historian John Strype, in his edition of Stow's *Survey*, inserted a story of the prior of Crutched Friars in London, who was found with a whore at eleven in the morning on a Friday ('a day of

114. The last Dean of St Stephen's College at Westminster added this two-storeyed cloister to the Chapel in 1526–9, i.e. at the same time as the building of Bridewell Palace. The quality of stonework to be found in royal buildings, such as Henry VII's Chapel, could be repeated elsewhere when finances permitted.

115. Part of the north wall of the garden of Thomas Pope's mansion in Bermondsey, the former Cluniac priory. These emblems in brick must be of early 16th-century date, a monastic fashion as at Charterhouse.

somewhat more mortification and devotion') by the agents of Cromwell. To conceal this incontinency, the surprised prior 'distributed £30 presently [i.e. at once] among them, and promised £30 more. All of which was certified to Cromwell in a letter. These scandalous crimes hastened the Dissolution of these monasteries'.

But there were other, more important reasons. It was a supremely materialist age; the aim of all ambitious men was material prosperity, land, hard cash and high place. Henry's early years as monarch had been an expensive and continual show of wealth. Shrinking government revenues, the king's extravagance in building his palaces, troubles in Scotland and Ireland, and later military preparations in case of foreign anger over Henry's divorce, all combined to make some form of action inevitable.

The great majority of the population supported the king's anti-papal measures. The king was unable to persuade Pope Clement VII to annul his marriage with Katherine of Aragon; so he declared himself Supreme Head of the Church in England and obtained his annulment from the Archbishop of Canterbury. Supported further by a strong feeling against the monasteries among the middle class who formed his parliament, Henry and his agent Cromwell instituted a campaign of wholesale confiscation of monasteries and their property in 1535–8 by persuasion, bribes and threats so that religious houses were surrendered 'of their own free will'.

In time, the middle class were to benefit enormously from the Dissolution, but not immediately. Three groups were the principal beneficiaries of the earliest sales or grants of the monastic houses: local landowners, often tenants of the former houses, who knew exactly what they wanted; individual courtiers in high favour or government agents; and officials of the Court of Augmentations which dealt with the property transfers. Thus Blackfriars passed to Sir Thomas Cawarden, Master of the Revels and Austin Friars to Sir William Paulet, lord treasurer, in April 1540. Paulet built a house on the site of the cloister, but the western half of the great church was given to the community of Dutch immigrants for their church, which ensured survival of the medieval structure up to the Second World War. Paulet's son, the Marquis of Winchester (hence the name Winchester Place), sold the monuments of many noble men, replaced the lead roof with tiles (though, says John Stow, this was not as profitable as he had hoped), and stabled horses in the church. Changes in other monastic houses were even more drastic.

From about 1542 there appeared a new class of buyers who bought and sold estates in bulk, probably acting as agents for principals; and either syndicates or private individuals buying for investment. St Helen's nunnery in Bishopsgate was partly saved because it was also a parish church. The nuns' hall and other buildings to the north of the church were sold first to Sir Richard Williams, nephew of Thomas Cromwell and great-grand-father of Oliver Cromwell; then to Thomas Kendall, leatherseller, who bought it on behalf of his company in 1544 – the Leathersellers' Company hall was built on top of the thirteenth-century dormitory undercroft. The Crown also disposed of the much more extensive urban property holdings of the monasteries, and some Londoners began to live as rentiers, purely from the management of property. Others, particularly those who were in a position to spot a bargain, dabbled in the market; Humphrey Brook, a notary public, for instance, was owner at his death in 1585–6 of much ex-monastic property, including a tenement within the Blackfriars, the Plough in Cornhill (which had belonged to the Charterhouse), two tenements in Soper Lane (Halliwell nunnery), a tenement in Old Fish Street (St Helen's), two tenements in Fenchurch Street (Holy Trinity Priory, Aldgate) and a tenement on the Southwark side of London Bridge (St Helen's again).

The most striking visible consequence of this largescale transference of ownership was undoubtedly the transformation in appearance of the monastic precincts themselves. Each has its own often peculiar story; only four will be used in this chapter to illustrate the most important social consequences of the Dissolution. These were, firstly, the adaptation or wholesale rebuilding of the monastic buildings into grand houses by the nobility, in imitation of the royal palaces of the time (Charterhouse, Bermondsey Abbey); secondly, the laying out of some precincts to form early upper-class housing estates (St Bartholomew's Priory, Smithfield); and thirdly, the soaking up of immigrants in small-scale housing within the skeletons of the old religious buildings by the end of the century (Holy Trinity Priory, Aldgate).

The Charterhouse had resisted dissolution and was forcibly suppressed in 1537, but its buildings stayed in royal hands until 1545, when it was granted to Sir Edward, later Lord, North, a privy councillor to the king. He began rebuilding and transforming the priory into a town house suitable for one who moved in royal circles; it was here that he entertained the young Queen Elizabeth in 1558 and 1561. His successor Thomas Howard, Duke of Norfolk, continued building between 1565 and 1571, and it is difficult to differentiate in the existing remains between the rebuildings by the two owners. Let us assume that their intentions were similar, and examine the house as left by Howard in 1571 [116].

The medieval priory consisted of a great square cloister surrounded by twenty-six cells, on the south side of which were grouped communal buildings and areas in a west-east axis: the recently rebuilt lay-brothers' quarters, the Little Cloister, and the church with the founder's tomb. There was a medium-sized frater dating from the fifteenth century, but it was buried in other buildings, stuck between two of the cells. Either North or Howard took the severely pragmatic attitude shown on many a monastic site throughout the country at this time. The lay-brothers' quarters, with their service rooms, were retained, though the cooking facilities seem to have been extended for the larger company expected at feasts. The little cloister was pulled down and drastically widened to form an impressive court of stone buildings to be entered from the south. The church, apart from its tower, was demolished, since the east range of the new court crossed it at right angles. The stonework of the priory building, and especially the doorways, was reused throughout the new work; some of Yevele's cell doorways found new homes upstairs in the grand house.

At the back of the new court lay the new hall, entered by a porch. Inside, much of the original woodwork survives as left by Howard: a hammerbeam roof with carved cherubs' heads, the carved oak screen bearing his initials T.H. and the date 1571 – though probably not the gallery above, which seems to be of early seventeenth-century date. A door at the dais end leads to a staircase of a new and grandiose design, only possible in new palatial buildings: surrounded by stone walls on three sides, two broad flights rise round square newel posts. It is predictably called the Great Staircase; the newels are carved with foliage, ribands, musical instruments, and trophies of war and of the chase. The parlour to which the stair should lead is not, however, immediately adjacent, but is reached by a corridor. Now restored after serious wartime damage, the Great Chamber is still largely decorated as it would have been in Howard's time: his arms and crest are much in evidence.

North and Howard transformed the priory into a great house with courtyards; in several ways the plan and arrangement of rooms followed that of the royal palaces of the day. An outer and inner courtyard, for instance, was now fashionable; the hall lay within the inner court. At Bermondsey Abbey, pulled down in 1540 by Sir Thomas Pope, first treasurer of the Court of Augmentations, the cloister itself naturally became a courtyard around which a range of buildings in stone, brick and new timber frames arose [117]. Pope demolished the large church to make his garden; the monastic yard with its subsidiary buildings was probably retained with comparatively little modification. An inner gatehouse of the priory survived intact until the early nineteenth century, and the right-hand side, with the jamb of the gateway, can still be seen in Grange Walk, Bermondsey. Though the Pope mansion has long since disappeared, and the site of the Norman monastic church is crossed by Tower Bridge Road, plentiful drawings of remains in the early nineteenth century show how bizarre and ruthless were the ambitions of Henry's assistants. Pope's mansion at Bermondsey, because of its rural position, survived into the nineteenth century; in contrast, the urban palaces only had short lives, for their extravagance was in the main overtaken by need for further change and subdivision as pressure for housing increased.

116. Plan of the Charterhouse in 1929, showing traces both of the medieval monastery and of the 16th-century mansion of North and Howard.

Before 1563 a contemporary historian wrote: 'fair houses in London were plenteous, and very easy to be had at low and small rents, and by reason of the late dissolution of religious houses many houses in London stood vacant, and not any man desirous to take them'. The accession of Elizabeth in 1558 and the adoption of a fierce and patriotic Protestantism encouraged an existing trickle of political refugees from France and the Netherlands which writers of the day (probably over-reacting) saw as one of the main causes of the remarkable increase in the city's population which followed. The newcomers were not always welcome; the ward of Billingsgate reported that aliens now occupied 150 houses within the ward, 30 in the small parish of St Botolph Billingsgate, where they would pay £20 a year for a house near the riverside which had formerly been let for £2 13s 4d; and whereas thirty years ago, the ward might collect £27 a year for the poor, it could now only manage £11, 'for the stranger will not contribute to such charges as other citizens do'. It might also be that dwindling generosity and rising rents were more to do with rapidly rising inflation; after a long period of stability, food prices had increased by 180 per cent between 1501 and 1550, and would rise to 437 per cent of 1501 prices by 1602.

Stow and other writers sympathised with the alarm of the city and national government about the growth of the capital. There was a great increase in building from the 1570s in response to the influx of migrants from the countryside and abroad; suburbs sprang up or rural hamlets sprouted houses, especially in Radcliffe, Limehouse, Shoreditch,

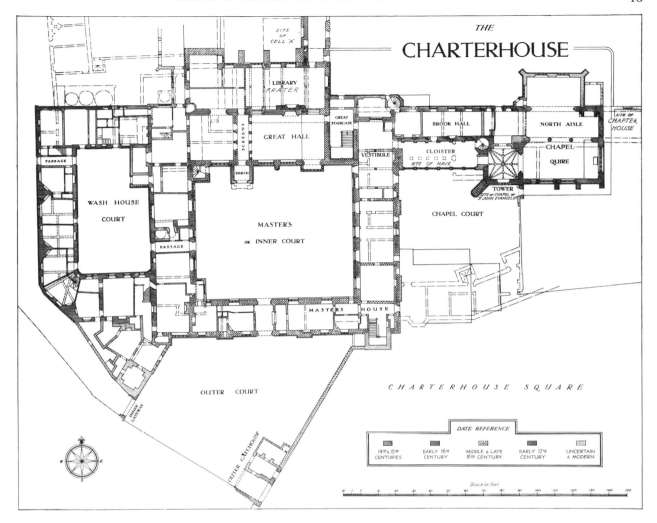

THE
CHARTERHOUSE

SITE OF CELL 'A'

LIBRARY
FRATER

GREAT STAIRCASE

BROOK HALL

NORTH AISLE

SITE OF CHAPTER HOUSE

SCREENS

GREAT HALL

VESTIBULE

CLOISTER
SITE OF NAVE

CHAPEL
QUIRE

PORCH

TOWER
SITE OF CHAPEL OF ST JOHN EVANGELIST

PASSAGE

WASH HOUSE
COURT

MASTER'S
OR INNER COURT

CHAPEL COURT

PASSAGE

MASTERS HOUSE

OUTER COURT

CHARTERHOUSE SQUARE

INNER GATEWAY

OUTER GATEHOUSE

DATE REFERENCE

14TH & 15TH CENTURIES	EARLY 16TH CENTURY	MIDDLE & LATE 16TH CENTURY	EARLY 17TH CENTURY	UNCERTAIN & MODERN

Scale of Feet

117. Sir Thomas Pope's house at Bermondsey: above the walls of the cloister rises a hotch-potch of timber framing. The serpentine braces are a common feature of the second quarter of the 16th century. The large window indicates a principal chamber, perhaps the hall.

Whitechapel and around St Katherine's Hospital – the East End of London was born. In 1580 a royal proclamation forbade any new buildings within three miles of the city; the Court of Common Council fought a vain campaign against subdivision of tenements, the increase of building and new foundations. Besides the danger of pestilence or civil disorder, the Privy Council pointed out that the growth of London caused the decay of other towns, and made the supply of the metropolis more difficult.

The demand for extra housing was met in a number of ways. First, the landlords and entrepreneurs of the city soaked up many of the remaining open spaces with buildings. Gardens were built over or subdivided to form smaller patches for the expanding tenements; some old inns were turned into housing schemes [118]. The owners of the former religious precincts were quick to profit from the rush of immigrants, though they preferred the upper-class end who could afford large new houses. Thus several of the convent sites sprouted four-storey houses, where there had been none before. Typical was the change at St Bartholomew's priory, which had passed to the first Lord Rich at the Dissolution. The third baron, coming into possession in 1581, began to develop the fairground on the northern side of the priory church and seems to have laid out several streets which survive today as Cloth Fair, Middle Street and Newbury Street. Several buildings from this private housing venture remained until the early twentieth century. Two-room houses 3½ or 4½ storeys high (that is, 3 or 4 storeys with garrets) encroached on to the site of the destroyed nave of the priory church, to the south of Cloth Fair, and others were built against the choir and Lady Chapel to the east. Facing them was Longtyled-house Row, of three storeys, built by 1598; the Dick Whittington pub, though claiming to date from the fifteenth century, was the end-house of this block [119].

118. *Below left:* Houses at Smithfield, surveyed by Ralph Treswell in 1612.

Ch   chamber
E   entry
K   kitchen
Sb   stable
Sd   shed
Sh   shop
Y   yard

119. *Below:* House in Longtyled Row, later the Dick Whittington pub, dating from 1598 but claiming a longer history. Beneath the corner jetties on the first floor are grotesque corbels (compare 127 and 136).

Secondly, the city authorities themselves submitted to mounting pressure to allow building on their own property; in particular on the city ditch, which was gradually obscured by the encroachment of yards and then buildings on the ditch-side edge of the extramural ring of streets. In the first half of the sixteenth century, as the bird's eye 'Agas' panorama shows, the outer edge of the ditch had been filled in over much of its length and used as drying grounds by clothworkers, who put up their wooden frames, or tenters, to stretch the cloth (see 52). By 1553 the ditch between Newgate and Aldersgate had been vaulted over, and leases to property in what is now Fore Street and Houndsditch become more common in the following decades. At first there was an attempt to keep some kind of ditch open as a token of defence; in 1588 the city decided to add a proviso to the leases, that if the ditch was to be dug out at any time, the spoil should be placed on the adjacent gardens, the tenants receiving a year's rent allowance in respect of it. As late as 1591 there was official concern about the sluices communicating beneath the causeways outside Bishopsgate and Aldgate. But it was a losing battle. In 1576 William Boxe, alderman, promised to maintain the banks of his garden alongside the ditch between Cripplegate and Moorgate, and to skim the filth from the ditch from time to time along all its length, the City finding a boat for the purpose; but two years later he was found to be encroaching over the ditch. This wish to expand was mirrored by those with property immediately inside the defences; owners of adjacent houses petitioned the city to be allowed to hire the bastions in order to build on them.

Along with the immediately extramural development of Fore Street and Houndsditch came the upgrading of the approach roads and thereby the suburbs, especially to the east. In 1572 the Lord Mayor and city surveyors viewed the street outside Aldgate 'which is to be paved and see what is to be done'; ten years later the city gateways were gravelled and Bishopsgate paved as far as the hospital of St Mary Spital, on the city boundary. The land between the city and Westminster, especially around the Inns of Court, had long ceased to have many large open spaces; but now the fields to the north and east of the city began to disappear under houses [120]. Along the newly-paved streets which led to the gates of Bishopsgate and Aldgate, a new generation of buildings arose (see 133); and at this time we hear of more inns for travellers on these extramural streets. Previously the centre of the hostelry trade was Fleet Street, with a remarkable total of fifty inns in 1384; two hundred years later, this preponderance was shared with several other locations.

The sweeping changes of the sixteenth century in the buildings of London are shown, above all, in the bizarre buildings cobbled together from parts of the monastic church at Holy Trinity Priory, surveyed in 1592 by John Symonds [121]. The community of Augustinian canons at Holy Trinity had in fact surrendered their house to King Henry in 1532, several years before the general Dissolution. The priory, once the richest in London, had been burdened by debt for some time. The canons were sent to other houses of the same order and the prior, after a period of personal uncertainty in the deserted precinct, as the creditors realised what was happening, was given a living in Kent. Henry granted the priory, among many other lands, to Thomas Audley, the self-made town clerk of Colchester who rose to be speaker of the House of Commons and in 1533

120. *Left:* Late 16th-century house in Sweedon's Passage, Grub Street, drawn by J. T. Smith in 1791. The structure on the right is an outside staircase, a common feature on the new houses. At first floor is a closet with a sink, as shown by the drain, though this may be a later insertion. Compare the form of the bay window with those of the restored Staple Inn [4].

121. *Right:* Holy Trinity Priory, Aldgate: reconstruction by Richard Lea of the east end of the priory church as it appeared in 1592, from plans by John Symonds. The choir and nave are roofless; around the courtyard formed by the choir jettied houses sprout from the early medieval chapels.

Lord Chancellor. At first Audley offered the priory church to the parishioners of St Katherine Cree, in exchange for their church, since he wished to develop the Leadenhall Street frontage. Perhaps because of their connection with the food-producing areas of Essex, the streets immediately within Aldgate were prospering; another local church, St Andrew Undershaft, had been totally rebuilt in the 1520s [122, 123]. But the parishioners of St Katherine's refused. Audley then began to dismantle the priory church, selling the peal of nine bells to Stepney church and to St Stephen Coleman Street, and removing the roof from the chancel and from the nave to form two courts. The north transept either was pushed down or it collapsed, making a diagonal access through into the cloister (later Mitre Square). John Stow records that Audley found great difficulty in getting rid of the stone, 'for all the buildings then made about the City were of brick and timber'. Audley also rebuilt some of the priory – probably the house which occupied the western range of the cloister and faced the great courtyard to the west. Audley died here in 1544, and the priory passed through his

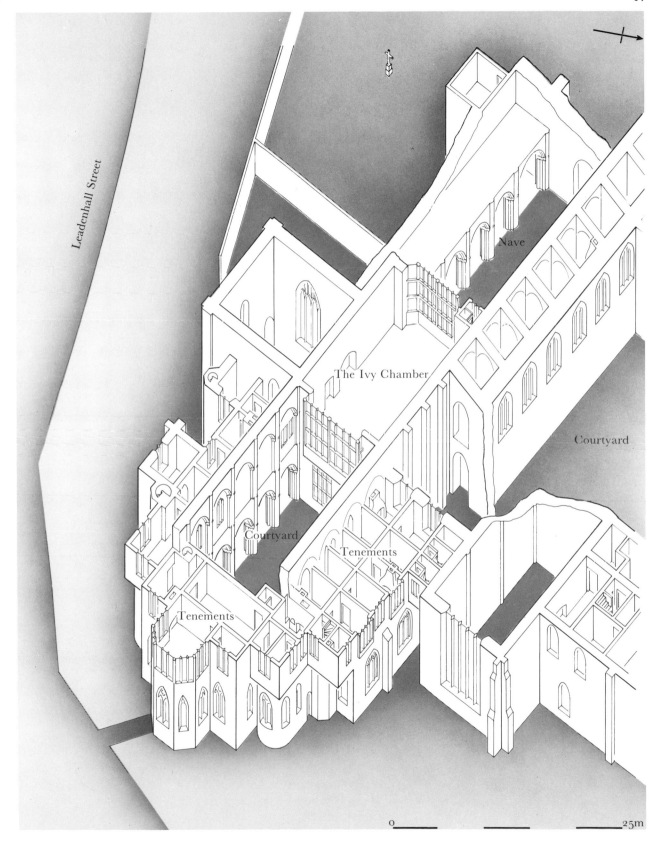

Leadenhall Street

Nave

The Ivy Chamber

Courtyard

Courtyard

Tenements

Tenements

0 25m

daughter to her husbands, the second of whom was Thomas Howard, Duke of Norfolk (whom we have already seen building at Charterhouse); the main house then became known as Duke's Place, commemorated now by the road which runs nearby along the line of the city wall from Aldgate to Bevis Marks. In 1800 Norfolk's crest, a demy-lion shot through the mouth with an arrow, could still be recalled on one of the buildings in Duke's Place.

Symonds's plan of the priory in 1592, drawn on both ground-floor and first-floor levels, shows not only the Norfolk mansion and its outbuildings taking up the great courtyard and western range of the cloister, but other houses carved out of the priory church. As at Charterhouse, we cannot tell if these were built by Howard or his predecessor, in this case Audley; they were probably the results of continuous adaptation throughout the century as rebuilding took place. The nave and chancel were left as unroofed courtyards, and between them a house called the Ivy Chamber, with large windows to east and west, was built in the crossing between the transepts (see 121). At first-floor level a gallery led from the Ivy Chamber along the north side of the roofless nave, looking down into the nave on one side and through the medieval windows of the church into the cloister on the other. The five chapels forming the east end of the chancel were rebuilt at first-floor level, with jettied windows, to make a pleasant suite of rooms just as Sir Richard Rich had converted the Lady Chapel at St Bartholomew's into a first-floor dwelling house in 1544. Smaller tenements sprouted from the sides of the choir, with medieval masonry below and timber-framing above: fireplaces, ovens and privies were grafted on to the Romanesque walls and arches. An entrance to the court from Aldgate was knocked through the former Lady Chapel on the ground floor. Here, perhaps, John Stow, who lived nearby, looked in as he collected material for his *Survey of London*, published in 1598. He lists the tombs and memorials of many famous Londoners buried in the priory. He may have been working from written records which have not survived, but he may also have wandered round the choir courtyard and found, still visible in the floor, the tombstones of two of the children of King Stephen, buried in the twelfth-century heyday of the priory.

Religious change was also to affect the parish church. By 1550, the parish churches of London were very largely concretions of parts of widely differing dates – a fifteenth-century tower, a thirteenth- or fourteenth-century aisle or chapel, a porch endowed by one parishioner and the roof or windows by others. In this state the majority lasted until the Great Fire of 1666; but two were rebuilt in the sixteenth century, and thus indicate what a church was meant to look like in the contemporary mind, if money and the will was available for wholesale reconstruction.

St Andrew Undershaft, at the corner of Leadenhall Street and St Mary Axe [122, 123] was rebuilt in 1520–32, largely at the expense of Stephen Gennings, merchant tailor and mayor. Other contributors left their arms in the glass of the windows; these were removed in the Second World War and are stored nearby. The tower and its door, through which (as in many London churches, see 89) one entered the church, are both fifteenth-century; but the rest of the three-aisled church is of one build and style. It seems that there was formerly no south aisle; a blocked-up window on the east side of the tower which can be seen from the south aisle would have

122. St Andrew
Undershaft, drawn in
1817 by R. Schnebbelie.
Some of the houses on
the left probably date
from the 16th century,
and survived into the
early modern period.

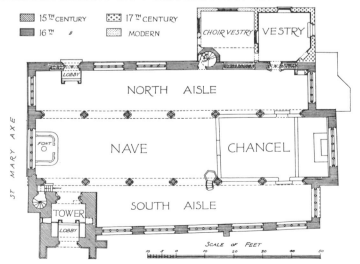

123. Plan of St Andrew Undershaft. The line of
the rood screen, marking the division between
nave and chancel, is shown by the position of
the rood-stair in the north wall.

looked outside, and the south arcade of piers passes close to the tower but does not connect with it, as would be the case if it was restating an earlier arcade. Perhaps the sixteenth-century piers were built just inside the old south wall, which was then demolished to be moved to its new position. A turret in the north wall allowed access to the rood which spanned the middle of the church.

Just outside Cripplegate, in a rapidly expanding suburb, St Giles Cripplegate was badly damaged by fire in 1545 and rebuilt, also incorporating an earlier tower. It, too, is a large church of three aisles. Though St Giles was traditional in form, its builders of 1545–50 were being overtaken by the surge of anti-Catholicism we call the Reformation. The wave of confiscations of monastic houses and property was only one part of a general urgent desire for change in all branches of the religious world. With the Dissolution of the Monasteries virtually over, and the monarch established as the Supreme Head of the English Church, reforming zeal turned on parish churches, with their stored-up wealth in plate and their glittering, but now idolatrous, images.

The rapid religious upheavals principally in the reign of Edward vi, the 'counter-Reformation' of Mary, and the final establishment of the Protestant faith of the reign of Elizabeth, all within a space of thirty years, had disturbing effects on the appearance and use of churches. The almost farcical experience of the churchwardens of St Michael Cornhill, one of the richest parish churches in medieval times, must have been typical. In 1548–9 the official assault upon imagery, the saints and the cult of the Virgin began. The churchwardens obediently paid a mason for cutting down the stones on which the images stood in the church, took down the statues of Mary and John in the rood loft, replaced the Shriving Pew (confessional) with an ordinary pew, and bought a copy of the paraphrase of the New Testament by Erasmus, which was to be placed in every parish church in England. They sold the church plate to a goldsmith for £80, and with the proceeds erected ten chambers in the churchyard. Six altars were removed from the body of the church and its chapels, the spaces being paved over with brick. The copes and vestments were sold; the churchwardens' accounts almost sigh as they detail the departing linen: a blue cope with ravens, a red vestment with a black cross and stars, an altar cloth of purple velvet and cloth of gold, eighteen copes, fourteen vestments, twenty-two little altar cloths and much more. Also sold off were the old choir books (to be replaced by eight psalters in English), a mass book, the cross of stone and the tomb of Mr Sutton, an old chest, an old aumbry (cupboard), the great press for the copes which stood in the vestry, forty feet of grave stone, two embroidered images, and the brasses of the choir and chapels. The stone forming the table of the high altar was taken down and moved into the cloister round the churchyard. Finally the rood and its loft were taken down. Inside three years the old religion had been overturned and the church disembowelled.

With the accession of Mary in 1553 official directives on religion took a complete about-turn, for the queen was a devout Catholic and intended to reinstate the old practices. What the churchwardens of St Michael's thought of this is not recorded. They desperately tried to conform, spending rather more money than they had coming in, so that individual churchwardens had to dip into their own pockets. They brought the high altar stone back in out of the churchyard and set it up again, rebuilding the altar and steps of the choir with two thousand bricks, mending various other places in the church which had been damaged by the reforming zeal of the previous months. New pews which had invaded the chancel were removed, so that the altar could be seen once more; wax candles and the equipment of the sacrament – a holy water sprinkler, a censor, a pax, and altar cloths – were bought afresh, along with antiphoners, hymnals, and a mass book, a psalter and a chalice, no doubt at higher prices than were obtained for the sale of the old ones only a couple of years before. A rood was built and put back up – the beam or large timber like a tie-beam was brought from St Giles and taken into the church on rollers. One Peter the joiner was paid £3 for a St Michael, presumably a wooden effigy, which took a mason four days to set up on a stone. By 1557, restored to something of its former splendour, the church could go as far as obtaining a veil or cloth to place over the crucifix during Lent, as is still practised in Anglican high church today.

The death of Mary and the accession of Elizabeth in the very next year must have caused consternation and then foreboding of yet another inevitable about-face. Other parish councils which had not gone so far to accommodate the changes of Mary's reign must have been relieved they had not imitated St Michael's. Now the churchwardens had to take down the high altar, on which the mortar can hardly have set, and finally sold off the altar stone, together with the new beam. St Michael and his foot of stone were again removed, and the holes made good. The remaining altar vestments were sold, together with the holy water stock and other communion vessels. A new set of books was bought: four new song books, two books sent by the Bishop, and 'a great paper book for the church to register the names of christenings and burials'. This time, understandably, the changes were slower in implementation; it was not until 1572 that the churchwardens agreed to buy appropriate texts, including the 'book of martyrs of Mr Fox and the paraphrases of Erasmus', this time to be tied with a chain to the Eagle of Brass (the lectern).

In sharp contrast to these scenes of destruction, confusion and rapid change in the city's hundred-odd churches, the three most important surviving buildings of Elizabeth's reign are traditionally medieval in form, though with some new details. These are the halls of the Inns of the legal profession: Middle Temple and Staple Inns, and the earliest of the three examples, Gray's Inn. Just beyond the city's western boundary lay the estate of the Gray family, the manor of Purtpool, in 1307. During the fourteenth century they leased out rooms to lawyers, and 'Gray's Inn', where Inn means 'town house', was well known as a lawyers' establishment by 1400. The earliest surviving buildings are the walls of the chapel, of the first half of the sixteenth century, and the hall, rebuilt in brick in 1556–60. The roof, now reconstructed after war damage, shows an uncertain blend of old and new styles: the lower spandrels are filled with Gothic tracery, but the higher ones have only simple moulded bars or mullions. The moulding of the sides of beams, whether curved or straight, is here the indicator of underlying change: at Middle Temple Hall, the roof of 1570 [106] is of double-hammerbeam construction as at Hampton Court, but the beams have Renaissance mouldings: a sunken slot or channel with a flat bottom, together with a quarter-round (one quarter of a circle in section) to round off the edges. The further development of these mouldings can be seen in the roof of Staple Inn (also much restored after being hit by a flying bomb in 1944), built in 1580–1, which is also of hammerbeam construction. Here the pendants are totally classical in outline.

The legal societies of the Inner and Middle Temple (their separate buildings could only be differentiated with difficulty, even by the residents) settled south of Fleet Street some time in the fourteenth century; they used the church of the former occupants, the Knights Templar, as their common chapel. The hall of the Inner Temple may well have been built at this time, since two fourteenth-century vaulted rooms, one on top of the other, survive at the west end of the ninteenth-century hall. As at Lincoln's Inn, the building complex included large gardens, through which Middle Temple Lane, the principal route through the Temple, reached a busy landing-stage at the point where the lane now meets the noisy modern traffic of the Victoria Embankment. The Great Fire only singed the Temple church, but fires of 1678–9 and 1683, together with heavy war damage, have drastically changed the appearance of the numerous little courts in which the students of law lived. To the south of the church was Cloister Court, which had rooms over the cloister walks; it was rebuilt in its present form by Wren, and augmented after the Second World War. The only pre-Fire building still substantially intact is Middle Temple Hall, which was built between 1562 and 1570 [124]. Like the new hall at Gray's Inn a few years before, it was built of brick, with stone dressings. The louvre and porch are modern. Inside, we have already spoken of the roof, almost the last of its type; but ultra-modern in 1570 was the decoration of

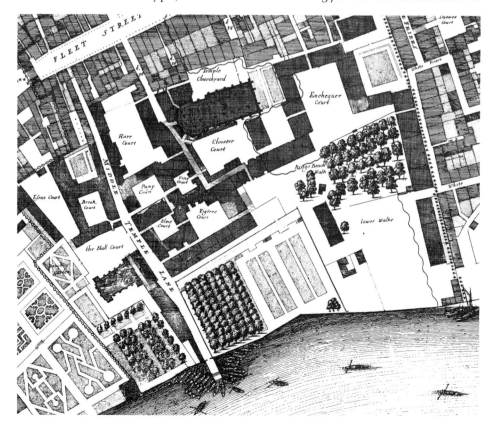

124. The Temple, from Ogilby and Morgan's map of 1677. The wavy line marks the limit of the Great Fire in 1666. In the top left, the original site of Wren's Temple Bar, marking the City boundary.

the great screen which gives entrance to the hall (see 106). To understand this fully we have to go back a few steps in time, almost to the cosmopolitan court of Henry VIII.

The Lord Protector Somerset (effectively regent of the young Edward VI) continued Henry VIII's policy of importing French and Italian elements of planning and decoration in his new houses: a mansion at Isleworth, on the Thames, and a house in the Strand, built in 1547–50. Like the previous Tudor palaces, it was a courtyard house, but with what has been called 'probably the first deliberate attempt to build in England a front composed altogether in the Classical taste': a two-storeyed range with windows and projecting bays arranged symmetrically round a central three-storey gatehouse. Within the court, the arcade, which was also borrowed from many continental houses, made an appearance [125].

Somerset died on the scaffold in 1550, and his new architectural movement died with him. But classical ideas were not long in coming by another route. The continental version of the public arcade, for instance, reappeared twenty years later in Thomas Gresham's Royal Exchange, built in 1566–70 between Cornhill and Threadneedle Street [126], where the present Royal Exchange stands. The intention was to take advantage of current religious upheavals in the Low Countries by establishing an exchange in imitation of the one at Antwerp, complete with a tower more at home in the Netherlands (though there seems to have been a taste for private towers in London from the 1530s – see 131).

Also from the Netherlands came fashions in woodwork and stone which invaded London before the middle of the sixteenth century. The style was promulgated partly by the circulation of Flemish and Dutch architectural text-books, but also by workmen fleeing from the Low Countries. At a high social level their work survives in three similar structures of about the same date: the woodwork over the screens passages at Gray's Inn Hall, North's hall at Charterhouse and Middle Temple Hall (see 106). The bones of each structure are Renaissance interpretations of classical orders – Ionic, Doric and Corinthian – with columns flanking arches which have a prominent key-block or corbel, either of a leaf-scroll or a lion's head. Where further vertical emphasis is required, classical figures – Hercules, other deities, or caryatids – grow out of pilasters or are placed in niches. Friezes, and sometimes the columns themselves, are covered with designs called simply and understandably *strapwork*.

Towards the end of the sixteenth century the corbels grew more and more grotesque [127], and in such forms were widely spread among newly-built houses in many towns. The simpler leaf-scroll corbel can still be seen in the frontage to Holborn at Staple Inn (1586); and two examples of the more grotesque are in the collection of the Museum of London, preserved by its predecessor the Guildhall Museum from the Dick Whittington tavern in Cloth Fair (1598; see 119).

It is in West Smithfield, near Cloth Fair, that we find one of the earliest surviving timber-framed house fronts: the frame above the west gateway into St Bartholomew's churchyard, once the west end of the priory church. This was built in 1595 by Philip Scudamore, a parishioner, and he included much reused timber, among which was a piece of a wooden screen from a church, possibly St Bartholomew's itself. The present windows, and the form of the timber framing, however date from a restoration of 1916

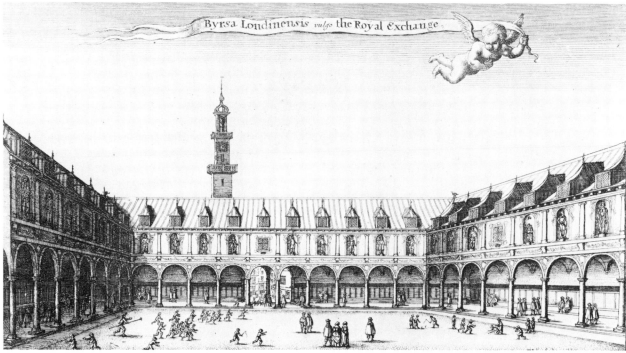

following damage in a Zeppelin raid. Before this date the front was covered
with bricks or tiles, and there were two sash windows on each floor, so the
accuracy of the framing cannot be guaranteed.

Similar doubts surround the present form of the frontage to Holborn of
Staple Inn [4]. Built in 1586 (the western part possibly before the rest), it
was restored in 1894 and 1936; in the first restoration the roof of the

127. *Right:* 'A magnificent mansion lately standing in Crutched Friars', drawn by J. T. Smith in 1792; a splendid display of 16th-century woodcarving skills. The shields around the first-floor jetty were of the twelve major livery companies. Continuous double-height windows seem to be a development of the years after 1550.

125. *Left:* East side of the internal courtyard of Somerset House, from a print of 1777.

126. *Left:* Interior of the courtyard of the Royal Exchange (1566–70). The arcade, a Renaissance feature, followed a precedent set at Somerset House.

westernmost house was made to conform with the remainder. Old photographs and engravings show that prior to 1894 the frontage had sash windows, and was plastered over. The present arrangement of close-set vertical timbers ('studs') is suspect since in many cases only every fifth one is pegged to the horizontals. It seems likely that the houses were originally decorated with panels only, and were never close-studded. Even so, the present appearance must represent that of many other London buildings of the late sixteenth century.

This chapter has been concerned with the sweeping changes of that century; the brief extravagance of Tudor palaces, the courtyard forms of the legal Inns, the Dissolution of the Monasteries and the new houses, of many shapes and sizes, both large and small, which sprang up in their place. Up to now we have been working largely with fragments, and an overview has rarely been possible. Shortly after 1600, however, the increase in evidence is such that we can for the first time enter the homes and workplaces of a wide range of London's residents.

To the Great Fire 1600-1666

7

The four-fold increase in population (from about 50,000 in 1550 to about 200,000 by 1630) in only three generations changed the medieval city of London into the early modern metropolis. The Dissolution of the Monasteries had released a flood of land for new building, in such quantity that whole areas could now be laid out as streets or squares, both for those who could afford town houses of quality (including an increasing number of country gentry requiring a place in town) and for artisan housing, later to be slums. This distinction encouraged the separation of people into stratified groups in society, and a radical change in the way they perceived their status and place in society's hierarchy. This change heralds the end of the medieval city.

To our great good fortune, this short period around 1600 produced two important surveys of London buildings by contemporary observers; one well known, the other not. John Stow's *Survey of London* (1598) is the starting-place for every student of London's medieval topography, social history and customs. He was born in 1525, and could just remember the prior of Holy Trinity riding in civic procession among his fellow aldermen; he recalled speaking with old men who remembered Richard III as a comely prince. Stow saw the city spread in every direction, and lamented the speed and brutality of the changes during his lifetime; he recorded with regret the breaking up of old buildings, though he also took pride in the increased prosperity of the Elizabethan city and the newer buildings which reflected that wealth. He walked round every ward and looked into every church to record what the Reformation had left, though he would not mention many new monuments 'because those men have been the defacers of monuments of others'. He tried to examine livery company records, but was rebuffed by that strong and ancient tradition of secrecy concerning records which has hampered researchers ever since. He also visited the sites of building or excavation works with an archaeological eye. In 1586, for instance, during the rebuilding of Aldgate near his house, he noted that the fabric produced a Hebrew inscription probably taken from one of the Jews' houses in 1215; in Leadenhall Street (then called Aldgate Street), in 1590, he inspected an excavation for a cellar and saw an arched gate, its hinges remaining, and square windows with bars of iron on each side, in a wall reaching to a depth of twelve feet below the street. He concluded these were the remains of a house destroyed in one of the fires of Stephen's reign, though it sounds more like the front wall of a later medieval undercroft, with central entrance and flanking windows.

Perhaps because of his minute observation and painstaking research, Stow's view of London is imbued with a love of the past and the vanished and disappearing city of his youth. A different view emerges from the work of Ralph Treswell (?c. 1540–c. 1616), who produced surveyed plans of a large number of houses belonging to two land-owning institutions: Christ's

128. An early photograph of the south door of St Helen's, Bishopsgate; on the left, the jetty of a building erected in the precinct soon after the Dissolution.

Hospital [132], the city's orphanage founded in 1552 (of which he was a governor), and the Clothworkers' Company, who paid him to survey their London property in 1612 [118, 131]. Treswell was by trade a Painter-Stainer; he painted banners and cloth hangings. In the 1580s he began producing surveys of rural estates, joining the expanding group of estate surveyors like Christopher Saxton who were developing the bird's-eye view or map, a particularly useful document when city institutions had rural property some distance from the estate office. In the few years before 1612 Treswell produced lease-plans for over 150 tenancies of the two institutions in the city. The surveys are ground-plans of buildings, with doors, stairs and chimneys carefully measured and drawn; but their value is increased since Treswell has added, in each of the two portfolios, a written description with measurements of all the rooms in the upper storeys of the majority of the buildings. Thus for the first time we can begin to reconstruct a large number of ordinary houses in three dimensions. Treswell's work complements that of Stow, for here is the professional surveyor measuring every wall, going down back alleys and recording privies, stables, warehouses and the everyday buildings which are not mentioned by Stow and only hinted at in the archaeological record.

The houses standing in the streets of London in 1612 were many different shapes and sizes, and of varying ages; but several types of house may be suggested from Treswell's surveys. The smallest houses, such as that of Widow Kinricke in Billiter Lane (now Billiter Street), had only one room on each floor [129]. Her ground-floor room, entered directly from the street, was 12 feet by 13 feet 6 inches; the total floor space in her house was only 556 square feet, made up of three rooms, one above the other. Each had an average size of 185 square feet, and two – the ground-floor and first-floor rooms – had chimneys; the room above was a garret, probably used for storage as there was no cellar. There was no built-in privy. The Clothworkers' records do not say when the house was built, but it was probably standing when their records begin in 1528. A more modern house with one room on each floor, built by the company in 1537, stood a few doors away down the Lane [129]; on a somewhat larger site, Thomas Hall's tenancy reached four storeys instead of three and boasted 1663 square feet of floor space, three times that of Widow Kinricke's. In this case all four rooms were heated, and the average room size was 356 square feet.

On the other side of Fenchurch Street, almost directly opposite the turning into Billiter Lane, lay a small block of four houses which backed on to Clothworkers' Hall itself [130]. They also seem to have been built before 1528, since the plentiful records of the Company do not mention rebuildings after that date. The three which formed the western half of the block were variants of the two-room design which we have already seen was widespread in medieval London on medium-sized properties – in this case, 70–80 feet long. Each house comprised, on the ground floor, a shop on the street side and a kitchen behind, though the middle house was also able to include a buttery by making the shop smaller. The third house, which was occupied by John Yeoman, a clothworker, had its kitchen chimney in one corner, rather than along one of the sides. The corner fireplace became widespread during the sixteenth century (occurring, for instance, in the early sixteenth-century buildings at Charterhouse; see 116). There was a second, larger fireplace in the 'shed', a building at the back of the yard,

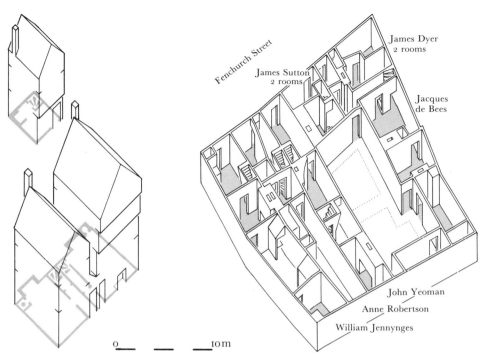

0 ___ ___ ___ 10m

129. *Above left:* Reconstruction of one-room plan houses in Billiter Lane in 1612, from Ralph Treswell's surveys: *above* the house of Widow Kinricke; *below* that of Thomas Hall.

130. *Above right:* Reconstruction of houses at 46–8 Fenchurch Street from a survey by Ralph Treswell in 1612.

which may have formerly been a separate kitchen; this would imply that the main house was old and had only recently been modernised. Although we cannot reconstruct the upper storeys with any certainty, Treswell's surveys enable us to say that the western of the three houses, that occupied by William Jennynges, was statistically nearest an 'average' two-room-plan house, with just over 1550 square feet of ground and floor space spread over four floors, with seven rooms. Only three of these were heated; the kitchen and two chambers above it. The hall, on the first floor next to the street, had no chimney; like the other two houses, Jennynges's house was heated only at the rear. There were also differences: the middle house, occupied by Anne Robertson, was one storey lower and, unlike the other two, had no cellar beneath the shop.

The larger house forming the eastern half of this group was split, in 1612, between three tenants. On the street frontage in the north-east corner James Dyer held two ground-floor rooms, a shop and a kitchen. Whether he lived there, or merely used the premises, we do not know. Across the passage which ran from Fenchurch Street to the large garden behind the frontage, James Sutton had a parlour and kitchen, with a suite of rooms upstairs: a hall lay over both his ground-floor rooms and thus could be heated; there were two chambers above the hall and two garrets above those. The rest of the ground floor, the garden, and the upper storeys above James Dyer's two rooms were occupied by one Jacques de Bees. We may take his tenancy as an example of a third type, the middle-sized house with several rooms on the ground floor. He had no street frontage at ground level, and his spacious hall was reached via the passage between the two front tenants. Beyond the hall lay a kitchen, and beyond that a 'water-house' with a privy. Over Dyer's shop de Bees had an imposing chamber 17 feet by 17½ feet, five other chambers on the first floor over the entry, hall and kitchen, and a garret over all on the second floor. His accommodation totalled over 3000 square feet, but still only four of his ten rooms had fireplaces in them. The number of fireplaces in a house evidently did not rise proportionately with the number of rooms; Widow Kinricke had two of her three rooms heated, or 66 per cent of her accommodation, whereas William Jennynges had only three out of seven rooms heated (43 per cent) and Jacques de Bees 40 per cent.

We can also say something about the functions and arrangement of the rooms in these houses, though research on the occupations of the tenants in 1612, when the surveys were made, has not yet come to fruition. At the front of most houses was the shop, still often entered directly from the street as in medieval times, but sometimes from a side door down a passage; this alternative entrance was to become more common in the later seventeenth century. The hall, if on the ground floor, had direct access to a courtyard or other open space (as in the case of Jacques de Bees); but often, as we have seen, the hall was on the first floor over the shop. In larger houses, inns and company halls a parlour would be found adjacent to the hall with a communicating door, but it was never entered directly from a courtyard. Usually the parlour had only one door for entrance and exit, unless there were stairs in a corner. Thus the parlour was the innermost room of the household, a private space for the family, often looking out over the garden. This contrasts with the status of the parlour in later years. By the eighteenth century, the parlour was the room to use for entertaining *other* families, and moved nearer the street. The nineteenth century saw the climax of this social movement when 'the vicar came to tea', and the parlour or front room developed into an almost sacred space where the family's best manners were observed. In my Yorkshire childhood in the 1950s the front room was referred to simply as *The Room*.

The kitchen in Treswell's plans, on the other hand, had different functions to perform. It usually communicated with the yard, and often had more than one entrance to allow circulation. On several of the surveys the kitchen block includes a privy (see 69), though it was partitioned off from the body of the kitchen and entered from the yard. Perhaps this was an intentional juxtaposition, for archaeologists find that many privies were used for the disposal of kitchen and meal waste. The peelings, it seems, went out of the kitchen and into the privy at the next doorway.

Treswell's survey of the Clothworkers' Company property at the corner of Fenchurch Street and Billiter Lane illustrates how large and small houses intermingled in early seventeenth-century London [131]. Here a large block of land belonged in the medieval period to the hospital of St Mary, Bishopsgate. Part of it had become the site of Ironmongers' Hall, and was thus not surveyed by Treswell. Fronting on to Fenchurch Street on the west side of the hall was a tenement called The Tennys Place, since down an alley leading from the street was a tennis court, first mentioned in 1549, and possibly first laid out then by the Clothworkers themselves. Our interest, however, centres on the buildings covering the rest of the ground to the east and north. Behind the row of small houses along Billiter Lane, which included the houses of Widow Kinricke and Thomas Hall, lay a large courtyard house which clearly retained many medieval elements. In 1520-5 it was briefly the hall of the Fullers' Company before they united with the Shearmen to form the Clothworkers' Company in 1528. As one of the larger company properties it attracted wealthy tenants throughout the

Sh
K
Sh
Y
tennis court
garden
garden
Fenchurch Street
Wh
K
tower
B
Ch.
B
Sh
walk
H
C
yard
P
K
gate
Thomas Hall
K
K Ch Ch Sh K K ?Sh Sh Sh Sh
Widow Kinricke
Billiter Lane
houses built in 1537
0   20 m

131. Plan of Clothworkers' Company property at Fenchurch Street and Billiter Lane, surveyed by Ralph Treswell in 1612.

B   buttery
C   cellar
Ch   chamber
H   hall
K   kitchen
P   parlour
Sh   shop
Wh   waterhouse
Y   yard.

sixteenth century, both company men and gentry. In the 1590s the main tenant was a Mr Blower, a rich clothworker; after his death his widow married Sir Edward Darcy in 1598, and Darcy is the tenant named in the survey of 1612. The house is a particularly fine example of the larger property which could serve both as a house of quality and a company hall, showing that the aspirations and social milieu of both largely coincided.

A visitor would enter usually from Fenchurch Street, beneath a four-storey range only one room wide (like the houses at Staple Inn) and then through a gatehouse into a yard in front of the hall. A second gatehouse to Billiter Lane had been carved out of two small houses in 1596. A semi-octagonal bay window emphasised the position of the hall, which was entered through a screens passage. On the domestic side of the screens were two butteries, stairs to the upper floors and a large kitchen. Around the yard was a gallery which gave access to some chambers on the upper floor. In contrast to the smaller houses along Fenchurch Street and Billiter Lane, there was only one upper floor over most of the buildings; thus the higher houses on the street frontage must have formed a screen up to three storeys higher than the larger house behind.

Several other features of Darcy's house are typical of Elizabethan houses in London. He had two large gardens. In the southern was a tower of brick, built against the boundary with Ironmongers' Hall. We cannot say when it was built, except that it appears in company records of 1593 when Blore's (Blower's) 'turret' was 'insufficient' (i.e. in need of repair). John Stow records the practice of several prominent citizens, beginning with the mayor of 1536, building towers of brick or timber, a vanity which he roundly condemns. In the northern, larger garden was a fountain, and on its west side, backing on to the Billiter Lane houses, a range which comprised a long ground-floor vault or cellar above which were three rooms including a parlour; above them on the second floor was a gallery sixty-eight feet long. The Fullers, in their brief use of the house for their hall in the 1520s, may have strolled contentedly in summer evenings either along the walk or in the gallery, savouring the perfumes of their own garden. Here too, perhaps, Sir Edward Darcy courted the rich widow of clothworker Mr Blower.

A specialised form of the courtyard house was the travellers' inn. There had been inns along Fleet Street and around Cheapside from at least the fourteenth century and no doubt before; the sixteenth century saw the development of further concentrations of inns around Smithfield and outside the eastern gates of Bishopsgate and Aldgate. Holy Trinity Priory originally owned all the land on both sides of what is now Aldgate High Street, but had a policy of selling it while retaining a small annual payment or *quit-rent*, recorded in a priory document which has survived. Thus we know that the house next to St Botolph's church, on the north side of Aldgate, was owned by William Cosyn, 'potter', in 1344, and by the Burford family, who made bells, in 1356 and 1399. A medieval bell-founding pit was found in the churchyard of St Botolph's during roadworks in 1959; perhaps the adjacent Burfords were responsible. There is a gap in the property's history until 1548, when it was in the hands of John Margettson, a brewer; in 1551 it is called the Crowne, and mention in a lease of 1569 of its five stables strongly suggests it was then an inn. The Crowne was bought for £100 in 1581 by William Couch, an innholder – i.e. one of the craft of inn-managers. He was buried under a stone with a brass inscription in the north aisle of St Botolph's in 1583, having left the 'reversion' of the Crowne to Christ's Hospital; it would pass to the hospital after the death of his widow Johanne. The survey made by Ralph Treswell in 1610 [132] probably shows the inn as Couch left it. Near the street lay the principal rooms, the hall ('14 panes of glass', notes the lease of 1569), parlour ('7 panes of glass, wainscotted around') and other drinking or social rooms. To the rear lay the stables, all with haylofts over, and a narrow back entrance to what was formerly the great extramural garden of the priory. This inn had two courtyards, separated by an inner gatehouse, which effectively cut off the public and guest rooms from the stable yard. Several of the other inns of Aldgate, but unfortunately not the Crowne, survived to be sketched in the nineteenth century before the coming of the underground railway [133]; Aldgate tube station now covers the site of the Crowne.

Although galleries are not mentioned in Treswell's survey of the Crowne, they may well have been present to enable circulation on upper storeys and to give single access to private chambers for the travellers. Such galleries are a feature of large houses, such as Darcy's tenancy in Fenchurch Street, and especially of inns of this period. No medieval inns survive today in London, and we must imagine them like the splendid New Inn at Gloucester or other inns surviving in smaller towns. Rarely, the detail of the gallery was noticed by those who recorded London inns during demolition. The majority of London inns survived to be recorded only in their early modern form, though in some cases probably dating from the late seventeenth century, about eighty years after Treswell's time. The only

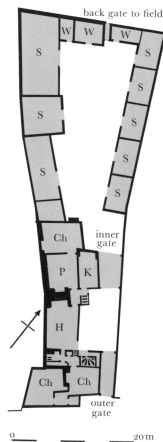

132. Plan of the Crowne Inn, Aldgate, from Ralph Treswell's survey of 1610 for Christ's Hospital.

Ch   chamber
H   hall
K   kitchen
P   parlour
S   stable
W   warehouse

back gate to field

inner gate

outer gate

0 ____ ____ ____ 20 m

133. The south side of Aldgate High Street in 1817, showing 16th- and 17th-century development of the suburb; watercolour by R. Schnebbelie.

survivor is the George Inn in Southwark, of which the south wing remains with its galleries, built after a fire in Southwark in 1676. It originally had galleries on three sides of a narrow courtyard [134]. It is built mostly in a softwood, pine; for such a large construction oak was clearly too expensive by the 1670s. The garrets or attics still possess their partitions, dividing the roof space into rooms for commercial travellers.

It is within the setting of such an inn courtyard, with its galleries providing plenty of space for onlookers, that Shakespeare and his colleagues developed the possibilities of dramatic performance. When specially built theatres were constructed during the latter part of Elizabeth's reign, they naturally adapted features of the galleried inns from which they sprang. The Globe Theatre in Southwark, and its colleague the Swan, are well known, partly through the drawing of the latter by Johannes de Witt. Other theatres were in Blackfriars and outside the city walls to the north, in Golden Lane (now appropriately opposite the Barbican Arts Centre). Here, in 1599, Philip Henslowe and Edward Alleyn, the famous actor and founder of Dulwich College, contracted with Peter Streete, carpenter, to build a theatre in terms which enable a reconstruction to be made [135]. The Fortune Theatre was to be three storeys high, on a low wall foundation of brick ('underpinning'). An open stage 43 feet by about 27 feet was to be surrounded by galleries, including four 'gentlemen's rooms' (? like boxes) and other 'twopennie rooms'. The stage, modelled on that of the Globe in Southwark, would have its pillars 'wroughte palasterwise [i.e. strapwork pilasters], with carved proporcions called satiers to be placed and set on the top of every of the same postes'. The reconstruction shows how the gallery, the essential feature of the new theatres, was copied from the inns, which in turn had adapted it from the large house.

In the ten years either side of 1600, strapwork and grotesques in timberwork assumed their most outlandish and vivacious forms [136]. At the same time classical motifs were used in panelling and on fire-places; the room would be crowned with a plaster ceiling, either in the lighter Elizabethan style (see 137) or a heavier Jacobean style with flat moulded

134. The George Inn, Southwark, drawn by J. C. Buckler in 1827, showing its original galleries. Now only the southern wing, to the right, remains.

135. Reconstruction of the Fortune Theatre, from the building contract of 1599, by Walter Godfrey.

136. House, possibly built in 1596, at the corner of Chancery Lane and Fleet Street, drawn by J. T. Smith in 1794. The exuberant grotesques spread along other buildings down the lane.

beams of plaster, exemplified by the surviving ceiling of 1610–11 at Prince Henry's Room, in Fleet Street. The house exterior could be a bravura performance of carpentry skills, either in exploiting a corner site by the use of jetties, which were already going out of fashion [136] or by incorporating in a two-storeyed front the most up-to-date window shapes and arrangements from contemporary country houses of brick and stone, as in the house-front of Sir Paul Pindar's house in Bishopsgate Street, now in the Victoria and Albert Museum.

James I, 'whom God hath honoured to be the first [king] of Britaine', decided that, 'as it was said of the first emperor of Rome, that he had found the city of Rome brick and left it of marble', he was determined to have it said of himself 'that we had found our Citie and suburbs of London of stickes, and left them of bricke, being a material far more durable, safe from fire and beautiful and magnificent'. He issued a proclamation in 1605 that houses were to be built of brick and stone, and not timber. This was soon modified to allow building in timber in narrow lanes, and thus brick

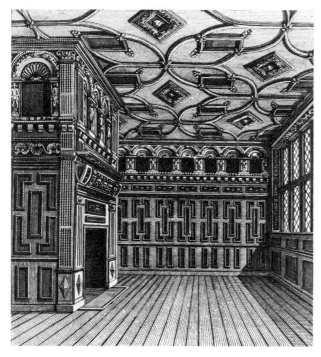

137. First-floor room in
the house in Hart Street,
Crutched Friars, shown
in 127. The fire-place
was dated 1609. The
ceiling may be a little
earlier.

became associated with house fronts, the main street and the front one
presented to the world. There are very few records of any houses built in
accordance with the proclamation; a few houses in Holborn and the Strand
in 1619, drawn by a visitor with an interest in architecture, show
apparently brick fronts surmounted by curved gables, topped by pediments, in a style imported from Amsterdam and the Netherlands. For
examples of this all-brick style we have to look to slightly later houses in
surrounding districts, such as The Presbytery in Croom Hill, Greenwich, of
about 1630, and Kew Palace, which was originally built as a country
residence of a Flemish London merchant, Samuel Fortrey, in 1631. At the
same time as this Netherlandish form of classicism was gaining ground, the
design of some royal and public buildings was taking a completely different
course, as Inigo Jones, London's first great 'architect' in the modern sense,
steps into the scene.

Inigo Jones was born in London in 1573; he died in 1652 and was buried
in the church of St Benet's, Paul's Wharf, which happily still stands as
rebuilt by Christopher Wren, the architect who followed in Jones's
footsteps. Jones travelled in Italy and on his return from an extensive tour
of that country from 1613 to 1614 found sympathetic patrons in James I
and, later, Charles I. In 1615 he was appointed Surveyor-General of the
King's Works, a post which he held until 1642, the eve of the Civil War.
Jones's style was formed by the influence of a single Renaissance theorist,
Andrea Palladio. The creators of the florid Elizabethan and Jacobean style
had applied Renaissance and classical motifs in a haphazard and purely
decorative way, taking Italian, as well as Flemish and German, text-books
as pattern-books. Palladio's intellectual and philosophical theories of
architecture, published in 1570 in his *Four Books of Architecture*, were based
on the study of classical buildings and monuments. Jones brought back to
England this intellectual thoroughness and coupled it with his natural

ability as an artist – his main occupation was as a designer of royal masques, in which he often co-operated with Ben Jonson. Jones's buildings were conceived as unified designs, based on the ideals of symmetry, harmony and proportion which he found in Palladio's work.

The first building designed by Jones as Surveyor of the King's Works was the Queen's House in Greenwich. Begun in 1616, it was not finished because of interruptions until 1629–35. The Queen's House was meant to be a small pleasure house in two sections flanking a road which originally passed through its middle; one part would be in Greenwich Park and the other in the grounds of Greenwich Palace, with a bridge over the road to connect the two sections. Jones's pupil John Webb filled in the gaps later.

The Queen's House should be compared with Jones's contemporary Banqueting House in Whitehall, built between 1619 and 1622 [138] – the only part of a projected new palace for Charles I ever built. The proportions of both buildings are based on the cube: the Banqueting House is a perfect double cube. The ground floors of both are rusticated (the pointing mortar has been left out to emphasise the joints between the blocks), giving the visual effect of a plinth supporting the first floor, the *piano nobile*. The south

138. Banqueting Hall, Whitehall, begun by Inigo Jones in 1619.

front of the Queen's House incorporates a loggia, a purely Italian recessed colonnade; masking the low roof is a balustrade. The two-storey façade of the Banqueting House (the interior hall rises through both storeys) is more ornate, divided into seven bays by columns and pilasters. The windows are topped with pediments – those of the upper storey uniformly square, but alternating round and triangular on the lower. Above runs a frieze consisting of swags of ornament, which became a favourite device of Wren's craftsmen.

In the 1620s, however, these buildings were totally alien to the man in the London street; the influence of Jones came to be felt only after his death in the latter years of the century. A hesitant classicism can be seen in the few churches rebuilt at the time, for example at St Katherine Cree (1628–31), where the medieval tower of 1504 was retained, but the body of the church rebuilt. Outside, except for the windows, it might still be medieval; but inside, the rib-vaults of plaster spring from round arches and Tuscan columns. An even more pedestrian classicism is found in the south door of St Helen's, Bishopsgate, replacing the medieval door in 1633 [128]. At other churches and chapels, such as the chapel of Lincoln's Inn, which may have been designed by Jones, classical ideas were mixed freely with the tail end of Perpendicular Gothic to produce lively if gawky vaulting. Jones himself was not above clothing the old styles in the new, as he demonstrated with considerable refacing of the nave and transepts of St Paul's about 1640, adding a classical portico to the west end [139].

In 1630 Jones was able to extend his ideas to town planning and new forms for ordinary houses. At the Dissolution the first Earl of Bedford had been granted the produce garden of Westminster Abbey called Covent (Convent) Garden. The fourth Earl employed Jones to design a square or piazza in Italian style as a high-class housing venture on the north side of Bedford House, which occupied part of the site. Terraces of brick houses with ground-floor loggias and stuccoed fronts occupied the east and north sides; on the west side Jones designed St Paul's church (1631–3), with a great Tuscan portico looking out on the square. Covent Garden was meant to be, and for a short time was, an aristocratic residential area; it became associated with a vegetable market only as fashion moved westwards and decline set in. But the essential point had been made. From the time of Inigo Jones, planners and builders began to think in terms of new streets and housing schemes for separate income groups almost regardless of profession or trade. In the West End, this was at first for the rich; in the East End, it was for the poor artisan. Thus the city of London, and its suburbs, began a long and slow change from a medieval city in which where and how people lived related to their trading groups to a city where zoning was based not on function but on wealth.

The new kind of house for the wealthy, exclusive square as envisaged by Inigo Jones or one of his avant-garde contemporaries – for the architect is not precisely known – can be seen in Lindsey House, built about 1640 on the west side of Lincoln's Inn Fields [140]. It was stuccoed at a later date, and would originally have had a brick façade. We have already met many of the architectural features of the new style: a rusticated ground storey, large windows with pediments on the first floor, two-storey pilasters and a balustrade at roof level. Also new is the idea of the house being fronted by a shallow courtyard entered directly from the street, instead of being behind

ECCLESIÆ CATHEDRALIS.
S. PAVLI
AB OCCIDENTE PROSPECTVS.

139. Western portico added to St Paul's by Inigo Jones, *c.* 1640.

a range of buildings as with the grander houses of the medieval city. This idea was to be taken up by the urban palaces of Bloomsbury and further points westward in London's later expansion.

For ordinary houses, the three decades before the Great Fire saw some aping of the new fashions, at least in detail; the basic structure of the late medieval house did not change at all. To the double-storeyed bay windows of the 1590s were added Corinthian pilasters [141], rising to support the jettied garret. Occasionally, an ambitious plasterer would try out Netherlandish motifs. The framing of such houses was becoming light and frail; the infilling was still of lath and plaster with some brick. The thin walls of the Treswell surveys, and the accounts of contemporary writers, suggest that very few buildings were of brick or stone in the seventeenth century. There were of course some fashionable houses in brick, such as one built in 1648 in Great St Helen's; but the trio of houses nearby in Bishopsgate [91], built in 1657, seem from their elaborate decoration to be of timber. They had pilasters, topped by Corinthian capitals, running through the two principal storeys of the façade, and bay windows typical also of the reign of Charles II. In this case the central bay had its windows crowned by a pediment in the new style, only to be over-topped by garrets in the medieval style of the previous centuries.

London's buildings, on the eve of the Great Fire of 1666, were thus a multitude of styles dating back in some parts three or four hundred years. Although there were many large houses in their own grounds away from the bustle of the streets, the buildings along the streets were high, often old, and jettied, which contributed to the narrowness of the streets themselves. Many of the houses and shops forming lucrative street frontages were owned by institutions, especially the livery companies and the city, whose tenants would not be inclined to put up large amounts of money to rebuild in new styles or with new materials. Most buildings, despite some small progress towards brick construction, were high, closely-packed, and timber-framed, a natural prey to fire (see 147).

The best witness of the disaster of 1666 was the diarist Samuel Pepys. About 3 am on Sunday 2 September, Pepys was called from his bed by a maid who pointed out a fire somewhere to the west of his house in Seething Lane. Pepys thought it was on the other side of Mark Lane, 'but being unused to such fires as followed, I thought it far enough off, and so went to bed again and to sleep'. In the morning, having been told that three hundred houses had been destroyed, he went to the Tower and from a vantage point saw the area around the bridge-head all on fire. He took a boat up through the bridge, and found the fire was almost at the Steelyard. People were flinging goods into lighters, or into the river; as the fire spread, they clambered from one river stair to another to avoid the flames. Goods were moved to friends' houses, only to be moved again and again as the fire spread and consumed everything. After lunch-time on the Sunday, goods removed to Cannon Street were being removed to Lombard Street. By the end of the day the fire appeared as an arch of flame a mile long [142].

140. Lindsey House, Lincoln's Inn Fields, built in 1640. A royal commission of 1618 noted, and encouraged, the spreading of 'dwellings and lodgings of noblemen and gentlemen of quality' round Lincoln's Inn Fields, thus formalising the square into its present layout. Inigo Jones is said to have drawn the ground-plot of the square with the exact dimensions of one of the pyramids of Egypt.

141. *Right:* Houses in Long Lane, West Smithfield, drawn by J. T. Smith in 1795. The long panels and thin braces of 17th-century timber-framing show how the houses surveyed by Treswell may have been constructed. Note the classical pilasters, suggesting a building date in the 1630s.

142. *Below:* The Great Fire of London, from a painting by Griffier, engraved in 1792. This may be an imaginative reconstruction, but appears to show Ludgate, to judge from the position of St Paul's behind.

143. Map of the fire-damaged area by Hollar,
using the street-plan of John Leake, 1666.
Though a few stone structures remained in part,
the area was devastated; pre-Fire buildings
were thereafter to be found only in the north
and eastern parts of the City. The churches of St
Ethelburga [91], St Helen's Bishopsgate [128]
and St Andrew Undershaft [122] are among the
small group that survives to the present day.

On Tuesday 4 September Tower Street, then quite narrow, was ablaze and Pepys began to fear both for his house in Seething Lane and the Navy Office where he worked in Mark Lane. A hardware shop had been emptied of its goods, and local people were frantically using the dishes, trays and shovels to speed water down the gutter in the middle of the street. On the other side of the city the whole of Fleet Street as far as the Temple was on fire, but there a higher proportion of brick building was checking its advance. Later in the day, when the mayor's authority was clearly not sufficient, the King and his brother the Duke of York gave the order for houses to be blown up at Temple Bar, near Smithfield and at other points to the north and east of the fire to create fire-breaks. By Thursday evening it was under control, though isolated outbreaks continued, and some well-fuelled fires had to burn themselves out. Clothworkers' Hall, Pepys noted, was strange to see, 'on fire these three days and nights in one body of flame – it being the cellar, full of oil'.

The extent of the Great Fire, and the official account of the rebuilding that followed, is given in full on its most enduring memorial: the pillar called simply The Monument which stands near the source of the fire in Pudding Lane. It was built in 1671–7 to the design of Sir Christopher Wren. Originally there were to be brass flames issuing from loopholes along its entire height, and a phoenix at the top. The Latin inscription on the north side summarises the disaster:

In the year of Christ 1666, the 2nd day of September, eastwards from hence, at the distance of 202 feet, the height of this column [i.e. where Pudding Lane is crossed by Monument Street, a late nineteenth-century creation] a terrible fire broke out about midnight; which driven on by a strong wind not only wasted the adjacent parts, but also very remote places, with incredible noise and fury. It consumed 89 churches, the city gates, Guildhall, many public structures, hospitals, schools, libraries, a vast number of stately edifices, 13,200 dwelling houses, 400 streets; of the 26 wards it utterly destroyed 15, and left eight others shattered and half burnt. The ruins of the city were 436 acres, from the Tower by the Thames side to the Temple church, and from the north-east along the city wall to Holborn bridge [see 143]. To the estates and fortunes of the citizens it was merciless, but to their lives very favourable, that it might in all things resemble the conflagration of the world. The destruction was sudden; for in a small space of time the city was seen most flourishing, and reduced to nothing. Three days after, when this fatal fire had baffled all human counsels and endeavours, in the opinion of all, it stopped, as it were, by a command from heaven, and was on every side extinguished. But papistical malice, which perpetrated such mischiefs, is not yet restrained.

Another inscription on the west side, attributing the fire to 'the treachery and malice of the popish faction', and 'their horrid plot of extirpating the protestant religion', was erased in the reign of James II, recut under William and Mary and finally removed in 1831. Attacking papists as culprits, though vehement at the time, was soon regarded as without foundation: Alexander Pope, in a famous couplet, likened the column to a tall bully rearing its head and telling lies. The inscription on the south side records the rebuilding of London:

Charles the Second, son of Charles the martyr, king of Great Britain, France and Ireland, defender of the faith, a most gracious prince, commiserating the deplorable state of things, whilst the ruins were yet smoking, provided for the comfort of his citizens, and the ornament of his city; remitted their taxes and referred the petitions of the magistrates and inhabitants to the parliament; who immediately passed an act, that public works should be restored to greater beauty, with public money, to be raised by an imposition on coal; that churches, and the cathedral of St Paul, shall be rebuilt from their foundations, with all magnificence; that the bridges, gates and prisons should be new made, the sewers cleansed, the streets made straight and regular, such as were steep levelled, and those too narrow made wider, markets and shambles removed to separate places. They also enacted, that every house should be built with party walls, and all in front raised of equal height, and those walls all of square stone or brick; and that no man should delay building beyond the space of seven years. Moreover, care was taken by law, to prevent all suits about their bounds [cases brought in court, delaying matters]. Also anniversary prayers were injoined; and to perpetuate the memory hereof to posterity, they caused this column to be erected. The work was carried on with diligence, and London is restored, but whether with greater speed or beauty, may be made a question [i.e. which was the greater, the speed of rebuilding or its beauty? It is not meant to be ironical]. For at three years' end, the world saw that finished, which was supposed to be the business of an age.

Also on the west front, a relief by Caius Cibber shows both destruction and restoration in allegory [145]. A female figure representing the city of London sits disconsolately on a pile of ruins. Time tries to raise her up; behind are goddesses of Plenty and Peace, and the citizens of London, all willing to lend a hand. A beehive at the City's feet symbolises that whole cities can be built by industry and hard work; below, the dragon from the city arms attempts to hold up the ruins. Opposite the City stands the King, in Roman costume; he directs three of his servants to help the young lady. The first attendant is Science, with Nature of the many breasts – ready to give assistance to all – in its hand. The second is Architecture, with plan, square and compasses; the third Liberty, waving a hat in the air. Behind the king stand his brother the Duke of York, Justice (with a coronet) and Fortitude with a reined lion.

The whole thing is gloriously absurd, for it was soon surrounded by only slightly wider streets of three- and four-storey houses in brick. The sculpture has been compared with paintings and tapestries glorifying Louis XIV, and it is one of the few relics of the intention of Wren and his circle to rebuild London, if they could, like the Paris of Louis. Broad avenues would radiate out from *rond-points*, the most imposing with a new Royal Exchange at its centre. Certainly some streets were widened; Thames Street and the lanes leading to it were heightened with fire rubble and the slope carefully lessened, and a New Quay was cleared along the riverfront, largely by cutting back the former building line. One new street was laid out from the Guildhall to the quay: King Street, and its continuation Queen Street, which now lead to Southwark Bridge (but originally only to the wharf). The height of houses was carefully regulated according to their positions on principal streets, major or minor alleys.

Spasmodic rebuilding started almost immediately, and within months the city set up courts and surveyors to set out property boundaries for building. The houses went up when the owner or tenant could afford to rebuild; and therefore the streets took shape only in fits and starts. Such was the speed of rebuilding, however, that by the time of Ogilby and Morgan's map of 1677, only some of the church sites remained unbuilt, awaiting the energy and vision of Christopher Wren who was to design fifty-one of them. This map of the post-Fire city [144] is paradoxically where students of medieval and Tudor London begin, for it records the

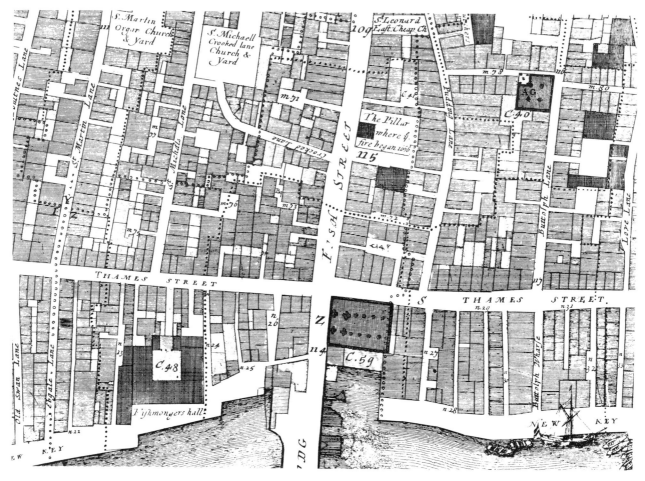

medieval city at the moment of its extinction. Not only outside the area of the fire, but in the larger area within the limit of the flames, the property boundaries of 1677 are those of the ancient town. Although a very different city of brick rose from the ashes, its structure of streets, alleys and properties was dictated by the underlying medieval topography. Such indeed is the conservative nature of the city's topography that many medieval, and sometimes in origin late Saxon, boundaries are obliterated only by building developments of our own century.

The Great Fire marks the end of our story; but the successor to the medieval and Tudor city, in appearance so different, was in its structure the product of development and decisions made over many previous generations.

144. *Above:* Where the Fire began, from Ogilby and Morgan's map of 1677. The Fire began in Pudding Lane and spread slowly at first until it reached Thames Street to the south. Then it became a major disaster.

145. *Right:* The Monument, photographed in the early 20th century, showing the main allegorical panel.

Postscript

The city explored in this book largely disappeared in the Great Fire of 1666, but by fitting together the scraps of evidence gathered from a variety of sources, we can begin to recreate on paper some of its buildings, and explain their uses and effects. We have, in part, been composing a guide to a city that no longer exists.

It is interesting, therefore, to compare this picture of medieval London with the present-day form of historic cities whose buildings have had better fortunes – with York, for instance. To wander round York today is to see in timber, brick and stone the kind of buildings we have been recreating on paper. In its history York is remarkably similar to London. Both were founded by the Romans within about twenty years of each other in the mid-first century. Until the sixteenth century York was often regarded as the capital of the north to balance London, and monarchs disaffected with London's power, such as Richard II and Charles I, toyed with the idea of making York the national capital. In the history of its site and buildings also, York has many parallels to offer. Christianity came with a Kentish princess in the early seventh century, as Kentish influence had brought it to London; the Roman city walls were retained, but internal fort walls lost to encroachment by the developing city. York was the only city outside London to have two Norman castles. But the importance of parallels is greatest for the individual buildings of medieval and Tudor York, which, transposed, could have stood in London streets. The Minster, though not on such a prominent site as St Paul's, can still give the effect of a large church dominating its town. The early fourteenth-century Lady Row in Goodramgate, and countless other timber-framed buildings, are models for the reconstruction of their long destroyed London counterparts. York has the largest surviving number of medieval guildhalls, equivalent to London's fifty company halls; and it retains a good number of fairly intact medieval churches with an unrivalled display of stained glass.

I make this point to suggest that London was, in many ways, a large medieval city [147] different only in degree, and not really in kind, from lesser towns. The reconstruction of the city's buildings, by archaeological excavation, study of engravings or contemporary ground-plans should be fleshed out by comparison with surviving buildings in other places, which were erected on the same principles, and by the same kind of people.

London was like York, or Norwich, or King's Lynn; but the degree of difference was at times acute. London, because of its position as an international port and as the seat of prelates, members of parliament and all those concerned with the machinery of government at Westminster, was the home and workplace of men with capital, a traditional capacity for extravagance in architecture and the will to indulge it. Thus London became the melting-pot where new styles, whether they actually began here or not, received their most influential boost. The pointed arches of the

146. A study in the intimacy of medieval buildings: houses on the north-east side of Southwark Cathedral in 1807. Beyond the 16th-century row lies the 14th-century chapel attached to the priory church of St Mary Overie (the tower of which appears top right).

Temple church may predate those of Canterbury Cathedral in the 1170s; William Ramsey's chapter-house at St Paul's is one of the first Perpendicular buildings in 1336. Through their connections with the court and other patrons, masons and carpenters based in London led the country; Henry Yevele and Hugh Herland, who built Westminster Hall in its present form and its roof respectively, probably lived within three-quarters of a mile of each other in Thames Street.

On a more mundane level, the city's rapidly growing size in the twelfth and thirteenth centuries resulted in the drawing up of building regulations against fire and governing certain aspects of drainage, privacy and encroachment. This led to a continuing concern with the standards of privies, chimneys and health hazards in general, so that London houses at most periods were probably among the best constructed and fitted out of any English city. Innovations of importance to the mass of the city's population, such as the widespread provision of stone or brick chimneys so much in evidence in Treswell's plans of 1612, or the construction of timber-framed buildings in four, five or even six storeys, probably also started first in London, because of the pressures caused by density of buildings, availability of capital generated by trade and the insistence of civic regulation. Further research may elucidate this process.

We would also like to know more about the interaction of major masons, who become distinguishable figures in the fourteenth century, with these smaller and everyday building operations in the city. Michael of Canterbury, designer of royal tombs, may well be the architect of the east end of St

Paul's; yet he was also one of the four 'viewers' of the city for the *Assize of Nuisance*, and found time to adjudicate a boundary dispute. John Croxton, building Guildhall, advised the Brewers' Company on details of their new almshouses, and sold them stone for one of their doorways. The existence of a large local building industry, a constant influx of materials such as Caen stone intended for grander buildings but sometimes side-tracked or resold, and master masons and carpenters of national repute and influence must have given a certain quality to all the buildings erected under their direction or with their advice.

How did the inhabitants of London, and all those who were drawn to the city, use its buildings? That is a very difficult question, for London meant many things to many people – the abbot or knight wanting an urban base to administer his estate or further his political career, the merchant storing his goods or entertaining foreign colleagues, the craftsman working in a single room, or the rural poor searching for work and a bed. We can understand these uses, and how they combined or clashed with each other, by studying the forms of the buildings, their materials, decoration and fittings. By assembling details of the chapels and altars in late medieval parish churches, for instance, we shall begin to understand the use of the parish church for expressions of piety, charity and personal status by the more prominent merchant and noble families. Or by reconstructing the form of the livery company hall, so often repeated throughout the city, we shall be able to see in its context the conservatism of the direction of trade and industry. Since ceremony and ritual were important components of public diplomacy and private negotiation, it would be interesting to find

147. Part of Hollar's panorama of the pre-Fire city, drawn in 1647. It shows the cathedral of St Paul, without its spire, still dominating the city as the minsters at York and Lincoln still do today.

Paulus wharfe   Queene hythe

out how the buildings of London were influenced by their ceremonial uses: the effect on the gates and main streets of the visits of kings or foreign princes, such as the coronation procession from the Tower instituted by Richard II, or the ceremonies of greeting and playing host to guests of the merchant aldermen.

At the heart of this enquiry, however, have been two simpler, more fundamental questions: how did London grow into its medieval and Tudor shape? And what did it look like? What we know of each stage of its growth has been outlined in the preceding chapters. I hope it has been possible to join together some of the scattered fragments of records, to form individual buildings or blocks of property, and thus obtain an impression of the medieval and Tudor townscape. As in York, the city contained many large and fine buildings, among which pride of place must go to Guildhall [87]; the size of these large constructions would be emphasised by the small scale of houses around them, especially in comparison to modern buildings. Streets and alleys were narrow; room sizes, as we have seen, were usually small. In many parts of the city and its suburbs, buildings crowded together so that the view down a court or alley would constantly bring together contrasts of stone and brick, the finely moulded and the vernacular, the secular and the religious [146].

The London that existed before the Great Fire must have been a fascinating place to explore. By fitting together fragmented pieces of evidence, we still have the means of forming an impression of the medieval and Tudor city, and gaining insights into one of the most formative periods of the capital's illustrious past.

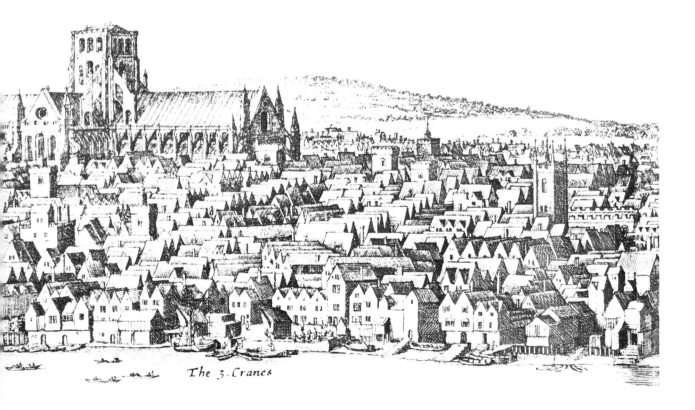

The 3. Cranes

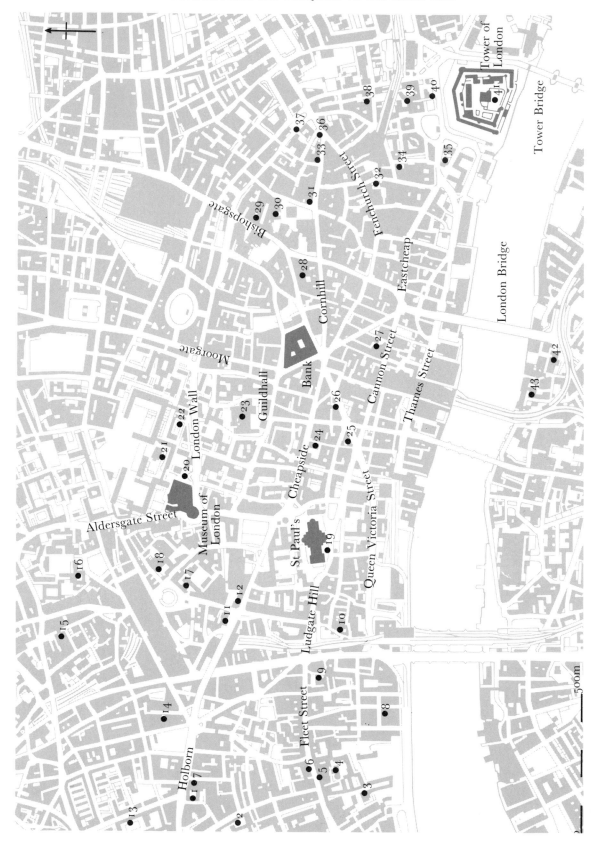

Tower of London

Tower Bridge

London Bridge

Bishopsgate

Fenchurch Street

Eastcheap

Moorgate

Cornhill

Bank

Guildhall

Cannon Street

Thames Street

London Wall

Aldersgate Street

Museum of London

Cheapside

St. Paul's

Queen Victoria Street

Ludgate Hill

Fleet Street

Holborn

500m

Gazetteer

The places marked on this map show main sites where the remains of the medieval and Tudor City of London can still be visited, with permission where necessary.

1. STAPLE INN, HOLBORN: hall, 1580; frontage to Holborn, 1586+.

2. LINCOLN'S INN: hall of 1490; gatehouse of 1518; courtyard ranges of 1520–1530.

3. MIDDLE TEMPLE HALL, MIDDLE TEMPLE LANE: hall, 1571.

4. TEMPLE: church, 12th century and later; two vaulted rooms of 14th century, attached to Inner Temple Hall.

5. INNER TEMPLE GATEWAY, 17 FLEET STREET: timber-framed front of 1610–11; inside on first floor Prince Henry's Room (plaster ceiling).

6. ST DUNSTAN'S PORCH, FLEET STREET: statues of King Lud and sons from Ludgate; above the entrance, statue of Elizabeth I (1586) from the same gate.

7. BARNARD'S HALL, HOLBORN: early 15th-century hall.

8. 4 BRITTON'S COURT: 14th-century vaulted undercroft, part of the Whitefriars.

9. ST BRIDE'S, FLEET STREET: Saxon and medieval church is laid out in the crypt, with a small museum of finds.

10. APOTHECARIES' HALL, BLACKFRIARS LANE: hall built partly on the guest house of the Blackfriars; a small amount of medieval stonework is visible.

11. ST SEPULCHRE, HOLBORN VIADUCT: 15th-century church and tower, thoroughly rebuilt in the 19th century.

12. GILTSPUR STREET: corner-tower of medieval city wall, beneath GPO buildings and yard.

13. GRAY'S INN, GRAY'S INN ROAD: 16th-century chapel; hall of 1560.

14. ST ETHELDREDA'S, ELY PLACE: chapel of the town house of Bishops of Ely, dating from 1290, with original carpentry in crypt.

15. ST JOHN, CLERKENWELL: remains of church, 12th century and later; monastic gate in St John's Lane, 1504.

16. CHARTERHOUSE, CHARTERHOUSE SQUARE: late 14th-century Carthusian monastery with 16th-century monastic and post-Dissolution building.

17. ST BARTHOLOMEW THE LESS: 15th-century church.

18. ST BARTHOLOMEW THE GREAT, WEST SMITHFIELD: Augustinian priory, 12th century and later.

19. ST PAUL'S CHAPTER-HOUSE, ST PAUL'S CHURCHYARD: foundations of chapter-house and cloister of 1336.

20. BARBICAN: a length of the city wall, with Bastions 11A, 12 (on the corner), 13 and 14, is preserved (best view from walkway by Bastion House).

21. ST GILES CRIPPLEGATE: 15th-century tower; church of c.1545–50.

22. LONDON WALL: remains of 14th-century crossing tower of hospital of Elsing Spital, later the parish church of St Alphege; to the north-west, a length of the city wall with brick additions of 1477.

23. GUILDHALL, GUILDHALL YARD: late 13th-century west undercroft; east undercroft, porch and hall of c.1411–c.1440.

24. ST MARY LE BOW, CHEAPSIDE: late 11th-century crypt.

25. ST MARY ALDERMARY, QUEEN VICTORIA STREET: lower stages of tower, 1511 and 1629.

26. 34 WATLING STREET: corner of a 14th-century vaulted undercroft preserved in basement.

27. ABCHURCH LANE: fragment of 14th-century vaulted undercroft (access via St Mary Abchurch).

28. MERCHANT TAYLORS' HALL, THREADNEEDLE STREET: 14th-century company hall, contemporary undercroft; 15th-century kitchen.

29. ST ETHELBURGA, BISHOPSGATE: 14th- and 15th-century church.

30. ST HELEN'S, BISHOPSGATE: parish church and Benedictine nunnery, 12th century and later.

31. ST ANDREW UNDERSHAFT, LEADENHALL STREET: 15th-century tower; church of 1520–32.

32. ALL HALLOWS STAINING, MARK LANE: 15th-century tower. Access through the tower (by permission of the Clothworkers' Company) to undercroft of St James's Hermitage (Lambe's Chapel).

33. ST KATHERINE CREE, LEADENHALL STREET: 16th-century tower; church of 1628–31.

34. ST OLAVE, HART STREET: 13th-century crypt: 15th-century church.

35. ALL HALLOWS BARKING, GREAT TOWER STREET: Saxon arch and north-west corner of church of reused Roman tiles; Saxon cross fragments in crypt; 14th- and 15th-century church above.

36. MITRE STREET: 14th- or 15th-century arch from entrance to chapel in church of Holy Trinity Priory (now bisected by street).

37. DUKE'S PLACE: pedestrian subway under Duke's Place has a mural showing the Roman and medieval city wall which was cut through for its construction.

38. 7–9 CROSSWALL: length of the Roman city wall, and foundation of Bastion 4A uncovered during redevelopment in 1979–80 and to be displayed in the new building.

39. COOPER'S ROW: length of city wall, (?) 12th-century apertures.

40. TOWER HILL: length of city wall, and Tower Postern.

41. THE TOWER OF LONDON: keep and fortifications of 11th–17th centuries.

42. SOUTHWARK CATHEDRAL: St Mary Overie, Augustinian priory, 12th century and later.

43. CLINK STREET: west gable of hall of Bishop of Winchester, with rose window, c.1330.

Bibliography

INTRODUCTION

The major edition of John Stow's *Survey of London* (1603) is by C. L. Kingsford (2 vols, 1908; repr. 1971). This reproduces Stow's addition to his text of William Fitzstephen's *Description of the Most Noble City of London* in Latin. For an English translation of Fitzstephen, see Stow's *Survey* edited by H. B. Wheatley, Everyman editions (1912; rev. 1956), 501–9. For surviving buildings, see N. Pevsner, *London I: The Cities of London and Westminster*, The Buildings of England Series (1957; 3rd edn rev. B. Cherry, 1973); for remaining (and many lost) churches, G. Cobb, *London City Churches* (1942; rev. 1977). Further reading on individual buildings is noted in the paragraphs below.

On the results of archaeological excavation since the Second World War, see W. F. Grimes, *The Excavation of Roman and Medieval London* (1968); J. Schofield and T. Dyson (eds) *Archaeology of the City of London* (1980) and two overall interim reports in journals: B. Hobley and J. Schofield, 'Excavations in the City of London, 1974–5: First Interim Report', *Antiquaries Journal* 57 (1977), 31–66, and T. Dyson and J. Schofield, 'Excavations in the City of London: Second Interim Report, 1974–1978', *Trans. Lon. Middx Arch. Soc.* 32 (1981), 24–81.

For the city records, see P. E. Jones and R. Smith, *A Guide to the Records in the Corporation of London Records Office and the Guildhall Library Muniment Room* (1951). Many illustrative extracts are collected by H. T. Riley (ed.) *Memorials of London Life in the XIII, XIV and XV Centuries, 1276–1419* (1868). For the *Assize of Nuisance*, see notes to chapter three. The Viewers' Certificates (currently being prepared for publication by Janet Loengaard) and the Repertories and Journals of the Court of Aldermen (card index of topographical references by Anne Sutton) are in the City of London Record Office. The Brewers' accounts of 1423 are printed in R. W. Chambers and M. Daunt (eds) *London English 1384–1425* (1931), 152–61. There are few studies of early representations of London or its buildings; for examples, see P. Glanville, *London in Maps* (1972); and A. M. Hind, *Wenceslaus Hollar and his Views of London* (1922).

1 ROMAN AND SAXON ORIGINS

For the Roman city, see R. Merrifield, *The Roman City of London* (1965) and P. Marsden, *Roman London* (1981). The most recent review of Saxon London is T. Dyson and J. Schofield, 'London' in J. Haslam (ed.) *Anglo-Saxon Towns of Southern England* (forthcoming). For the history of London at this period, see C. N. L. Brooke with G. Keir, *London 800–1216: the shaping of a city* (1975). For Saxon churches generally, see B. Cherry, 'Ecclesiastical Architecture' in D. Wilson (ed.) *The Archaeology of Anglo-Saxon England* (1973), 151–200; and for the Vikings, see Sir R. E. M. Wheeler, *London and the Vikings* (1927). For some of the detailed archaeological discoveries, see S. Roskams and J. Schofield, 'Milk Street excavations, 2', *London Archaeologist* 3 (1978), 227–34 (dark earth); G. Milne, 'Saxon Botolph Lane', *ibid.* 3(1980), 423–30; and L. Miller, 'New Fresh Wharf, 2: the Saxon and early medieval waterfronts', *ibid.* 3 (1977), 47–53.

2 NORMAN LONDON

The standard history is C. N. L. Brooke and G. Keir, *London 800–1216: the shaping of a city* (1975); see also Sir F. M. Stenton, *Norman London* (1934), available in D. M. Stenton (ed.) *Preparatory to Anglo-Saxon England* (1970), 23–47. On the Tower of London, Westminster Abbey and Westminster Palace, see Royal Commission on Historical Monuments, *London, Vol. V (East London)* (1930), *Vol. III (Westminster Abbey)* (1924) and *Vol. II (West London)* (1925) respectively; summarised and discussed in R. Allen Brown, H. M. Colvin and A. J. Taylor (eds) *History of the King's Works*, vol. 1 (1963). For St Paul's, see W. Longman, *A History of the three cathedrals dedicated to St Paul in London* (1873), and G. H. Cook, *Old St Paul's Cathedral* (1955); Bermondsey Abbey (priory), A. R. Martin, 'On the topography of the Cluniac Abbey of St Saviour at Bermondsey', *Journ. Brit. Arch. Ass.* 32 (1926), 192–228, and W. F. Grimes, *The Excavation of Roman and Medieval London* (1968), 210–17; the work on the reconstruction of Holy Trinity Priory is by the author and Richard Lea of the Museum of London (the Symonds plan was published by W. R. Lethaby, 'The Priory of Holy Trinity, Aldgate' in *Home Counties Magazine* 11, 1900, 45–53). On hospitals, nunneries and other religious houses see C. N. L. Brooke and G. Keir, *London 800–1216: the shaping of a city* (1975), 310–37. Fig. 35 is from 'St John of Jerusalem, Clerkenwell' in A. W. Clapham and W. Godfrey, *Some Famous Buildings and their*

Story, (1913), 165–78. The town houses at London Bridge and Corbet Court are reported in *Archaeologia* 23 (1831), 299–308 and *Journ. Brit. Arch. Ass.* 1st series, 28 (1872), 176–9. For the Milk Street house, see S. Roskams and J. Schofield, 'Milk Street excavations, 2', *London Archaeologist* 3 (1978), 227–34.

3   THE EMERGENT CITY

The standard work on London Bridge is G. Home, *Old London Bridge* (1931). For building at Westminster Abbey, Palace and the Tower see *King's Works* and H. M. Colvin (ed.) *Building Accounts of King Henry III* (1971). The houses on the Strand, and Ely Place, are described among many others by C. L. Kingsford in his series of articles, 'Historical Notes on Medieval London Houses', *Lon. Top. Rec.* 10 (1916), 44–144; 11 (1917), 28–81; 12 (1920), 1–66. For St Paul's, see W. Longman, *A History of three cathedrals dedicated to St. Paul in London* (1873) and G. H. Cook, *Old St Paul's Cathedral* (1955). The building regulations of 1212 are discussed in H. M. Chew and W. Kellaway (eds) *London Assize of Nuisance 1301–1431*, Lond. Rec. Soc. (1973) (hereafter *Assize of Nuisance*), 9–30; the Eyre of 1244 in H. M. Chew and M. Weinbaum (eds) *The London Eyre of 1244*, Lond. Rec. Soc. (1970). For the technique of dating carpentry joints, see C. Hewett, *The Development of English Carpentry, 1200–1700: an Essex Study* (1969) and *English Historic Carpentry* (1980).

4   THE LONDON OF YEVELE AND CHAUCER

For the Bishop of Winchester's house and the rose window, see H. Roberts and W. H. Godfrey (eds) *Survey of London: xxii, Bankside* (1950), 45–56. For St Stephens, the spread of Perpendicular architecture and the careers of Yevele and his associates, J. Harvey, *The Perpendicular Style 1330–1485* (1978). The Packman's Wharf lcase and the contracts mentioned in this chapter are reproduced in L. F. Salzman, *Building in England down to 1540: a documentary study* (1952; rev. 1967), the standard work on the medieval building industry. The discussion of domestic buildings is based on the author's research, aided by R. R. Sharpe (ed.) *Calendar of the Coroners' Rolls of the City of London, A.D. 1300–1378* (1913), P. Eames, *Medieval Furniture* (1977) and the *Assize of Nuisance*. Several archaeologists and historians are now working on the London waterfront; the Trig Lane material is from G. & C. Milne, 'Excavations on the Thames

waterfront at Trig Lane, London, 1974–6', *Med. Arch.* 22 (1978), 84–104 and *Medieval waterfront development at Trig Lane*, Lon. Middx Arch. Soc. Special Paper (forthcoming), incorporating the documentary work of Tony Dyson; see also V. Harding, 'The Two Coldharbours of the City of London', *Lon. Top. Rec.* 24 (1980), 11–30; T. Tatton-Brown, 'Excavations at the Custom House site, City of London, 1973', *Trans. Lon. Middx Arch. Soc.* 25 (1974), 117–219 and 26 (1975), 103–70; for a summary of waterfront buildings, J. Schofield, 'Medieval waterfront buildings in the City of London' in B. Hobley and G. Milne (eds) *Waterfront archaeology in Britain and northern Europe*, (1981), 24–31.

5   STABILITY AND CONSOLIDATION

The Guildhall has been studied by C. Barron, *The Medieval Guildhall of London* (1974), with further suggestions on the form of the roof by G. Wilson, 'The Original Design of the City of London Guildhall', *Journ. Brit. Arch. Ass.* 129 (1976), 1–14. For the bequests of Richard Whittington, see J. Imray, *The Charity of Richard Whittington* (1968). The survey of late medieval churches here is based on churchwardens' accounts and R. R. Sharpe (ed.) *Calendar of Wills proved and enrolled in the Court of Husting, London* (2 vols, 1889–90), and for the copperplate map, A. Prockter and R. Taylor, *The A to Z of Elizabethan London* (1979). The list of relics of St Margaret Bridge is in Guildhall Library Ms. 1174; the register of the Fraternity of Holy Trinity is now published by P. Basing (ed.) *Parish Fraternity Register*, Lon. Rec. Soc. (1982). For the livery companies and their halls, see G. Unwin, *The Gilds and Companies of London* (1908), modified by more recent individual company histories: e.g. P. Metcalf, *The Halls of the Fishmongers' Company* (1977), A. Crawford, *A History of the Vintners' Company* (1977). For Merchant Taylors' Hall, see C. M. Clode (ed.) *Memorials of the Guild of Merchant Taylors* (1875) and Royal Commission on Historical Monuments, *London: IV (City)* (1929), 34–7. For the waterfront installations, see Schofield, *op. cit.* in notes to chapter 4. Crosby Hall is described in detail in P. Norman, *Survey of London: ix, Crosby Place* (1907) and C. Goss, *Crosby Hall* (1908); its removal to Chelsea in A. Clapham and W. Godfrey, *Some Famous Buildings and their Story* (1913), 119–38. Eltham Palace is described in Royal Commission on Historical Monuments, *London: V (East London)* (1930), 103–8; and discussed in the context of a late-sixteenth century plan of the palace and its outer courtyard in *Some Famous Buildings*, 47–66.

6 LONDON IN THE 16TH CENTURY

Baynard's Castle is the subject of a forthcoming archaeological report by its excavator, P. Marsden; for Bridewell, see D. Gadd and T. Dyson, 'Bridewell Palace', *Post. Med. Archaeol.* 15 (1981), 1–79. The description of Lincoln's Inn and Charterhouse (both before and after the Dissolution) is based on Royal Commission on Historical Monuments, *London II (West London)* (1925), 45–52 and 21–30; for Staple Inn, *ibid.*, 57–9; for Gray's Inn, *ibid.*, 53–7; for Middle Temple, *London IV (City)* (1929), 147–56. Rich's building at St Bartholomew's is described by E. A. Webb in *The Records of St Bartholomew's Priory* (2 vols, 1922); that of Audley and the Duke of Norfolk at Holy Trinity Priory is based on unpublished work by the author and R. Lea. The Counter-Reformation as experienced by the churchwardens of St Michael's is based on W. H. Overall, *The Accounts of the churchwardens of St Michael, Cornhill, 1456–1608* (1871).

7 TO THE GREAT FIRE

For Stow, see notes to chapter 1; for Treswell, J. Schofield, 'Ralph Treswell's surveys of London houses, c. 1612', in S. Tyacke (ed.) *English Map-Making 1500–1650* (1983), 85–92. The plans of Clothworkers' Company property are from a plan book of *c.* 1612 in the company archives; those of Christ's Hospital property in Guildhall Library Ms 12805. The section on function of rooms draws on the research of Frank Brown. For the Fortune Theatre, see 'The Fortune Theatre, London (1600)', in A. Clapham and W. Godfrey, *Some Famous Buildings and their Story* (1913), 13–28. For Pepys's account of the Fire, see R. Latham and W. Matthews (eds) *The Diary of Samuel Pepys, vii: 1666* (1972), 267–81.

Acknowledgements

The author and publishers are grateful to the following individuals and institutions for permission to reproduce illustrations:

Ashmolean Museum, Oxford 44;

T. Ball and C. Barron 88;

T. Ball and R. Gem 27;

British Library Board frontispiece; 43, 98;

Trustees of the British Museum 25, 139;

Christ's Hospital 132;

Worshipful Company of Clothworkers 118, 131, illustration on p. x;

Department of Environment 48;

Guildhall Library 2, 28, 41–5, 63, 78, 85–6, 88, 114–15, 117, 124, 133–4, 143, 146–7, illustrations on pp. vi, viii–ix;

Bibliothèque Nationale, Paris 73;

Master and Fellows of Magdalene College, Cambridge 107;

Museum of London 1, 3–23, 26, 29, 31–5, 37–40, 42, 47, 49–56, 58–60, 62, 66–7, 72, 75–7, 79–84, 89, 91–2, 94–5, 97, 99–100, 104–5, 108–13, 120–21, 125–30, 135–7, 139, 141–4;

Royal Commission on Historical Monuments (National Monuments Record) 24, 30, 36, 46, 57, 70, 90, 93, 96, 101–3, 116, 119, 122–3, 140, 145;

Walter Scott (Bradford) 61;

Woodmansterne Ltd (Nicholas Servian FIIP) 74.

Index

References in italic type are to illustrations; those in Roman figures refer to the preliminary pages.

Abbeys 21,37,52,141,142; see also Westminster Abbey
Abchurch Lane 69
Addle Street 28;21
Agas, Ralph, map of 111;viii–ix
Aldermanbury 29;21
Aldermanbury Square 115
Aldermen 5,11,30,79,115
Aldersgate 24,44,129,145
Aldersgate Street 85,115
Aldgate 4,24,46,69,104,121,129,145,146,157
Aldgate (street) 141,148,157,162;5,133
Aldgate High Street 162;132
Alfred, King of Wessex 15,24,25,37
All Hallows Barking 7,32,114;14,22
All Hallows on the Wall 21,69–70,117
All Hallows Staining 56
All Hallows the Great 83
All Saints, Fulham 113;91
Alleys 9,29,88,91,97,102,103,158,160,176;80
Almshouses 12,110,118,180
Arcades 41,76,110,121–3,153;98,126
Archaeological excavations 1,6,8,10,13
Architecture: Romanesque 37,40,41,42–4,47,52,56,65,113; Norman 37,40,41,42,50; Gothic 50,65,81–2,151; Perpendicular 84,99,113,129,132,168,179; Elizabethan 131,163,166; Renaissance 132,151,153,166;126; Jacobean 163–5,166; classical influences 153,163,166,168,169;106,141; Continental influences 37,40,45,56,65,82,132,153,166,168,169,175
Arundel House 23;68
Assize of Nuisance 11,79,115,180
Audley, Thomas 145–6,148
Augustinians 45,46,47,49,145
Austin Friars' (Augustinian) church 70,82,88,127,140;63

Bake-houses 28,29
Baltic 98,110
Banqueting House, Whitehall 167,168;138
Barbican development 24,68,163;53
Barking Abbey 21
Barnard's Inn 98,107; Hall 6;86
Barns 28,76
Bartholomew Fair 65
Basing Lane 78;60,76

Basingahaga 29
Basinghall Street 29
Bastions 20,21,38,56,68,69,70,145;x,52,53,56
Bath-houses 18,19,20
Battlements 68,81,112,113,127;105
Bay window 93–5,124,161,169;120; see also oriel windows
Baynards Castle (pre-1275) 38,40,70,132;26
Baynards Castle (post-1275) 132–4,136;108
Becket, St Thomas 1,49,59,115
Bedford House 168
Bellfounding 162
Benedictines 45,72
Bermondsey Priory, later Abbey 45,52,141,142;115,117
Bernard, Lionel 107; see also Barnard's Inn
Billingsgate 9,20,25,29,32,77,88,103,118,121,142;98,99
Billiter Street 158,160,161,162;129
Bishopsgate 49,69,129,145,162;52
Bishopsgate (street) 25,97,123,124,145,169
Black Prince, son of Edward III 54,85
Blackfriars (Dominicans) 38,40,67,70–2,126,140,163;54,55,56
Blackfriars (area) 100
Bloomsbury 169
Boats 16,17,25,33,120,145;17; see also shipping; transport
Boothby Pagnell, Lincs 52
Bosse Alley 102
Botolph Lane 25,28,93
Boudiccan rebellion 16,17
Boundaries, establishment of 11,30,31,32,38
Boundaries, property 29,54,75,76,88,93,96,97,100,102,161,175,176;59
Boundary, City 1,17,49,148,151
Bow Lane 8,25,28,29,44
Bowyer Row (Ludgate Hill) 88
Bread Street 28;19
Brewers 79,103,121,162
Brewers' Company 12,115,117,118,180; Hall of 12,115
Brewing 95,97
Bricett, Jordan of 50
Brick buildings 121,126,127,129,132,134,135,136,137,138,142,146,152,161,165,166,168,169,174,175;103
Brick kilns 126,136
Brickearth 16,17,129,136
Bricks 10,17,52,95,97,126–7,129,135,136,150,154,163,166,179;10,115

Brickmaking 17,126,127,129,136
Bride Lane 136
Bridewell Palace 129,132,134–6,137;109,110,111
Bridges 10,18,59,120,126,167,175; see also London Bridge
Bristol 75,81
Broad Street 70,82,88
Brothel 89
Budge Row 88,111,112
Building accounts 11,12,62,85,97,126,132
Building materials 10,12,20,22,25,32,33,55,62,76,95,126,129,171,180; see also stone; tiles; timber
Building regulations 9,11,75–6,92,93,95,144,165,175,179; see also Assize of Nuisance
Building techniques 9,17,28,29,32,42,135; see also masonry
Building types 9–10,28,50–2,54,56,86–90,97,115,131,141,144,155,157,158–9,160–2,167,168–9;69,80,129
Buildings: Roman 15,16,17,18,19,20;10,12; Saxon 24,25,27–33,76;19; see also brick buildings; monastic buildings; stone buildings; timber buildings; waterfront buildings
Burghley, Lord 46,162
Burhs 24,29
Burials 15,20,46,70,111,151,162
Butteries 88,93,117,158,161;131
Byres 28,29

Cannon Street 15,17,28,78,103,120,171;19,60
Canterbury, Archbishop of 21,64,70,81,127,136,140
Canterbury, Kent 1,21,24,59,76,85; Cathedral 50,85,179
Carpenters 11,12,62,79,84,98,163,180
Carpenters' Company 126; Hall of 118
Carpentry 10,12,17,28,76,77,85,98,100,126,165
Carter Lane 40
Carthusians 85
Castles 37,38,40,52,70,95,132,134,178; see also Tower of London
Ceilings 72,123,124,163–5;137
Cellars 9,28,55,77,88,97,158,159,162;6,79,131
Cemeteries 20,72
Ceolmundingchaga 24
Cesspits 9,10,76,77,96,99
Chambers 38,41,62,64,76,88,89,90,91,95,104,117,118,142,150,159,161,162;118,131,133
Chancery Lane 107,137;136
Chapels 44,46,47,49,54,56,59–60,64,65,81,85,95,100,110,111,112,114,117,124,131;x,24,49,85,121,146
Chapter-houses 45,47,60,64,72,82;65
Charitable works and bequests 59,107,110–11,112,115,118,121

Charles I 166,178
Charles II 169,174
Charterhouse 6,85,120,137,141,142,148,153,158;116
Charterhouse Square 85
Chaucer, Geoffrey 69,97,103–4
Cheapside 24,28,44,49,56,59,76,79,89,121,162
Chequerwork 85,99,120;79
Chertsey Abbey, Surrey 21
Chimneys 12,62,90,91,92,95–6,127,158,159,179
Christ's Hospital 157–8,162
Churches 37,45,47,56,59,112,114,151,174,175; guild 111; interior details 42–4,56,63,65,69,70,72,73,82,110,112–15,150–1; monastic 7,37,40,43,44,45,46,47,70,72–3,81,84,131,141,142,145,146,148;35,57,121; parish 4,31,32,59,72,73,81,107,111,112,114–15,131,140,146,148,150,151,180;57,89; Saxon 21,22,23,28,32;14,23; timber 32
Churchman, John 104,110
Churchyards 111,123,150,151,153,162
Cistercians 56,84
Cisterns 96,97
Civic amenities, provision of 10–11,45,79,97,145,175
Clay 18,63,92,95
Clerkenwell 50,54,137
Cloisters 12,46,49,60,65,72,82,85,141,142,152;49,61,65,114,117
Cloth Fair 144,153
Clothworkers 56,88,145,158,161
Clothworkers' Company 56,158,160–1;97; Hall of 118,158,160–2,174
Cluniacs 45,52
Cobbles 25,97
Coldharbour 63,103;83
Colechurch, Peter de 59
College Hill 110–11
Colleges 127,132,137
Company Halls, see Livery Company Halls
Conduits 72,79,97
Coneyhope Lane 123
Cooper's Row 24,67
Corbet Court 52
Cordwainers' Hall 116
Cornhill 15,97,110,112,117,141,150,153
Corporation of the City of London 59,95
Cottages 126
Counter-Reformation 131,150,151
Courts 11,175; see also Hustings, court of
Courtyards 95,97,126,127,132,137,141,146,148,160,162,163,168,181;49,109,112,125,126
Covent Garden 168
Craft companies, see guilds
Craftsmen 12,60,62,82,88,126,132,180
Cranes 85,120,121
Creed Lane 40
Cripplegate 20,23,56,68,69,129,145,150;104

Cromwell, Thomas 138–40
Crosby, Sir John 107,123,124, 129
Crosby Hall 107,124,126,127, 137;*7,100,101*
Crosby Place 123–4, 126
Crowne Inn, Aldgate High Street 162;*133*
Croxton (Crowston), John 12, 108,129,180
Crutched (Crossed) Friars 72, 138
Crutched Friars (street) 72;*127*
Crypts 44–5,50,52,64,66,72,77, 82,108;*30,51,87*
Custom House 64,100,103,104, 110,118,123

'Dark earth' 19,23,29
Daub 12,25,29,95,97
Dean's House, Westminster Abbey 85;*71*
Defences: Roman 16,20,38;*8,9*; Saxon 23,24,67;*17*; medieval 65–70,129,145; *see also* walls, city; ditch, city
Dendrochronology 10,29;*77*
Desebourne Lane 103
Diaper work 129,137,138;*103, 113*
Dick Whittington Tavern, Cloth Fair *118*
Dissolution of the Monasteries 81,138–42,144,145,150,155, 157,168
Ditch, City 70,129,145
Ditches 38,40,70
Docks 38,121,126,132; *see also* quays; wharves
Documentary evidence 1,11,12,13
Doors 13,28,85,89,95,112,126, 137,158;*128*
Doorways 12,52,64,65,86,124, 137,168;*33,50*; *see also* posterns
Dowgate 9,32,62,121
Drains 10,18,62,96,98,104, 136,175,179
Drapers 110,111
Drapers' Company 118,129; Hall of 118,126
Dukes Place, mansion of 148
Dyeing 97
Dyers 103

East End 168
East Smithfield 63,84
Eastcheap 25,62,121
Ecclesiastical building projects 44,59,64–5,70,136
Edward the Confessor 30,40, 41,44,45,60,66,115
Edward I 63,77,82
Edward II 38
Edward III 81,103
Edward IV 124,132
Edward VI 131,132,150,153
Elizabeth I 132,141,142,150,151
Elsinge, William de 81
Eltham Palace 86,124–6, *102*
Ely, Bishop of 64–65,77,127
Ely Place, Holborn 65,*49*
Embankment 25,29,32,*17,20 see also* reclamation; revetments; waterfronts

Estates, urban 29,30,108;*21*
Etheredeshythe, *see* Queenhithe
Eyre, Simon 107,110
Eyres 76,90

Fairs 47,65,144
Farming 23,97
Fences 9,29,97
Fenchurch Street 158,159,160, 161,162;*130–1*
Financial Times, Cannon Street 28;*19*
Fire, 'Great' (1666) 6,9,174–6, 181;*124,142,143,145*
Fire-places 95,117,124,148, 158,160,163;*137*
Fires 16,37,38,42,46,49,54,66, 75,76,91,132,134,135,150, 179;*10*
Fishmongers 79,88,93,103,111, 123
Fishmongers' Hall 100,103
Fissyngwharf Lane 97
Fitzailwin, Henry 75
Fixtures and fittings (interior decor) 12,64,72,91,92–5,98, 116,150,180
Fleet River 15,70,134,135,136
Fleet Street 70,89,134,145,152, 162,165;*136*
Floors 9,28,44,64,70,77,95,98, 135,148;*6*
Food supply 19,97,110,121,146; *see also* farming; market places
Fore Street 145
Forge 91
Fort, Roman (Cripplegate) 16, 23,28,29,30;*9,21*
Forum 16,21,25,52;*9*
Foster Lane 44–5,116
Foundations 9,10,17,20,38,55, 63, 99, 100, 117, 135, 136, 163; *78*
Fraternities 59,115; *see also* guilds
Fraternity of the Holy Trinity, Aldersgate Street 115;*93–4*
Fraternity of the Holy Trinity, Leadenhall 110
Fraunceys, Adam 88
Friaries 70,72,73; *see also* houses of the individual orders
Friars 54,59,70,72
Friday Street 89
Frier Lane 111
Fulham Palace 136;*112*
Fullers' Hall 160–2
Furniture 28,64,72,91,92–5, 98, 118,150;*72*
Furnival's Inn 107
Fyfield Hall, Essex 76

Galleries 38,41,120,124,135, 141,148,161,162;*134*
Gardens 8,65,72,97,118,120, 123,127,132,142,152,159,161, 168
Gatehouses 30,45,60,63,85,88, 127, 137, 142, 153, 161, 162; *103*
Gates 11,16,30,32,44,46,67–9, 132,137,174,175;*113*; see also Aldgate; Aldersgate; Bishopsgate; Cripplegate; Ludgate; Moorgate; Newgate

General Post Office, Newgate Street (GPO site) 8,23,29, 72;*1,10*
George Inn, Southwark 163;*134*
Gerard's Hall, Basing Lane 78, 89;*60*
Gildhalls, York 107,178
Glass; stained 72,73,82,111, 114,124,178;*3*; window 18,63, 64,70,72,73,93,95,132,148,162
Glaziers 62
Goldsmiths' Company 12,95, 129; Hall of 116,117
Gracechurch Street 25,52,56,79
Granary ('garner') 108,110,121
Graveley, Edmund 126
Gray's Inn 107,151; Chapel 151; Hall 6,116,152,153
Great Fire, *see* Fire, 'Great'
Great St Helen's 169
Great Tower Street 22,63,64, 174
Greenwich Palace 132, 167
Gresham, Thomas 153
Greyfriars (Franciscans) 70,72, 79,110
Grocers' Company 123,124; Hall of 123
Guildhall (of the City of London) 30,76,89,93,108, 110,137,174,181;*79,87,88*; Chapel *88*;Library 110
Guildhall (of Cologne merchants, Steelyard) 118–20
Guildhalls 60,107,118–20; *see also* gildhalls
Guilds 5–6,12,59,107,111, 115–18,129; *see also* Livery Companies; Livery Company halls; halls of the individual companies; fraternities
Gutters 75–6,96,174

Hagas 24,29
Halls 24,37,38,41,46,52,63,65, 72,76,78,81,86,88,89,90,91,92, 93,95,107,108,110,115,116, 120,124,126,134,137,141,142, 151,152,153,159,160,162, 168;*49,68,70,94,131,133*; *see also* halls of the individual companies
Hampton Court Palace 86,131, 132,136,151
Hampton Court, Kings Lynn 121
Hart Street *137*
Hatfield House 127
Hearths 25,28,91
Henry I 38,40,46
Henry III 37,41,60,63,68,69
Henry V 126
Henry VI 132
Henry VII 126,131,132
Henry VIII 126,127,131,132, 134,137,138,140,145,153
Herland, Hugh 85,86,179;*67*
Holborn 6,65,70,89,98,107,153, 154,166
Holborn Bridge 174
Hollar, Wenceslaus 42,84,111, 120;*25,28,29,62,65,68,84,97, 143,147*
Holy Trinity Priory, Aldgate 46,65,72,145–8,162;*31,32,121*

Honey Lane 54
Hospital, leper 49
Hospitals 11,37,47,49,81,110, 144,145,157,158,160
Houndsditch 70,145
Houses: courtyard 85,86,88, 103,115,123,132,134,142,153, 155,160,162,163;*68,112*; 'Jews' 52,67,157; 'stone' 52,54,55,56,76,98,140;*37,39, 46,71*; 'town' 29,52,65,81,98, 131,141,142,148,151,157;*37*
Housing developments 141, 144,157,168
Howard, Thomas, Duke of Norfolk 141,142,148;*116*
Husting, court of 11,33

Immigrants 10,126,131,140, 141,142,144,153
Industries 6,11,64,95,97,103, 118,145,180
Inner Temple 152; Hall 152
Inns 17,144,145,160,162,163; *see also* taverns
Inns: of Chancery 98,107; of Court 107,116,132,145,151, 155
Interior decor 18,64,72,82,93, 95,124,132,153,180; *see also* fixtures and fittings
Ironmongers' Hall 160,161
Ironwork 12,60,62,72,95,137, 157;*75*
Isleworth, mansion at 153

James I 117,165,166
Jetties (of houses) 11,76,89,90, 148,165,169,171;*119,122, 127,128*
Jetty (riverside) 25;*17*
Jews 52,56,67
Jocelin, Sir Ralph 129
John, King 40,67,70
Jones, Inigo 66,166–8;*138–40*
Jurdan, Thomas 126

Kendall, Thomas 140
Kennington Palace 85,117,126
Kew Palace 166
Kilns 126,136
King Edward Street 68,70,72
King Street 175
King's Works 104,126,166,167; *see also* royal building projects
Kings Lynn 107,108,120–1,178; Steelyard 120–1
Kitchens 12,63,88,91,92,96,97, 117,158,159,160,161;*72,118, 131,133*
Knightrider Street 95
Knights Templar 152

Lambe's Chapel, *see* St James on the Wall
Lambeth Hill 31
Lambeth Palace 64,81,98,127, 137;*70,103*
Lanes 25,97,165,175
Laths 12,95,97,118,169
Latrines 40,96,104
Lead 62,66,72,79,96,110,112, 140
Leadenhall 107,108–10;*85*
Leadenhall Street 114,146,148, 157;*5*

Leake, John 38,40;*143*
Leathersellers' Hall 140
Lewes, house of the Prior of 52,54,88;*37,38,40*
Lime 62,95
Lime Street 117
Lincoln, Earl of (Henry de Lacey) 137
Lincoln's Inn 107,127,137,152; Chapel 168; Fields 137,168; *140*; Gate 127,137;*113*; Hall 6,137
Lindsey House 168; *140*
Litigation 11,91,92,96,97
Livery Companies 12,115–18, 129,157,170; *see also* guilds
Livery Company Halls 93,103, 111,115–18,160,161–2,178; *see also* halls of the individual companies
Lombard Street 171
London, Bishop of 136,151
London: development of 1, 15–16,23,32,59,79,142,144, 168,175–6,180; economy of 22,23,32,59,81,82,107, 142,157; expansion of 10,79, 142–45,157,169,179; extent of extra-mural occupation 66,142,144,145; extent of intra-mural occupation 24,66,70,97; prehistoric 15
London Bridge 21,25,32,33, 59–60;*44,45,107*
London Wall (street) 82,118
Long Lane *141*
Longtyled-house Row 144;*119*
Lovat Lane 8
Ludgate 3,11,22,24,38,40,68,69, 70,100;*2,142*
Ludgate Hill 38,88

Manor of the Rose 81;*83*
Mansion House 110
Maps (bird's eye views, panoramas, plans, views, etc.) 12,13,111;*43,143*
Marble 18,70,72,98,165; Purbeck 50,65,73,98–9;*36*
Mark Lane 56,171,174
Market places 10,11,21,24,56, 79,108,110,121,123,168,175
Masonry 9–10,32,40,42,44,67, 85,99–100,167;*79*
Masons 11,12,60,79,84,98,104, 108,126,150,151,179,180
Matilda, wife of Henry I 46,49
Matilda, wife of King Stephen 49
Mayors (Lord), of the City of London 11,75,79,81,110,111, 112,115,124,129,145,148,174
Mercers 81,95,110,111
Merchandise, storage of 69,77, 78,88,121,123; *see also* warehouses
Merchant Taylors' Company 117,118; Hall of 81,95,116, 117,124;*78,95,96*
Merchants 5–6,21,62,110,111, 123,124; foreign 23,32–3,56, 77,79,81,118,120,123,166
Merchants' marks 72,124
Middle Street 144
Middle Temple 6,93,151,152; Hall 116,151,152,153;*106*

Middle Temple Lane 152
Middlesex Guildhall 60
Milk Street 25,28,29,54,89; *19,39*
Mitre Square 146
Monasteries 37,40,44–50,59,70, 79,84–5,110;*32*; *see also* Dissolution
Monastic buildings 40,45–50, 65,78,89,137,141–2,148; *32,116*
Monkwell Street 56;*x*
Montfichet's Tower 38,40,70;*26*
Monument, the 115,174;*144*
Moor Lane 11
Moor Park, Rickmansworth 127
Moorfields 15,110
Moorgate 110,129,145
Mortar 10,42,92,95,97,167
Morton's Tower, Lambeth Palace 127,129,137
Munfichet, William de 40

New Fresh Wharf 25,77,97;*6, 11,17,20,59,79,80*
New Inn, Gloucester 162
New Quay 175
Newbury Street 144
Newgate 69,70,72,145
Newgate Street 8,23,29,38
North, Lord Edward 141,142
North's Hall, Charterhouse 141,153
Nunneries 37,49,50,54,72,73, 97,123,140,141

Offa, King of Mercia 23,40
Ogilby and Morgan's Survey of London (1677) 12,175–6;*124, 145*
Old Bailey 70
Old Fish Street 121,141
Old Jewry 54
Old Square, Lincoln's Inn 137
Oriel windows 93,117,126, 137;*7*; *see also* bay windows
Ovens 25,148

Painted Chamber, Westminster Palace 41
Pakeman's Wharf, Thames Street 88
Palaces 16,17,64,127,136,142, 169; Royal 29,30,41,85,107, 126,129,131,132,134,135, 136,141,142
Palladio, Andrea 166,167
Panelling 95
Pantries 93,117
Parishes 29,30–2,38,45,52, 115,127
Parliament, Houses of 82,145;*47*
Parlours 88,91,110,116,117, 124, 142, 159, 160, 162; *71, 131, 133*
Paulet, Sir Thomas 140
Paving 12,70,72,79,90,97,145, 150
Penshurst Place, Kent 81,82,93
Pepys, Samuel 170
Peter and Paul Tavern, Paternoster Row 95
Pewterers' Hall 117
Philpot Lane 127
Pig-sties 79
Pindar, Sir Paul (house of) 165

Pits, rubbish 8,10,23,29,55;*12*; *see also* cesspits
Plague (Black Death) 84,85, 112,117,144
Plaster 18,76,92,95,99,163–5, 168,169
Plumbing 12,62,79
Pope, Sir Thomas 142;*115*
Population 82,142,157
Porches 28,52,76,93,108,114, 141,148,152;*39,84,88,112*
Posterns 30,67,110,129
Potters 29,95,162
Pottery 15,21,23,27,68,95
Poultry (street) 123
Pountney Lane 81
Presbytery, Greenwich 166
Prince Henry's Room, Fleet Street 6,165
Priories 37,45–7,50,52,114, 141,142,144,148
Prisons 11,69,79,110,175
Privies 10,12,38,64,75,76,79,96, 111,148,158,159,160,179;*76*
Properties, plans of 11,12,13, 88,145,148,157–62,169,179; *x,118,131,133*
Pudding Lane 174;*145*
Puddle Dock 38
Pultney, Sir John 81, 82, 103

Quarries 17,32,98,99,126,129
Quays, 9,17,20,22,25,32,64,103, 175;*11,82*; *see also* revetments; wharves
Queen Street 111,175
Queen's House, Greenwich 167–8
Queenhithe 25,46,60,96, 103,118,121

Ramsey, William 82,84,179; *61,65*
Reclamation 9,10,17,32,72, 100–3,120,134;*20,81*; *see also* embankments; revetments
Reformation 113,114,140,142, 148,150,151,157; *see also* Counter-Reformation
Revetments 10,17,100–3;*82*; *see also* embankments; quays; reclamation; wharves
Rich, Lord Richard 144,148
Richard I 54,56
Richard II 41,178,181
Richard III 115,123,124,132,157
Richmond Palace 132
Roads 9,11,25,145,148,167; Roman 15,21,29; *see also* streets
Rood 114,150,151;*123*
Roofs 28,41,42,54,75,76,85,86, 89,98,108,112,117,124,126, 137,140,141,151,152;*7,67,94*
Rows 88,144,178;*146*
Royal Exchange 153,175;*126*
Royal building projects 37–8, 40,59–60,82,84,85,86,126, 131,179; *see also* King's Works
Rubbish, disposal of 10,11,23, *8,79,121,160*; *see also* pits

Saddlers' Hall 116
St Alban Wood Street 23
St Alphege, London Wall 67–8, 81–2,129

St Andrew, Castle Baynard (now, by the Wardrobe), parish of 38
St Andrew Holborn 32,107
St Andrew Undershaft 7,14, 146,148,150;*89,122,123,143*
St Andrew's Hill 38,40
St Antholin 111,112;*89*
St Augustine Watling Street 22
St Bartholomew by the Exchange 112;*89*
St Bartholomew the Great, Smithfield; building above churchyard entrance 6, 153–4;*50*; priory 6,43,47,65, 81,100,137,144,153;*50*
St Bartholomew the Less 47
St Bartholomew, Hospital of 20,47,110
St Benet Gracechurch *89*
St Benet Paul's Wharf 134,166
St Benet Sherehog *89*
St Botolph Aldersgate 32,115
St Botolph Aldgate 32,162
St Botolph Billingsgate 142
St Botolph Bishopsgate 32
St Dunstan in the East 85,103, 112,113;*58,89*
St Ethelburga 112,113;*89,90, 92,143*
St Etheldreda 65,77,98;*49*
St Faith 66
St Gabriel Fenchurch *89*
St Giles Cripplegate 150,151;*53*
St Giles in the Fields, leper hospital 49
St Gregory 22
St Helen's Bishopsgate, nunnery and parish church 73,82,100,112,114,124,140, 168;*57,89,128,143*
St James Cripplegate (on the Wall) 56;*x,41,105*
St John of Jerusalem, Clerkenwell, priory and Hospital 7,50,137;*35*
St John the Baptist, Cloak Lane *89*
St John's Chapel, White Tower 38; *24*
St Katherine Cree 146,168
St Katherine by the Tower, Hospital of 49,144
St Lawrence Pountney 113
St Laurence Wharf 103
St Magnus the Martyr 85,104; *89*
St Margaret Bridge 115
St Martin le Grand 44,65
St Martin Ludgate 22
St Martin Outwich 112
St Martin Vintry: church 112; *89*; parish 111
St Mary Aldermanbury 30
St Mary at Hill: church 112, 114; parish 103
St Mary Clerkenwell, nunnery 50,54
St Mary Colechurch 59
St Mary Graces 84–5
St Mary Magdelene, Bermondsey 46
St Mary Mounthaw 32
St Mary Overie, priory (Southwark Cathedral) 7, 47–9,65,75,81,129,137;*33,146*

St Mary Somerset 32,100
St Mary Spital, Bishopsgate 49,
  145,160;*34*
St Mary Staining 29
St Mary-le-Bow 44,45,52;*30*
St Mary's chapel, Westminster
  82
St Michael Cornhill 112, 150–1
St Michael Crooked Lane 111
St Michael Paternoster Royal
  110
St Mildred 28
St Nicholas Cole Abbey 121
St Nicholas Shambles 1
St Olave Hart Street 7,33,72
St Paul Covent Garden 168
St Paul's Cathedral 21,38,41,
  44,65–6,168,175,179;*26,28,*
  42,43,51,65,107,139,147;
  Chapter-House 82,84;*65;*
  Churchyard 11;*22*
St Peter Cornhill 4
St Peter, Tower of London 63
St Peter, Westminster, *see*
  Westminster Abbey
St Stephen Coleman Street 146
St Stephen Walbrook 93
St Stephen's Chapel,
  Westminster 41,82–4,98;*3,*
  64,114
St Swithin London Stone 111
St Thomas Apostle 111
St Thomas of Acre (Acon),
  Hospital of 49
St Thomas's Hospital,
  Southwark 49,110
St Thomas's Chapel, London
  Bridge 59–60,85;*44*
Sanitation 64,79,95;*76*
Savoy 33
Scaffolding 32,62,85
Schools 131
Scotland Yard 40
Screen's passage 86,117,124,
  153,161
Seal House 100
Seething Lane 170,174
Shaa, Edward 129
Shingles 62,63,76
Shipping 23,31,32–3,60,103,
  121; *see also* boats; transport
Shops 60,88,89,91,96,121,158,
  159,160,170;*44,90,118,131*
Shrines and relics 21,60,66,114,
  115
Skinners 90,93,95
Skinners' Company 129; Hall of
  116
Smithfield (West) 6,65,153,162,
  174;*118,141*
Sokes 29,38
Solars 76,88,89,90,91,96
Somerset, Lord 'Protector' 153
Somerset House 153;*124*
Southampton 23,40,75,76
Southwark 15,21,25,33,52,60,
  88,110,137,163;*vi*
Southwark Cathedral, *see* St
  Mary Overie
Squares 85,157
Stables 140,158,162;*118,133*
Staeningahaga 29

Stair, river 100,120,121,170;*97*
Staircases 91,136,141–2;*120*
Stairs 38,52,55,68,91,93,135,
  137,141,158,161;*30,120*
Stair-turrets 44,113,114,129,
  134,137,150;*109*
Staple Inn 6,89,107,151,153,
  154,155,161;*4;* Hall 6,89,
  116,152
Steelyard, London 103,118,
  120,121,170;*97;* Kings Lynn
  120,121
Stinking Lane 72
Stockfishmonger Row, Thames
  Street 88
Stone 16,25,32,75,76,91,95,96,
  97,100,102–3,127,137,141,
  165,175,179; buildings 8,9,
  10,16,18,41,55,75,76,88,89,
  117,121,124,141,169,178;*6,*
  37; supply of 12,16,32,52,60,
  62,67,70,98–9,103,146,180
Stonework 44,46,52,56,68,73,
  82,84,99,108,126,138,141;
  13,22,36,38,41,58,80,85
Store-houses 28,45,46,69,93,108
Stow, John 1,5,132,146,148,157
Strand 23,64,66,107,153,166
Strapwork 153
Streams 10,20,31,38,40
Street clearance 11,79
Street frontages (relationship to
  buildings) 9,11,28–9,52,76,
  86,88,90,97,123,158–60,
  162,165–6,168,170
Street plans 24,37,40,97,175,
  176;*16,21*
Street repairs 79,145
Street surfaces 25,97,145
Streets 29,43,70,170,175;*16;*
  Roman 28,31; Saxon 24,25,
  28,29,31,70,148;*16*
Suburbs 6,23,32,45,49,50,64,66,
  107,127,142,145,150,168
Surveyors 12,145,157–162,169,
  175
Sweedon's Passage, Grub Street
  120
Symonds, John 148; *32, 121*
Synagogues 54

Tanners 79
Taverns 78,95,107,153; *see also*
  inns
Taxes 67,79,97,103,104
Temple, *see* Inner and Middle
  Temples
Temple Bar 174;*124*
Temple Church 6,50,65,75,
  152,174,179;*36*
Tennis courts 160
Tenters 145
Thames, River 9,11,15,103
Thames Street 9,32,64,100,
  103,120,175;*145*
Thatch 75
Thavy's (David's) Inn 107
Theatres 163;*135*
Threadneedle Street 81,117,153
Tiles 10,12,16,17,22,32,44,72,
  95,97;*14;* floor 64,72;*46;* roof
  10,63,76,95,126,140,153

Timber: structures of 33,41,76,
  96,100,104,113,124,135,161;
  supply of 33,60,70,98,153
Timber-framed buildings 6,9,
  11,17,46,76,77,95,100,117,
  121,131,142,148,153–4,169,
  178,179;*4,10,68,117,141*
Tolls 23,32,79
Tower Hill 24,67;*8*
Tower of London 15,37–8,59,
  63–4,67,85,95,126,134;*24,25,*
  43,48,98
Tower postern 67
Towers 40,81,120,132,153,
  161;*83*
Towers (of churches) 56,65,66,
  81,100,113–14,141,148,150,
  168;*83,91*
Towns 1,18,19,37,70; planned
  24,59
Trade 5,16,23,25,98,104,118,
  121,123; foreign 5,16,21,32–3,
  56,77,78,81,95,97,98,100,
  110,118,121; regulations 11,
  32,33,121
Trade guilds, *see* guilds
Transport 32,62,82,85,97,98,
  99,136
Treswell, Ralph 13,88,157–62,
  169,179;*x,69,118,129–31,133,*
  141
Trig, William 97,100
Trig Lane 97,100–2;*81,82,108*
Trinity Hall Aldersgate, *see*
  Fraternity of the Holy Trinity
Tudor Street 135
Tykenedleswharf 103
Tyler, Wat 50,111
Tyryngton, John 84,85

Undercrofts 8,45,47,52,55,56,
  78,81,89,108,117,124,127,
  137,140;*5,37,40,41,55,60,96*

Vaulting 43,47,50,52,56,85,
  117,126,129,137,152,168;
  37,38
Vaults 38,46,56,65,72,77,121,
  123,124,162
Viking raids 24,33,38
Villas 19
Vintners' Hall 103
Vintry 77,111

Walbrook 15,20,21,31,68,
  111,121
Wall construction techniques,
  see masonry
Wall, City 11,16,19,20,54,
  66–70,79,126,129;*x,8,52,105;*
  Roman riverside 9,20,25,63;
  13
Walls 9,10,12,33,52,75,85,96,
  99,102,103,120,175;*10*
Walworth, William 111
Ward meetings 115,117
Wards 29,30,31,35,46,69,79,
  117,132,142,157,174
Warehouses 16,20,91,120,123,
  158;*133; see also* storehouses

Warenne, Earl de 52,*37*
Wash basins 72,95;*120*
Water supply 10,11,18,45,75–6,
  79,96,97; *see also* conduits
Waterfront buildings 8,9,17,
  77–8,88,96,97,100,102–4,118,
  120,121,123;*6,59,80*
Waterfronts 17,19,25,64;*83,98;*
  see also embankments; quays;
  reclamation; revetments
Watergates 64,132
Watermills 104
Watling Court 28;*19,76*
Watling Street 91
Wattle (and daub) 25
Well Court, Bow Lane 8–9,29,
  44;*19*
Wells 10,43,77,79,97,99,111,
  117
West Cheap (Cheapside) 25
West End 168
Westminster 40,42,107;*43*
Westminster Abbey, St Peter's
  40,60,82,85,131;*27,61,84;*
  Chapter-House 64; monastic
  buildings 82,85;*61*
Westminster Hall 37,41,82,
  85;*27,66,67*
Westminster, Royal Palace of
  30,37,41,62;*27*
Wharves 9,17,18,29,77,88,103,
  121,132,175;*20; see also* docks;
  quays
White Tower, Tower of London
  37–8,63,96;*25*
Whitefriars (Carmelites) 70,72;
  95
Whitehall 23,167,168
Whittington, Richard 107,
  110–11
William the Conqueror 33,37,
  45,52,67
William II (Rufus) 37,40,41,
  45,46,76,82
Winchester, Bishop of 47,137
Winchester, Hampshire 25,50,
  66,75
Winchester House, Southwark
  47,81;*62,74*
Winchester Place 140
Windgoose Lane 120
Window shutters 35,93,95
Windows 41,44,64,65,69,73,75,
  82,84,89,95,108,110,131,
  132,137,148,153,168;*4,25,62,*
  63,74,95,117,127; see also bay
  window; oriel windows
Wolsey, Cardinal 127,132
Woodwork 75,85,98,112,114,
  124,137,141–2,150,151–2,
  153,163,167;*106,117,119,127,*
  136
Wren, Sir Christopher 42,43,
  44,114,152,166,174,175
Wyngaerde 111,121;*44,83,99*

Yakesley, John 81,117
Yards 9,12,86,111,117,142,
  145,158,160,161,162;*118,131*
Yevele, Henry 84,85,86,99,
  104,108,112,113,141;*66,84*
York 81,98,100,107,178,181